185 THE MALTA SQUADRON

185 THE MALTA SQUADRON

EDITED BY
ANTHONY ROGERS

Cover illustrations all from the photograph album of Ernie Broad.

First published by Spellmount, 2005
This paperback edition first published 2016

The History Press
The Mill, Brimscombe Port
Stroud, Gloucestershire, GL5 2QG
www.thehistorypress.co.uk

British Library Cataloguing in Publication Data.
A catalogue record for this book is available from the British Library.

ISBN 978 0 7509 6610 8

Typesetting and origination by The History Press
Printed and bound by CPI Group (UK) Ltd

Contents

Introduction and Acknowledgements

The original diary of 185 Squadron may be viewed by special request at The National Archives (formerly the Public Record Office) at Kew, in England. Copies of both volumes are also available in the archive's microfilm reading room (reference AIR 27/1142 and 1143). Such a diary, or 'line book', should not be confused with an Operations Record Book (ORB). The latter is an official day-by-day account of the activities of a unit or station, whereas the former is an unofficial and often humorous series of anecdotes by squadron members. As such, it provides a more personal insight into the lives of those who flew and fought in a bygone era.

What follows is a reproduction of the diary in its entirety for the period 1941–43. Some later entries, consisting mainly of repetitious one-liners recording little more than practice flights or uneventful scrambles, have been omitted.

When the diary is compared with an ORB it is perhaps inevitable that there will be discrepancies, not least in regard to pilots' claims for enemy aircraft destroyed. This is especially evident in entries for May 1942. It is only through post-war research of Luftwaffe records that we now know that neither document can be relied on to provide an accurate tally.

Nevertheless, with the exception of spelling mistakes and obvious grammatical errors, diary entries remain as they were written. Each diarist had his own unique style. I have preserved this by resisting the temptation to over-punctuate. This will explain the sometimes unusual sentence structure such as that of Pilot Officer (later Flying Officer) Peter Thompson, to which he himself alludes in the entry for 24 October 1941! Nevertheless, some adjustments were necessary, often to maintain a degree of consistency – for example, adopting a single method of dating for each entry. Generally, the same spelling has been retained for place names, such as Ta' Qali/Ta Kali/Takali and Valetta/Valletta, all of which were in use at the time. As a minor concession I have in most cases adopted the modern method where abbreviations occur in diary entries, such as HQ as opposed to H.Q. Excerpts from combat reports and other official sources were corrected for spelling only. There has been no attempt to define, and possibly misinterpret, any passages which are unclear.

Editorial notes and comments are italicised, together with a running commentary intended to provide the reader with a clearer understanding of events during the period covered by the diary.

Thanks are due to The National Archives for access to the original diary. The majority of images are from the photograph album of the late Ernie Broad, courtesy of Mrs Joan Broad and Mrs Penny Duke; additional material was provided by Matt Reid, Bill Nurse, Bill Stretch and Mrs M.C. 'Mimi' Thompson.

Of the nineteen diarists, thirteen have been identified, four of whom did not survive the war: Wing Commander Hugh William Eliot, DSO, DFC (killed 4 March 1945), Flight Lieutenant John William Yarra, DFM (killed 10 December 1942), Pilot Officer Gordon Russell Tweedale, DFM (killed 9 May 1942) and Flight Lieutenant Frank Thomas Holliman (killed 23 April 1945).

Anthony Rogers
Bavaria, 2016

Glossary and Abbreviations

AA, ack-ack	*Anti-aircraft*
A/c	*Aircraft*
Adj	*Adjutant*
AOC	*Air Officer Commanding*
ASI	*Air speed indicator*
Bandits	*Enemy aircraft*
Beaus	*Beaufighters*
Bofors	*40mm anti-aircraft gun*
C in C	*Commander in Chief*
CO	*Commanding Officer*
DH	*Direct hit*
E/a	*Enemy aircraft*
GAF	*German Air Force* (Luftwaffe)
GCI	*Ground controlled interception*
GL	*Gun laying*
Glen Martin	*Martin Maryland (aircraft)*
Gondar	*Fighter control*
Groupy	*Group Captain*
HSRL	*High speed rescue launch*
IFF	*Identification Friend or Foe*
IO	*Intelligence officer*
Kala	*Kalafrana*
LAA	*Light anti-aircraft*
Lamp:	*Lampedusa*
Lib	*Consolidated Liberator (aircraft)*
Maggy/Maggie	*Miles Magister (aircraft)*
MG, mg, m/g	*Machine-gun(s)*
ME	*Middle East*
MV	*Merchant vessel*
MNFU	*Malta Night Fighter Unit*
Ops/opps	*Operations*
ORB	*Operations Record Book*
OTU	*Operational training unit*

Pancake	*Return and land (an aircraft)*
Pant.	*Pantellaria*
Pongo	*Soldier (Army)*
PRU	*Photographic Reconnaissance Unit*
RDF	*Radio direction finding*
Recco	*Reconnaissance*
RNAS	*Royal Naval Air Service*
R/T	*Radio telephone*
Scramble	*Take off*
SFA	*Sweet Fanny Adams/sweet fuck-all*
Sing Sing	*Code name for Grand Harbour*
SNCO	*Senior non commissioned officer*
TA	*Target area*
Tally Ho!	*Enemy sighted!*
TO	*Take-off*
U/c, undercart	*Undercarriage*
U/s	*Unserviceable*
VHF	*Very high frequency*
Vic	*V-shape flight formation*
VNM	*Very near miss*
Wimpy	*Vickers Wellington (aircraft)*
Wingco	*Wing Commander*
Zambuk	*Code name for St Paul's Bay*

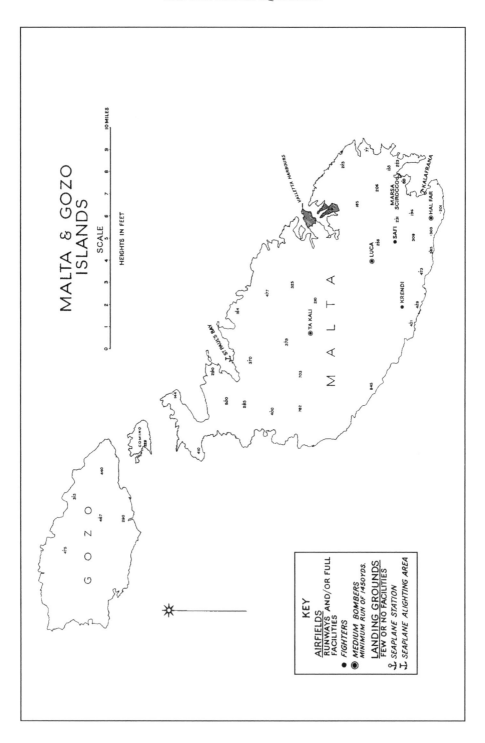

MALTA & GOZO
ISLANDS

SCALE
0   1   2   3   4   5   6   7   8   9   10 MILES
HEIGHTS IN FEET

GOZO
475
313
460
467
290

COMINO
289

440
144
290
350
285
400
782
703
370
379
164
477
385
290
845

ST PAUL'S BAY

MALTA

TA KALI

VALLETTA HARBOURS

KRENDI
LUCA
266
SAFI
231
MARSA
SCIROCCO
194
308
283
451
420
472
203
200
165
253
68
HAL FAR
KALAFRANA
206
185
225
71

KEY
AIRFIELDS
● RUNWAYS AND/OR FULL
   FACILITIES
◉ FIGHTERS
◉ MEDIUM BOMBERS
   MINIMUM RUN OF 1450 YDS.
LANDING GROUNDS
FEW OR NO FACILITIES
⚓ SEAPLANE STATION
⚓ SEAPLANE ALIGHTING AREA

Malta 1940–1941

Malta measures just seventeen and a half miles by eight and a quarter and is the largest of three main islands. These are situated in the middle of the Mediterranean south of Sicily and almost equidistant from Gibraltar in the western approaches and Suez in the east. The island, with a superb natural anchorage at Grand Harbour, has provided a succession of rulers with an enviably dominant position. In 1814 Malta freely became part of the British Empire, serving as an ideal base for the Royal Navy, the British Army and, eventually, for the Royal Air Force.

In the summer of 1939 the Committee of Imperial Defence approved a long-term air defence programme in recognition of Malta's strategic importance. The plan was designed to improve existing anti-aircraft capabilities and also took into account the requirement for fighter aircraft. Malta had already been provided with its first Radio Direction Finding (radar) station; there was an airfield at Hal Far and an airport at Ta' Qali and construction on a third aerodrome near Luqa was also well underway. In addition, there was a seaplane station at Kalafrana and seaplane facilities at Marsaxlokk and Saint Paul's Bay.

On 10 June 1940 Italy entered the war against Britain and France. Luqa aerodrome was soon to become operational, but there were still only thirty-four heavy anti-aircraft guns, eight Bofors and twenty-four searchlights available, together with several Royal Navy Gloster Sea Gladiators recently taken over by the RAF. At dawn on 11 June 2ᵃ Squadra Aerea of the Regia Aeronautica – the Italian Airforce – commenced operations against Malta, eighteen Macchi C.200s escorting some fifty-five Savoia Marchetti S.79s across the sixty miles of sea that separates the island from Sicily. Hal Far, Kalafrana and the Grand Harbour's Dockyard area were each targeted. The raiders were intercepted by three of Malta's Gladiators in this, the first of many aerial engagements during the next two and a half years.

The Fighter Flight's outdated biplanes were Malta's sole air defence for nearly two weeks following Italy's declaration of war. Eventually, they would be immortalised as 'Faith, Hope and Charity' (notwithstanding the fact that there were at least four aircraft on strength and others stored in crates). Reinforcements did not arrive until 21 June when two Hawker Hurricanes were assigned to the Fighter Flight after landing at Luqa en-route to the Middle East. On the 22nd six more Hurricanes arrived, three of which were retained in Malta.

1

It was also on 22 June that the RAF achieved its first victory when Flight Lieutenant George Burges, flying a Gladiator, was credited with destroying an S.79; there were two survivors, both of whom became prisoners of war. Air battles continued throughout July, with losses on both sides. On the morning of 3 July Flying Officer John Waters chased and shot down an S.79 before his own aircraft was attacked by FIAT CR 42s. Waters crash-landed as a result, but survived unhurt. His Hurricane was written-off. The first RAF fatality occurred on 16 July, when CR 42s shot down a Hurricane piloted by Flight Lieutenant Peter Keeble. On 31 July the only Malta Gladiator to be lost in combat crashed in flames following a dogfight over the south-east coast. Flying Officer Peter Hartley baled out into the sea from where he was rescued and rushed to Mtarfa Military Hospital suffering from severe burns.

The Maltese were only too aware that their island urgently needed more fighters and on 30 July 'The Fighter Plane Fund, Malta' was launched to enable the public to purchase their own aircraft for the islands' defence. In three months, enough was raised to pay for two Supermarine Spitfires. These were duly assembled and christened 'Malta' and 'Ghawdex', the latter after the Maltese name for the neighbouring island of Gozo. Ironically, neither machine ever reached Malta. Both were released to 74 Squadron in May 1941; W3210 'Malta' was reported missing during a sortie over northern France on 27 June 1941, while W3212 'Ghawdex' was eventually transferred to the Royal Navy.

Malta had been at war for nearly two months before an operation was launched to reinforce the island's fighter force. On 2 August twelve Hurricane Mark Is of 418 Flight left the aircraft carrier HMS Argus to be flown 380 miles to Luqa where they joined the surviving fighters to form 261 Squadron.

Malta was to experience a new mode of aerial attack when 96° Gruppo Bombardamento a Tuffo became the first Italian unit to be equipped with Junkers Ju 87Bs. Operations against the island commenced on 4 September with the dive-bombing of Delimara by five of the Italian-crewed Picchiatelli.

At the end of October 1940 Headquarters and Maintenance staff from RAF Luqa were dispatched to Ta' Qali preparatory to its transition as a fighter base.

On 17 November HMS Argus again dispatched to Malta twelve Hurricanes, this time accompanied by two Fleet Air Arm Blackburn Skuas. Tragically, eight of the RAF fighters ran out of fuel and seven pilots were lost (the other was rescued), while one of the Skuas was shot down by anti-aircraft fire after becoming hopelessly lost and flying over Sicily.

Malta's fighter pilots were extremely courageous men whose achievements cannot be over-emphasised, but in addition to its fighters, Malta also provided a base for other machines including flyingboats, bombers, torpedo and reconnaissance aircraft, all of which were kept operational due to the skill and dedication of the often overworked maintenance crews. Nor should one forget the magnificent efforts of the Royal Navy and Merchant Navy, or the heroism of Malta's land forces, particularly the anti-aircraft gunners. All would play a vital role throughout the siege.

Mussolini's offensive against Malta, the North African campaign and Italy's invasion of Greece finally led Hitler to send reinforcements to his ally in the Mediterranean. Towards the end of 1940 elements of the Luftwaffe's X Fliegerkorps, *commanded by* Generalleutnant Hans-Ferdinand Geisler, *began to arrive in Sicily from Norway. By mid-January 1941 the Luftwaffe had gathered in Sicily a formidable array of front-line aircraft that included Junkers Ju 87s and 88s, Heinkel He 111s and Messerschmitt Bf 110s. For Malta, the war was about to begin in earnest.*

In January 1941 Operation 'Excess' delivered to the island troops, supplies and a number of crated Hurricanes, though not without cost. The destroyer HMS Gallant *was severely damaged by a mine, while the carrier* Illustrious *was singled out for attack by the Germans during the debut of the* Luftwaffe *over the central Mediterranean. At 12:38 hours on 10 January, following an attack by Italian S.79s, German Ju 87 Stukas arrived overhead and moments later achieved the first of six direct hits. The assault lasted just six and a half minutes and was later described by the carrier's Captain Denis Boyd as very severe and brilliantly executed.*

Despite further attacks by both the Regia Aeronautica *and the* Luftwaffe, *during which she was struck yet again, the badly damaged* Illustrious *was able to limp into Grand Harbour during the evening of the 10th. Incredibly, the carrier was virtually ignored by the enemy until 16 January, when she was targeted by a combined force of some forty-four Ju 87s and seventeen Ju 88s escorted by Bf 110s, CR 42s and Macchi C.200s. But the defenders, having learned much from previous raids by Italian dive-bombers, had prepared a formidable 'box barrage'. The attackers also had to contend with the island's fighters, supplemented by Fulmars off the* Illustrious. *It is recorded that during one of the raids, a Fulmar followed a bomber through the barrage to level out at only fifteen feet before shooting down the German machine just beyond the harbour entrance.*

Two days later, the German bombers returned, this time concentrating on the airfields at Hal Far and Luqa. On Sunday 19 January Illustrious *was again subjected to a day of intensive bombing, with the attackers having to face a terrifying repetition of Thursday's barrage.*

On the 23rd the carrier slipped her moorings and quietly left Grand Harbour on the first stage of her journey to the shipyards of the United States. Her remaining Fulmars stayed as welcome reinforcements for the island's air force.

Events in Libya led to the departure between January and March of a number of Axis aircraft from Sicily (though some Ju 88s would return in early April). Early in February Messerschmitt Bf 109Es of 7/JG 26 were also transferred from Germany to Gela, in Sicily, under the command of Oberleutnant Joachim Müncheberg, *whose outstanding performance had already gained him twenty-three victories and earned him the coveted* Ritterkreuz *(Knight's Cross).*

At the end of January, six more Hurricanes arrived in Malta from North Africa. However, the Hurricane was no match for the faster, cannon-equipped Messerschmitt Bf 109E. During the next four months, 7/JG 26 would claim at least forty-two air victories, twenty of which were credited to Müncheberg (including one during his unit's brief involvement in the invasion of Yugoslavia) and all without a single operational loss.

Notwithstanding German efforts to neutralise Malta, the island was still able to provide the Royal Navy with a base from which to strike at Axis shipping, thus creating a constant drain on the enemy's Mediterranean supply routes.

The island's fighter strength was sustained by occasional reinforcements from North Africa coupled with the constant attention of RAF ground personnel. On 3 April Malta received its first Hurricane IIAs in the first of three major naval operations up to the end of May when the carriers Ark Royal *and* Furious *flew off a total of eighty-one Hurricanes, although many were to continue to the desert after refuelling. During this time – mid 1941 – the air forces on both sides in the central Mediterranean underwent some reorganising. April and May saw the arrival in Malta of the first Blenheim and Beaufighter units. Number 185 Squadron, which had been disbanded in the United Kingdom the previous year, was also re-formed as a fighter unit from pilots of the resident 261 Squadron.*

Book 1

185 SQUADRON.

30th April. 1941.

The following is a list of pilots posted from 261 Squadron to Hal Far for the purpose of forming a new fighter squadron to be known as No. 185 Squadron. These were commanded by F/Lt. P.W.O. Mould. D.F.C., and were divided into Flights as follows.

X. Flight.	Y. Flight.
F/O Eliot.	F/O Westmacott
F/Lt. Jeffries	F/Lt. Hancock.
P/O Hamilton	P/O Bailey
P/O Innes.	P/O Thompson.
P/O Hall	P/O DREDGE.
Sgt Bamberger.	Sgt Branson
Sgt Ottey	Sgt Hodson
Sgt Walmsley	Sgt Jolly.
Sgt Wynne	P/O Gray
Sgt Burton	

All aircraft in the Squadron are to be Mark II Hurricanes and during the afternoon these were all ferried over from Ta-Kali without incident. The Squadron goes on "readiness" for the first time at dawn tomorrow and much organization has been going on to prepare for this event.

At the moment we are known as "C" Flight 261 Squadron but we are all looking forward to the time when our new number is officially allotted to us. and we can become the rivals of our friends at Ta Kali.

1941

185 SQUADRON

Wednesday 30 April

The following is a list of pilots posted from 261 Squadron to Hal Far for the purpose of forming a new fighter squadron to be known as No. 185 Squadron. These were commanded by F/LT P.W.O. Mould DFC, and were divided into Flights as follows.

X Flight.	Y Flight.
F/O Eliot.	F/O Westmacott.
F/LT Jeffries	F/LT Hancock.
P/O Hamilton	P/O Bailey
P/O Innes.	P/O Thanson [sic].
P/O Hall	P/O DREDGE.
Sgt Bamberger.	Sgt Branson
Sgt Ottey	Sgt Hodson
Sgt Walmsley	Sgt Jolly.
Sgt Wynne	P/O Gray
Sgt Burton	

All aircraft in the Squadron are to be Mark II Hurricanes and during the afternoon these were all ferried over from Ta-Kali without incident. The Squadron goes on "readiness" for the first time at dawn tomorrow and much organization has been going on to prepare for this event.

At the moment we are known as "C" Flight 261 Squadron but we are all looking forward to the time when our new number is officially allotted to us and we can become the rivals of our friends at Ta Kali.

Thursday 1 May

Our first day of operations. During the morning some ME 109s were seen but they had the advantage of height and sun but made no effort to attack.

During the early evening, the Squadron was on patrol and was attacked by 6 ME 109s. These again had the advantage of height and caused us to break up in all directions. Unfortunately Sgt Walmsley didn't move quite fast enough and had to bale out as a result of damage to his aeroplane. P/O Innes was injured in his foot but not seriously. This was not discovered until he started to climb out of his cockpit. As he trod on the injured foot, he gave a loud howl and subsided onto the firing button which had been left to fire position and a hail of lead was forthwith projected over to hangars much to the alarm and consternation of all.

Taken all round – not a brilliant start but we hope better may be expected!

Friday 2 May

Bad luck again. An unfortunate accident this morning which no one can explain and which was just one of those things which happen at times for no apparent reason. The loss of Sgt Ottey under these circumstances is mourned by all. *[The ORB of RAF Station, Hal-Far records that Sergeant Ottey's Hurricane 'crashed from great height on approaching aerodrome and burst into flames. Pilot killed outright.' Sergeant Raymond Ottey has no known grave and is commemorated on the Malta memorial at Floriana.]*

Nothing of note occurred when the Squadron was scrambled *[ordered to take off]* on two occasions. Our aircraft situation is not too good but we still have six operating. Oh for the day when there will be twelve or even more.

P/O Hamilton did a forced landing from 32.000 ft when his engine stopped going. He got in all right and there are rumours that he had been flying on a gravity tank containing one quarter of a gallon of petrol! Needless to say this was vigorously denied by the gentleman in question!

Saturday 3 May

A little success at last. For some time the regular visits of Ju 88 on reconnaissance has been a source of irritation to all. Today one was probably destroyed by F/LT Jeffries and P/O Hall. Although it was not confirmed, the presence of a search party some time afterwards suggests that it did not "return to its base". P/O Hall's aircraft was hit by an AA *[anti-aircraft]* shell aimed at the E/A *[enemy aircraft]*. In spite of this and the fact that he was wounded in his left arm, he managed to land safely and so save his aeroplane. We all congratulate him on a very good show, and also F/LT Jeffries as well for being the first to draw blood for the new Squadron. We hope there will be many more to come – or rather go the same way.

The remainder of the day proved uneventful and a lively game of pontoon was indulged in, to "while away the weary hours".

Sunday 4 May

The weather has taken a turn for the worse which is perhaps a good thing! It at least gives us a little breathing space to sort one or two things out.

It must be the first time in some weeks that a day has passed without a scramble. This fact needless to say is not bemoaned by anyone, and a quiet game of cards constituted our day's activity.

Monday 5 May

Two ME 109s were seen skulking about at fairly low altitude by F/O Westmacott. These were pursued for some way until they finally disappeared into cloud. The weather is still "ten-tenths" [overcast] and the Hun apparently had no wish to play for the rest of the day.

We are still maintaining six aircraft on readiness which says much for the efficiency of our ground crews and maintenance party who are under the very competent supervision of Sgt Westbrook.

MAY 5th.

SQUADRON PILOTS ON "ACTIVE" LIST IS NOW AS FOLLOWS. TWO NEW MEMBERS HAVING BEEN RECRUITED FROM TA-KALI.

F/LT MOULD. DFC

X FLIGHT.		Y Flight.
F/O ELIOT.		F/O WESTMACOTT
F/LT JEFFRIES		F/LT HANCOCK.
P/O HAMILTON.		P/O BAILEY
Sgt BAMBERGER.		P/O THOMPSON.
Sgt BURTON		P/O GRAY.
Sgt WYNNE		Sgt BRANSON
Sgt VARDY	ARRIVED FROM	Sgt JOLLY
Sgt SHEPPARD	261 SQDN 5.5.41.	Sgt HODSON.

Tuesday 6 May

It never rains but it pours! After our previous misfortunes we were at least hoping to turn the tables on our friends across in Sicily. Today they certainly did not mean us to! A fairly small bombing force comprising 6 He 111s was escorted by a considerably larger fighter force said to number between thirty and forty ME 109s. The boys got amongst them but were hopelessly outnumbered and only as could be expected, we suffered in consequence.

Although we lost four aircraft, only one pilot was injured. P/O Dredge, after a gallant attempt to force land after being shot up, unfortunately over-ran the aerodrome and crashed. His aircraft burst into flames but the prompt action of the fire tender crew probably saved him from much worse.

Sgt Branson and P/O Gray both baled out one in the sea and the latter on the roof of a house! Both are quite unhurt and returned to the Squadron during the evening, in high fettle.

At about six o'clock in the evening, the Hun again tried his hand. This time, with only three serviceable aircraft in the air, F/O Westmacott, F/LT Hancock and P/O Bailey managed to intercept the bombers before the escorting ME 109s had fully woken up to what was going on. A certain amount of damage was inflicted before our three Hurricanes had to break off and deal with the escort. One HE 111 was definitely seen to be damaged and a second was possibly damaged.

This time we sustained no damage ourselves and altogether, after the morning show, it was indeed a very good effort.

Wednesday 7 May

During the morning one of our three remaining aeroplanes broke a tail wheel and so now we only have two rather lonely looking Hurricanes sitting outside our dispersal building.

The weather has gone back to "ten-tenths" again more or less and what with that and our small number of aeroplanes everyone is having an easy time.

May 7th.

```
HAL FAR TA KALI
NR5            4

GR63          TO  TA  KALI  HAL  FAR
              FROM HQ MED
OPS22 7/5 PERSONAL FROM AOC. I SHOULD LIKE C FLIGHT 261 SQDN TO KNOW
THAT I CONSIDER LYGON AIRCRAFT PUT UP A MAGNIFICENT SHOW ON TWO
OCCASIONS YESTERDAY AGAINST VERY HEAVY ODDS. ALTHOUGH INJURIES
TO PERSONNEL AND LOSSES OF AIRCRAFT WERE UNFORTUNATE THE SPIRIT
DISPLAYED IS A CONSIDERABLE COMPENSATION AND SHOULD UNDOUBTEDLY
ENSURE SUCCESS IN THE FUTURE AGAINST THE ENEMY= = = 0735 GMT

AM      VA  R0755  GMT     HF        TK       FONE PLEASE OFF
```

The above signal was received from the AOC [Air Officer Commanding] today in recognition of our effort against superior forces yesterday. It is appreciated by all personnel and is very encouraging to the pilots.

Thursday 8 May

We woke up to find pouring rain and the Squadron was put to 15 minutes availability. Most people took advantage of this and a general exodus towards Valetta was observed.

During the evening a party developed in the Monico when F/O Eliot put up one of his infrequent "blacks" and got horribly drunk!

P/O Hamilton and several others also appeared to be in a bad way in the Mess and altogether a good time was had by all.

Friday 9 May

Large convoy in today but weather is still very thick.

During a scramble in the morning, P/O Hamilton found a stray brace of Ju 87s which he warmed up to the extent of several hundred rounds of ammunition before they made off in cloud. He was credited with one probably destroyed. On his way home he sighted a submarine in close proximity to some of our destroyers and just to show there was no ill feeling he delivered a burst at its conning tower.

The submarine promptly crash-dived with great speed so it may be assumed it was of a hostile nature.

The rest of the day brought forth nothing and the weather is still bad. We were pleased to hear about the arrival of over a hundred troops for our new Squadron and some more aeroplanes which we badly need.

Saturday 10 May

This morning, it came to light that the submarine which was shot up by "Hamish" yesterday has been identified as HMS Utmost! Presumably no damage was done to it as no mention of the attack was made by the ship in question. However we really must put a stop to this indiscriminate shooting up of under-water craft!

We heard with great delight during the afternoon that nine Beaufighters were over strafing Catania and Comiso. This is the first time this has ever happened and is a sign that Malta is at last taking the offensive and paying off a few old scores.

Hardly had the "Beaus" returned when half a dozen ME 109s came to return the compliment and while five engaged "X-ray" Squadron, one detached himself and carrying out a very nice dive attack, succeeded in completely writing off a Sunderland which was moored in the Bay off Kalafrana.

Our Squadron did not engage this time and there were no casualties to either side.

Sunday 11 May

Early this morning the Squadron was scrambled and an aircraft was sighted flying low just off Delimara Point. Anti aircraft bursts were seen in the vicinity of this aircraft, and led by P/O Hamilton the boys gave chase. For twenty minutes, having pulled everything in sight to try and get an extra mile per hour, the chase continued. After nearly a hundred miles very little progress had been made and the leader gave it up.

Sgt Wynne however with great gusto continued the chase single handed and eventually closed to firing range. After putting all his ammunition into what he supposed to be a Ju 88, he returned to land and reported he had damaged the aircraft in question.

All well and good – one probable Ju 88 to the credit of the Squadron – but more to come! Some little time later an irate Glen Martin [*Maryland*] crew arrived looking for the Hurricane who had chased them half way to Crete! After a good deal of explaining and apologies everything was settled and a party ensued during which everyone concerned became very light hearted about the whole issue.

The evening ended with handshakes all round and a promise from the Glen Martin crew to enter in their log book – "Affiliation exercises with Hurricanes"! Needless to say not one hole was shot anywhere in the Glen Martin!

Monday 12 May

Today the Squadron is officially born and we are now a separate unit to 261 Squadron. Signals of good wishes for the future were received – one from the AOC which appears opposite [*see below*].

Although on its first day, the Squadron did quite a lot of flying, no engagements took place, and we passed a fairly peaceful day. During the evening a party got going in celebration, and our CO [*Commanding Officer*] made a good start by getting very drunk!

```
HAL FAR
HQ MED NR3

GR28                    TO:- HAL FAR
                            FROM:- HQ MED
OPS49 12/5/41. PERSONAL FROM A.O.C.   .    PLEASE GIVE O.C. 185 SQDN
MY VERY BEST WISHES FOR A MOST SUCCESSFUL RECORD FOR HIS SQUADRON
WHICH IS OFFICIALLY BORN TODAY = = = = = = = = = = = = = = = = = 0735 GMT

PEGG    VA    V    R 0802    GMT    ES    VA
```

```
HAL FAR
HQ MED  NR7                   I M P O R T A N T

GR84                         TO:- KALAFRANA   HAL FAR   LUQA   TA/KALI
                             FROM :- HQ MED

O: 142 12/5 . FURTHER PARA 3 THIS HEADQUARTERS INTERNAL CIRCULAR
MEMORANDA SERIAL NUMBER 38 DATED MAY 3RD . NUMBER 185 SQUADRON
```

FORMED AT R.A.F. STATION HAL FAR WITH EFFECT FROM MAY 12TH FROM
"C" FLIGHT NUMBER 261 SQUADRON WHICH CEASED TO EXIST WITH
EFFECT FROM SAME DATE . NUMBER 185 SQUADRON IS PLACED UNDER THE
ORDERS OF THE OFFICER COMMANDING R.A.F. STATION HAL FAR FOR
OPERATIONS AND ADMINISTRATIONS . F/ LT P.W.O. MOULD IS APPOINTED
TO THE COMMAND OF NUMBER 185 SQUADRON WITH EFFECT FROM DATE
OF FORMATION = = = = = = = = = = = = = 1230. G.M.T.

Tuesday 13 May

We are now confronted with a problem which so far has not been met
in Malta. Our friends the ME 109s are now dropping bombs and instead
of doing their bombing as before with Ju 88s etc, we now have to contend
with large formations of ME 109s some fighters – some bombers. These all
become fighters as soon as they release their bombs and it is going to be a
tricky problem knowing just how to deal with the situation.

During the afternoon F/O Westmacott when signalling the rest of his
formation to close up suddenly found they had square wing tips. At this
moment things began to happen and his aeroplane tried to do all sorts of
things which were quite unusual and so he thought it was time to aban-
don ship.

Fortunately he landed safely and only suffered from a slight injury to
his arm.

Wednesday 14 May

Two large raids by ME 109s were made during the day. No casualties
were sustained during the first one which occurred about 08.00 hrs. F/LT
Jeffries was observed to be having some fun and games with two ME 109s
at very low altitude. In spite of their determined efforts, he managed to
outwit them and had not so much as one hole when he landed.

Our second party was at 4.40 in the afternoon. This time luck was
against us and as usual the odds were very heavy. It is with great sorrow
that we put on record the loss of one of Malta's oldest and most experienced fighter boys – P/O Hamilton. Known throughout the Island and
among his friends as "Hamish" he was the only representative of the Auxiliary Air Force and probably the most popular member of the Squadron
both in "185" and in "261". He had destroyed five enemy aircraft and we
shall miss him very much both as a friend and as a leader.

Thursday 15 May

After the usual early morning "recco" [reconnaissance] which of course
we failed to catch, there was a quiet pause after which things began to
happen. To start with the Squadron could only produce two of its four
aircraft in a serviceable state.

At about noon a plot of "plus 24" appeared and our aircraft were
scrambled to rendezvous with 261 Squadron over their base. After about

ten minutes large numbers of ME 109s appeared – some carrying bombs, some not.

After they had done their stuff, the Hurricanes came in for some attention and before long another of ours was shot down. This time it was Sgt Wynne to go. Sgt Bamberger who was leading was lucky enough to get away with it.

Once again we have to express our regret at the loss of a very valuable pilot who although he had only been with us a short time had showed promise of future success.

During the afternoon S/Ldr Mould as he now is and several other pilots went for a talk with the "powers that be".

It was agreed that under the circumstances we could only be strictly on the defensive against enemy fighters until such time as the Squadron was up to full strength.

Friday 16 May

This morning our aerodrome was bombed by a fair sized formation of ME 109s.

Various records for sprinting were established and F/O Eliot rather shook the Sergeants Mess by hurdling over a large stone wall on his way to earth.

Only three bombs actually landed on the aerodrome and no damage was caused with the exception of one empty hangar which got a few holes in it.

This was all too close for our liking and we trust the Hun will in future confine his activities to other spheres.

Saturday 17 May

This morning a "recco" was nearly caught! The wretched wireless decided to stop working at the critical moment and rather spoilt things. These little things are so annoying when they happen at just the wrong moment.

Two funerals were attended this morning by members of the Squadron. A very depressing business but everything went smoothly and no hitches occurred much to the relief of those present.

Owing to the fact that two of our three aeroplane [sic] were due for thirty hour inspections the Squadron was released at 13.00 hrs for the rest of the day. Obviously a party was indicated especially as it was a Saturday.

Most of the officers went to Valetta where they were entertained by our American friend Lt/Cdr Moorhouse US Navy who is spending a few days in Malta and whom we have got to know very well.

The celebrations were mostly in honour of the birth of a daughter to the wife of our CO S/Ldr Mould. This bouncing infant weighs 8½ pounds and apparently is taking after her father in size!

Sunday 18 May

Today was one of the quieter days again. Everybody of course likes these days very much and it is noticeable that towards the end of a "readiness" period when there has been no "scramble" the "morale" of the pilots is very noticeably high!

We are expecting a busy time in a few days as it is rumoured that large numbers of Hurricanes are on their way to go to Middle East. It is hoped that the Huns don't get wise – or life won't be worth living here when they arrive! After the ME 109s bombing the aerodrome a day or two ago we no longer have people standing about gazing up and saying "Oh – it's only another fighter sweep!"

As we ourselves have so few aeroplanes, let us hope that this anticipated stream of Hurricanes will bring forth a pleasant surprise for 185 Squadron.

Monday 19 May

Our numbers grow smaller and smaller as the days go by. We are back to operating two aeroplanes now which are the sad remnants of eighteen Hurricane IIs which have been at Malta.

The day passed peacefully enough and except for two standing patrols nothing happened. It appears that No. 249 Squadron are on their way to reinforce us which is very good news. We have long been in need of some new blood on the Island and we wish them every success when they commence operating.

P/O Hall and F/LT Westmacott have both been along to see us from Imtarfa where they are at the moment in residence while having sundry small pieces of shrapnel removed from their persons.

Tuesday 20 May

Today, a large number of enemy aircraft approached the Island and everyone was expecting the usual fighter-bomber raid. The plot which started as +20 and ended up as +50 did not however cross the Island, (sighs of relief from those in the air!) and nothing materialised.

What the Hun is playing at is very difficult to surmise but he seems to be in the habit of doing this sort of thing – all of which is of course is [sic] very unnerving to our "gallant pilots" who suffer very frequently from an ailment known as "twitch"!

Later in the evening a plot of "+15" did come across and planted some nifty bombs on Luqa. 261 Squadron were engaged and suffered one casualty but our aircraft were so high that they were not able to pick up the raiders (They must have been very high!) F/LT Hancock who was leading ran out of main tanks and couldn't turn on reserve as his petrol cock had stuck. After wrestling with it several times he decided to land with no engine. This is always a bit tricky and as luck would have it, he "pranged" neatly on a wall at the edge of the aerodrome, and did his aircraft no good at all although luckily he was unhurt himself.

On 21 May Hurricanes of 213, 229 and 249 Squadrons took off from aircraft carriers for the Middle East. When they landed to refuel at Malta, those in 249 Squadron learned that they would be staying as replacements for 261 Squadron whose pilots then departed leaving their old Mk Is in exchange for 249's new fighters.

Wednesday 21 May

This was a great day as 48 Hurricanes went through on their way to Middle East. We were all very busy with refuelling both aircraft and pilots and it was a great feat that although the first visitor did not land until nearly 09.45 they were all ready and on their way by half past one.

No raids occurred to cause confusion except a solitary "recco" first thing in the morning. All the Hurricanes reached their destination safely with one exception.

We are pleased to hear that most of 249 Squadron pilots are here, and their place has been taken by members of 261 Squadron who took their aircraft on to Egypt for them. All that remains now is for some more Hurricane IIs to arrive for both us and 249.

The present situation as regards aircraft is that we are left with about thirty odd Hurricanes (MK I) which we shall fly alternately with 249 Squadron for the next week or two.

Thursday 22 May

For the first time 185 Squadron operated as a complete unit of twelve aircraft flying from Ta-Kali. Owing to bad weather no flying actually took place but we had hopes of trying out a new formation for patrol which we intend to use if it is found successful.

249 Squadron came to readiness for the first time today but were not initiated owing to the continuation of the bad weather. What with that and the fact that the [German] invasion of Crete is in full swing, the Huns seem to be leaving us alone for a time. How long this period of comparative quiet will last we don't know, but the longer the better.

Friday 23 May

The weather slightly improved today and we were able to practice the new formation. It seems moderately successful but needs a good bit of practice before everyone is "word perfect". When we have really got it "taped" it should provide the enemy with a very difficult target to attack besides giving us the maximum amount of flexibility and enabling us to keep a very good look out in all directions. Added to this is the ease in which all the formations of the formation can break as violently as they like without losing height.

No operational flying was done for the second day in succession which is a good thing as we are having the chance to do some much needed practice flying.

249 Squadron had a short scramble but nothing was engaged. They seem to have some big ideas about what they are going to do and we only hope that they don't have any surprises in store for them! We of course also have ideas and the same applies to us. With the pilots we have at the moment, none of whom lack experience or ability we should indeed do well given the average amount of luck.

Saturday 24 May

While we were up on a practice this morning a plot came on the board and we got an opportunity to see how the formation would work under actual patrol conditions when looking about and searching are necessary. We were all pleasantly surprised and as soon as it was announced over the R/T [radio telephone] that some ME 109s were on the way, everyone came to life with a bang and the formation went like clockwork.

Sunday 25 May

While on patrol this morning a small number of ME 109s were seen. As there was 10/10th cloud at about 15.000 feet and we were sitting just below it, the enemy after appearing suddenly out of this disappeared back into it almost as quickly. If nothing else we feel we won a "moral victory"! Our present system of operation, involves a daily trip to and from Ta-Kali but as we only do the morning stand-by it enables us to get into Valletta fairly early most evenings where a good time is had by all.

Most of the officer pilots can be found in the "Monico" bar almost any time and no doubt the sergeants have their pet haunts as well. Occasionally the weekly dances at Sliema are attended with the usual result that our squadron car brings half the people back to Valletta! The record for a "Ford 8" must be held by us with eleven up which would take some beating.

Monday 26 May

The Squadron was only scrambled once this morning and nothing was encountered. The squadron air drill and formation is improving day by day and it is quite a pleasure to watch 185 take off and land [and] another day or two should see us as perfect as is practically possible.

After the Squadron had stood down and 249 had taken over, an incident occurred which only goes to show that we should be on the "qui vive" the whole time we are on the aerodrome. Three ME 109s detached themselves from a formation of about 9 aircraft and the main part of this went out northwards. The three which had detached themselves were not detected by the "cuckoo" and when they came down and shot up the aerodrome not an aircraft was in the air. It was very lucky that only two persons were injured and then not seriously. Several aircraft were badly damaged and two written off completely. It was some time before order was restored on the aerodrome and sundry fires were got under control. Needless to say No 249 Squadron were not a little shaken by this but given time they will get accustomed to these little things which occur fairly frequently in Malta!

Tuesday 27 May

In spite of the number of aircraft rendered unserviceable by yesterday's low flying attack we were able to put up eleven aircraft when the Squadron was scrambled just after nine o'clock this morning. Nothing was engaged although one bomber accompanied by the usual bevy of ME 109s was seen far above. We of course had not sufficient height to do anything about it and after their departure we returned and landed. It was noted that the squadron closed up very appreciably upon sighting the enemy! We have now got our "patrol" formation going as well as can ever be expected and it seems to be a very satisfactory formation from all points of view. However it has yet to be tried in action but we hope in the near future that we shall have the opportunity of doing this.

Wednesday 28 May

It has now been decided that the two squadrons will operate on alternate days from Hal Far and Ta Kali. This is presumably to fox the Hun (?) (Is such a thing possible?) Anyway we turned out at dawn this morning and had only one scramble which was never more than a few troop carriers on their way to Libya. 249 Squadron came by road and took over at 9 o'clock for the remainder of the day giving us an opportunity for a little shopping and so forth during the morning and afternoon. A little quiet drinking was also indulged in during the latter part of the evening.

Thursday 29 May

There was little aerial activity today. The Hun must be throwing everything into a last desperate effort to gain Crete. The fate of that Island seems assured now and it cannot hope to hold out any longer, against the weight of air attack which is being employed against it.

The only visit the ME 109s paid us today was very short and at one time it looked as though we might have been in a position to attack. We put on our best aggressive air and with great determination pointed our noses in the direction of twenty ME 109s which were slightly above on our beam. As usual we lacked height and the enemy pushed off without more ado. However if we had been three thousand feet higher it might have been a different story.

Friday 30 May

We turned out for dawn stand-by with thirteen serviceable aircraft which included our two remaining MK IIs. No scrambles occurred and we went off duty at 9 o'clock feeling that a hard day's work had been well done!

Having nothing to do for the rest of the day, the squadron went en masse on a swimming party. A very enjoyable picnic lunch was packed into the Humber utility car – that invaluable vehicle of which we are now the possessors, and led by S/Ldr Mould we made for Ghain-Tuffehia [sic: Ghajn Tuffieha] where we made ourselves very sore for the next few days with sunburn.

The party ended up in the evening at the Monico for a "quickie" before finally going home feeling slightly fitter than usual.

Saturday 31 May

Except for a miserable "+3" which came on the board this morning we again had a "hard day's work"! It was pretty agonising wearing a parachute over our burnt shoulders and turning round in the cock pit was almost impossible.

During the morning, after we had come off readiness much time was spent in dabbing sunburn lotion on each other's backs. The stuff doesn't seem to do much good and it will be a few days before we lose that light pink colour which indicates one's first exposure to the sun.

Just lately we have been having a bout of sickness amongst the Squadron. Luckily it has never affected two people at a time but even two off the list makes it difficult. Fortunately all our ailments have been of a very minor nature and have usually only lasted for two days or so.

On 1 June Air Vice-Marshal Forster Maynard, Malta's Air Officer Commanding since the start of hostilities, was relieved by Air Vice-Marshal Hugh Lloyd. A few days later, Malta was reinforced with Hurricane IIs and an influx of pilots from 46 Squadron. Additional Hurricanes, including the latest four-cannon IICs, arrived during the month. The Allied build-up in Malta coincided with the run-down of the Luftwaffe *in Sicily. Most of its aircraft were withdrawn in May for Operation 'Barbarossa', the German invasion of Russia. In June 7/JG 26 also left, flying south to Libya.*

Sunday 1 June

We again did dawn stand-by this morning. Four of us chased off after a lone troop carrier which was going South fairly slowly. After getting within a few miles of it we unfortunately failed to locate it and as visibility was very bad, we returned to the Island.

Another Squadron of Hurricane IIs is expected shortly and we are wondering what is going to happen to us. At present we have no aeroplanes we can call our own and if the new Squadron came they will not want to part with theirs.

During the past week, not one engagement has taken place although the enemy has been sighted several times. 249 Squadron probably still think this is a rest-cure but so far they have been lucky. Any moment now things are liable to brighten up!

Monday 2 June

We are now starting night flying. Last night was the first day and owing to weather nothing happened.

Two small plots came on during the morning when the Squadron was standing by. It was scrambled and it is worth noting that the standard of air drill is now splendid. To watch the Squadron get off the ground is a real pleasure to one with an eye for such things.

Tuesday 3 June

S/L Mould and F/LT Jeffries held the fort during the night. One or two illuminations were held but the CO had bad luck and was not able to get to grips.

We are now dispersing aircraft up at SAFI which is a landing strip some miles from the aerodrome. This means that whichever Squadron is on at dawn has the job of going by road to this strip and collecting aeroplanes. This job is not looked upon with favour by those who have to get up half an hour early and wait until nearly six o'clock for their eggs and bacon!

We again went off duty at 9 o'clock having done very little to earn our day's pay except recline on a bed for a few hours!

Wednesday 4 June

The Squadron carried out an interception this morning which for Malta is almost an unknown thing. Some ME 109s came over the Island while we were still climbing up and after they had passed over, we climbed out in a North Westerly direction while the bandits [enemy aircraft] were orbiting South of the Island. We were by very good controlling able to cut across their path home at a greater height than they were. All this occurred about fifty miles off the Island which shows what can be done by first class controlling. After having got so far the enemy slipped through our fingers because of bad visibility and the fact that when sighted they were nearly over Sicily going in the opposite direction to ourselves. We were most disappointed but very encouraged by the fact that we did actually see them at any rate, and the next time – woe betide the poor ME 109s if they find themselves below us!

Thursday 5 June

Nothing occurred during the night owing to weather and the Squadron went to Ta Kali to operate this morning from 09.00 until lunch time. A quiet time was had and the usual game of cards took place.

It has been noted lately that large sums of money are at stake and several people seem to have lost rather a lot (notably the writer). The CO seldom takes part in this heavy gambling, but then he is a married man!

The usual flapping is going on at the moment as the next batch of Hurricanes are arriving tomorrow. We hope that the usual hot reception will not be forthcoming for them.

Sgt Bamberger is leaving us for a very well earned rest. Until his return to UK, he has been appointed to a position of "chief overseer of maintenance crews" at Ta Kali. Just what this involves no one quite knows. We all wish Sgt Bamberger a speedy return home after a stay in Malta which has hardly been a bed of roses.

The above is the last entry by the original diarist, Flight Lieutenant H.W. 'Chubby' Eliot. Subsequently, various writers assumed responsibility for the diary for several days or weeks at a time. It has not been possible to identify each individual, but Sergeant H. 'Stanley' Burton appears to have compiled most of the following entries up to the middle of August 1941.

June 6th and general report up to the end of the month. We have to record that F/Lt Eliot and Sgt Bamberger have now left us. The former to control us from the mine of Malta *[underground war rooms, Valletta]*, the latter squeezing his war trophies into a Sunderland and going home to his grey haired mother in a place called England – said to be a country in Europe still unoccupied by the enemy.

Both have done sterling work. Mr Eliot as a Flight commander showing great enthusiasm and ability in leading against the Hun in the sun and Sgt Bamberger as an unassuming and proficient pilot always ready to do more than his share and au fait with all the mannerisms of 109s.

The next three weeks – waiting for reinforcements – can be summarised as routine night flying patrols against the odd Italian bomber.

Coming over in small numbers at about 18000 ft they caused great distress to the fish round the Gem of the Med – tho' they have hit the island once or twice and helped the farmers to scatter the good seed over the land.

It has been proved conclusively that the IFF *[Identification Friend or Foe]* does explode when a Hurricane is forced into a hangar. Sgt Burton spent a fortnight in Mtarfa thinking out the results of this expensive experiment and the CO does not wish for any repetition as results were quite successful.

Most nights Gremlins were active on the flare path; not only setting fire to P/O Gray's A/C *[aircraft]* (he was not smoking in the cock-pit at that time), but also attacking with vans and backs of lorries the tail units of the CO's and F/Lt Jeffries' planes.

Other incidents – obviously emanating from tampering with the powers of Darkness – such as Sgt Algernon (I've been here six months) Hodson's preference for landing at Luca and P/O Gray making an approach on the Sunderland flare path in the Bay have filled in the time.

Coincident with the rise of the moon other squadrons braved the night air and dispersed at Sarfi [sic: Safi]. They will shortly take their share in night flying and it is hoped that 185 will meet their quota of Macchis on returning to day operations.

Sgt Jolly destroyed a Macchi 200; P/O Bailey and Sgt Sheppard shared in the destruction of others. These three have returned to us after temporary loan to 46 and 249 Sqdns.

Undated:

No 185. [(Malta) Night Fighter] Squadron!!

S/Ldr Mould

'A' Flight	'B' Flight
F/Lt Jeffries.	F/Lt Hancock
P/O Gray.	P/O Thompson.
Sgt Burton.	Sgt Branson
Sgt Vardy.	Sgt Hodson.

We are occasionally reminded that F/Lt Hancock can claim the distinction of being the only pilot to have an engagement at night ... naturally.

Considering the usual standard of searchlight effectiveness we were unlucky to operate when "illuminations" were rare and brief.

Friday 27 June and Monday 30 June

About 30 planes (some with 4 hat racks sticking out in front) landed on the Gem of the Med.

Since the diary only respects the truth it must be written that the landings at Hal Far were bloody. Gremlins pushed up and pulled down the surface of the 'drome as the pilots 'held off' and maintenance crews were seen dashing their heads against brick walls. Technical reasons were given and accepted for the landings made.

In July twelve Hurricane IIs were allocated for a new night fighter unit. Malta's defences were further improved following the arrival of extra troops and the delivery of more AA guns and ammunition.

Tuesday 1 July

Sqdn Ldr Mould had an informal chat with all the pilots today; giving 'gen' peculiar to the Gem of the Med and replying to questions of the new pilots who have been detailed to flights as per the opposite page *[see below].*

Afterwards F/Lt Jeffries and F/Lt Hancock collected their respective flights and had a pow-wow on various subjects – mostly about flying. The diarist listened to learned discussion on aerodynamics etc. until a word seemingly like 'Shag' – this from a notorious oil-splashed motorcyclist – jarred on his cultured ear and he blushingly retired.

There was a successful practice flight by 'B' Flight in the afternoon. Although it is too early to form an opinion; the formation was quite good in the air for a first trip, – the take off not too bad and the landings far too irregular.

Undated:

<u>No 185 Squadron</u>

<u>Squadron Commander</u>

× <u>S/Ldr P.W.O. Mould. DFC</u>

<u>"A" Flight</u>		<u>"B" Flight</u>	
F/Lt Jeffries.	×	F/Lt Hancock.	×
F/Lt Pike.	×	P/O Thompson.	×
P/O Gray.	×	P/O Bailey.	×
P/O Veitch.	×	P/O Winton.	×
P/O Allardice.		P/O Barnwell.	×
P/O Oliver.		P/O Woodsend.	×
Sgt Jolly.	×	Sgt Hodson.	×
Sgt Sheppard.	×	Sgt Branson.	×
Sgt Vardy.	×	Sgt Nurse.	×
Sgt Sutherland.		Sgt Ream.	×
Sgt Bates.		Sgt Alderson.	
Sgt Hunton.		Sgt Westcott.	
Sgt Hayes.	×	Sgt Forth.	×
Sgt Horsey.	×	Sgt Ellis.	
Sgt Knight.	×	Sgt Cousens.	×
Sgt Swire.	×	Sgt Lillywhite.	
Sgt Wren.	×		

Sgts Walmsley × and Burton × to be allocated to Flights when fit for operational duties.

Wednesday 2 July

During the morning watch 'A' Flight took off in good style for a practice flip. It seems that their formation flying and station keeping could do with buttoning up before the flight commander will be satisfied.

Coming in to land P/O Allardice in 2329 [Yellow 2] might have thought that the red light was a Red Lamp; consequently, as becomes an officer and a gentleman, he ignored it and, after an enforced run on one wheel ran gently into 2514 (P/O Gray – Yellow 1 – in the seat). 2514 is serviceable again and 2329 will be sent, when removed from its undignified position, to Kalafrana [*presumably to the aircraft dump located there*].

Later in the day the CO led 'B' Flight in 2 scrambles against (a) 1 bomber [*and*] 9 fighters. 60 miles. NE: and (b) +3. 50 miles but, since the Italians would not play and went home too quickly, no engagement took place.

Thursday 3 July

'A' Flight had a practice scramble at an hour when all decent [*sic*] are still in bed and F/Lt Jeffries took them to have a look at Sicily "from a new angle". It looked quite nice and we might as well have it.

There were two plots on the board when 'B' Flight were on duty today. Scrambled each time; the 1st was +2. 35 miles N going North (perhaps Italian Admirals having a look at their own lake) and the 2nd was an inoffensive PRU [*photographic reconnaissance unit*] Hurricane returning on completion of its legitimate business. No engagements took place.

Sgt Walmsley went up in 'Maggy' [*Miles Magister*] after being earth-bound for two months. He is now test-pilot for the Squadron and will resume operational flying shortly.

It is noticeable that the Squadron flying is much neater – even after the few trips made – and this augers well for future dates with the Regina [*sic*] Aeronautica.

Friday 4 July

Following a scramble at 06.30 against +2. 20 miles by 'B' Flight with no engagement, 'A' Flight scrambled four of their planes against +1. 40 miles and sent off two additional planes to keep a fatherly eye on a Catalina flying boat in in [*sic*] bay.

The +1 faded and, as sometimes happens – due to the mysteries of Radio Location – became +9 at 75 miles; +12. 56 miles; +20. 30 miles; +25 at 20 miles. Shortly after the last tit-bit had been given F/Lt (Jeff) Jeffries shouted the official equivalent of his "ere t'is" and led Sgt Sutherland as his R2 and Sgts Jolly and Bates (White 1 and 2) into the attack.

With favourable odds of 6 to 1 the Italians might have put up a better show but they preferred to read about their attack in their own pet newspaper – next day.

Mr Jeffries, using cannon, shot one down and attacked two others, probably damaging them. Sgt Jolly shot down his 2nd Macchi in a week or so, – the pilot being fished out of the sea, and Sgts Sutherland and Bates entered the fray vigorously and, though not getting any confirmed, warmed the Italians on the way back to Sicily with bags of .303.

Thus with two shot down and some damaged without loss to ourselves a profitable use was made of the petrol and we warmly congratulate the pilots concerned on their splendid show.

Saturday 5 July

This morning 'B' Flight scrambled 12 planes against a +12 plot 60 miles north moving south. Fifty miles from the island the E/A split into two sections; 6 planes travelling NE and 6 travelling N. As they did not linger we had no chance to intercept and the Flight came back in creditable formation.

There was no further activity until the evening watch, when a +1. 60 miles north came on the board. Once again 'B' Flight were defending the Right to be Free; four Hurricanes took off and wended their way back when the plot faded.

We do not know if the two pairs were not persona grata with each other but have to record that they approached the filling points about a mile apart, before dropping in for their still lemonade.

Sunday 6 July

We did not interrupt the morning Sicily–North African mail, when a +9 at 70 miles was proceeding SW. Ten A/C from 'A' Flight defied gravity but could not be vectored in time and no engagement took place.

To cover an attack by the Blenheim Sqdrn on the Palermo Harbour, 'B' Flight took off this afternoon and patrolled the south coast of Sicily. Incidentally, the Blenheim boys gave the shipping in the Harbour a thorough pasting and, such was the complete surprise of the attack, no opposition – either ground defence or fighter aircraft – was experienced.

A practice scramble in the evening by 'A' Flight testifies that conscientious work brings results and the formation was quite pleasing.

Monday 7 July

Following a night of nuisance raids – single E/A operating over the island every ¼ hour for a few hours – 'A' Flight came on the dawn watch and were sleeping in various ungainly postures when, at 8 o'clock their peace was abruptly disrupted by a +2. 50 miles NNE.

From his couch of parachutes F/Lt Jeffries ordered off three sections of sleepy beauties and it was not until he was airborne that Sgt Hayes realised he was too keen or something and had not been included in those detailed. The plot faded and all returned to rest.

The Teller's records show the following entries during 'B' Flight's morning watch today.

10.45   Two A/C to cover Flying boat in Bay.

10.50   +15. 53 miles NE course SW.

10.58   Air Raid.

11.05   9 Hurricanes airborne.

That record covers a situation that could well have terminated in the unnecessary loss of 12 Hurricanes.

We know that down the mine of Malta they have cornered the market for spare white women on the Gem and we suppose the ladies carry out their work efficiently etc. etc. and their presence etc. etc. Nevertheless, from our somewhat exposed position, we cannot look placidly at an Italian bomber plus a dozen fighters, stooge gently over our particular back-yard, when our own planes are still lining up to take off. By chance only, the bomber was a recco' that didn't happen to possess the odd bomb.

Someone had got their finger(s) up, right up; either our planes should be up with the enemy by the time they reach the island or they should be dispersed and the ground crews near a shelter – no doubt this will be so in the future. Our 'planes just had time to climb to 18000´ when the E/A were approaching their own coast.

Before the end of their morning watch 'B' Flight sent up 6 planes to investigate a +2 which were orbiting 40 miles north of Grand Harbour – perhaps an enemy fighter from the previous tour had dropped his knitting in the sea –, the two planes hurried away before contact could be made.

A concert near the dispersal hut was attended by most of us and passed 'B' Flight's evening watch along. Four planes were sent up by S/Ldr Mould to intercept a friendly plane during one of the less vulgar turns and everyone seemed to enjoy themselves. The acts would not have been snatched up by George Black, but no one anticipated elaborate scenes and the evening was at least as remunerative as most of those spent in the hut, where learned discourse on philosophy or the arts – except one – seem at a discount.

Tuesday 8 July

No enemy activity to report today. F/Lt Pike, for the first time, led 'A' Flight on practice formation flying this afternoon.

He took them towards Sicily; nothing came on the board, and the trip was uneventful.

Sgt Branson ('Doc') started four days compulsory rest at St Paul's Bay. He needed it.

Wednesday 9 July

Six 'A' Flight lads took off during the dawn watch when +6 were vaguely plotted somewhere near Sicily. They received "await further instructions" soon after taking off.

P/O Bailey and P/O Winton led Sgts Alderson [*written above name:* Combat 36] and Westcott against a couple of seaplanes and a few Macchi 200s about 40–50 miles north of Grand Harbour.

P/O Bailey damaged a Macchi and Sgt Westcott a sea-plane. Back in the dispersal hut the former indulged in light raillery at the expense of Sgt Alderson who "may have" warmed up eight Brownings in his direction. No Hurricanes were hit in the encounter. [*An addendum, apparently signed by Bailey, reads:* NOTE. DELETE "may have"]

P/O Winton allowed a Red Cross plane to go on its lawful (???) business; an action which received general approval. He could have had a poop at it – as Sgt Westcott did – since escort was nearby, but preferred to await a worthier object. Unfortunately no Macchi, (which is not quite as primordial as we first believed – tho' quite easy meat –) came his way.

P.M. The Boys From Syracuse

Comment is unnecessary, save that the snap shows them taking off, regarding the most successful and energetic beat-up of the sea-plane base at Syracuse. [*The 'snap' refers to an attached photograph – not included here – captioned:* +800 cannon shells were contributed to this, our latest war effort. Light coastal batteries opened up on the 4 Hurricanes as they went out to sea, causing no damage but slight ring twitch.]

Our industrious CO and F/Lt Jeffries went with the CO and Sgt Mackie of 46 Squadron.

NT 1   from the CO's official report – – – –

> We approached the harbour from the East: entered the harbour through the entrance at about 50 feet and immediately did a steep right hand turn and slipped out into echelon port and opened fire at a cluster of three seaplanes. (Cant) I was then at about 5 feet off the water. I saw my shells going low to start with and after raising my aim one of the three seaplanes caught fire, the tail fell off another and I could see my shells going into the third machine. I then turned slightly and saw the remainder of my shells go into the hangar, but no definite damage was seen. I nearly hit one of the seaplanes and then the hangar and eventually nearly removed my starboard wing on some large building. There was quite a lot of A.A. but all bursting at about 250 feet this started just before I started breaking away.

COMB
34   from F/Lt Jeffries' official report – – – –

> I, F/Lt. Jeffries was following S/Ldr. Mould, we approached Syracuse harbour from the East, I saw several seaplanes on the water. I opened fire on the nearest one [and] I observed several strikes. I then concentrated my fire on the slipway on which there were about five aircraft. I saw one floatplane burst into flames as my shots entered it. I sprayed the other a/c and then fired a long burst into the hangar. Several men working there scattered. As I flew over the slipway I observed about 3 a/c on fire. A huge pall of smoke hung over the harbour as we flew out to sea.

In the evening 'B' Flight scrambled 10 Hurricanes against plus 12. 38 miles NE. The E/A were travelling away from the island and no engagement elapsed [sic].

F/Lt Hancock's Maltese Dog had pups during the day.

On the facing page there are three more 'combat cuts' or 'pilot's lines' (main part of a pilot's combat report). These evidently refer to events that occurred two days later.

~~9/7/41~~ or 11?

S/LDR MOULD

> At 2000 ft. I noticed that someone in the formation had left his transmitter 'ON' I carried on climbing, very fast and when at 15,500 ft. managed to receive a message from "Banjo" saying 15 – plus 10 miles North of Zambuck [sic: Zambuk – code name for St Paul's Bay]. I was then just South of Zambuck. Within one minute I saw the enemy aircraft about 1000 ft. below and just in front of us. We were not well positioned for a decent formation attack, so I broke my formation up and dived into the middle of the rear formation. I aimed at the outside one of a vic of three, and they immediately broke in all directions. I followed the one E/A in a steep diving spiral firing bursts at intervals, at ranges varying from 75 to 20 yards., when I had to break away. I did not see the enemy aircraft hit the water, but I am sure that I damaged it badly. (Position 15–20 miles N.E. Grand Harbour) – I lost sight of E/A when I had to break away. I then chased another Macchi 200 and fired several bursts into it from varying ranges with no visible result. I was then about 30–35 miles N.E. Grand Harbour. I returned home after finishing my ammunition. All my Squadron machines returned safely.

I was yellow 1 flying with the Squadron at 16000 due West when I saw 4 Macchis going East. The Squadron Leader turned and followed them. I then saw about 12 more 10 miles East going North. At the same time I saw about 20 below at about 50–500 feet. I dived on these giving a short squirt full beam allowing too much deflection. I then attacked another which did a stall turn. I opened fire about 150 yards from below. My shots went into it raking it from just behind the cockpit to the tail It could not hold on to the position owing to the height. I then attacked another from slight port quarter to astern some pieces came off as my shots entered the fuselage. I had run out of ammo and had no further interest in the proceedings.

An armed trawler which witnessed the above fired at me as I was returning.

F/LT PIKE

I saw 4 or 5 Macchis in loose formation flying North over the Island about 3,000 ft., below, and two formations of Macchis 200's flying South about 2,000 ft., below. I attacked Macchi 200 flying North firing several bursts of cannon seeing one hit in the fuselage just forward of the tail. I followed it out to sea at sea level but could not gain on it so broke off attack.

Thursday 10 July

Today was a day of rest, with the exception of one flap when 'A' Flight put up six Hurricanes against a +3. 50 miles NE during the afternoon.

Evening report: the two Boys from Syracuse have not been drunk during the last twelve hours.

Friday 11 July

As is customary, when not flying, "A" and "B" Flights – during the first 2 watches today – were eating huge quantities of unpaid for sandwiches and mechanically drinking jar-after-jar of unpaid for lemonade, while our foe was preparing for publication a report on " ... one of the greatest battles amongst air forces ... that has ever been fought in the central Medi-terranean ... " that was, in fact, to be fought later in the day.

12 Hurricanes from 'A' Flight were scrambled about 1 o'clock against +3. 70 miles north coming towards the Gem of the Med.

Due to a dreamy pilot leaving his transmitter on the R/T information received clearly was very scanty and may have saved ½ doz. Macchis. Dreamy pilot please note.

The +3 became +9. 35 miles North and then +16. 20 miles north together with +2. 50 miles north. No doubt the size of the latter plot increased as the planes came in.

From the pilots' lines we can say that at least 40 E/A came over the island and, from a most trustworthy source, that 8 Macchis essayed a low flying attack on Luqa, where one Wellington was set on fire and two others damaged.

The Italians went home quickly, leaving three Macchi pilots, and their machines, in the drink, north of Grand Harbour. This is confirmed by the Navy, who did the necessary fishing.

Since this was essentially a Squadron effort the pilots' reports are given without special mention of any individual effort.

The modest Italian report is given herewith [*from the RAF Daily Intelligence Summary, No. 22, dated 13 July 1941*].

ON LUQA

"The great offensive activity of the enemy has met effective reply in the daring action carried out by our light forces against the principal airport in Malta...................... Five twin engined bombers of the WICKER [sic: VICKERS] WELLINGTON type were set on fire one of which loaded with ammunition blew up into the air...............our escorting aircraft were engaged by Hurricanes from above in the course of the most violent combats four enemy machines were shot down, two at Hal Far and the other two crashed into the water ten kilometres East of Marsaxlohk [sic: *Marsaxlokk*] ....this encounter in which more than 100 machines were engaged is one of the greatest battles among air forces composed of fighters that has ever been fought in the Central Mediterranean ....none of our planes were lost................the total enemy losses amount to nine machines besides an unascertained number of others.........................."

Notes: (i) probably more than the 3 Macchis confirmed failed to get home.

(ii) a squadron without effective R/T is handicapped and loses most of its fighting efficiency.

(iii) the two squadrons 126 – this was the old 46 – and 249, which are resting at Ta Kali, would have enjoyed the trip if they had been allowed up. They put up two Hurricanes to protect their planes.

(iv) the practice of bouncing .303 ammo off another Hurricane to hit a Macchi, not held in the sights, will be gently discouraged.

(v) pilots should pay for their own expensive bun-feasts down at flights.

There were two other scrambles later in the day; "A" Flight sent up six Hurricanes against +1. 60 miles North and 'B' Flight, in the evening, put up 10 Hurricanes against a +6 40 miles ENE which was reported 'going out' when they had been airborne for 5 mins or so.

Five combat cuts are attached to the facing page.

F/LT JEFFRIES   Combat 42

I, Green one, sighted approximately 30 Macchi's. Due to the fact that a transmitter had been left on I turned to attack, without informing the leader, Squadron Leader Mould, hoping that he would follow. I engaged a Macchi [and] gave him a short burst. He tried evasive action [and] I let him go. I engaged two more Macchi, without any visible results. I then picked on one aircraft and gave him five seconds firing. He broke away going down. I was firing from about 50 yards range.

I then engaged another Macchi at sea level closing to about 100 yards, I fired about 5 seconds bursts into this A/C. I am claiming this aircraft as damaged. My bullets were plainly visible as they entered the fuselage. The other A/C. mentioned before I claim as probable. it should have crashed 30–35 miles North East of Delimara.

Flying White 1, I first sighted E/A slightly below, at about 16,000 ft. Our leader turned to the left and dived upon the E/A. Being on outside of turn I was left behind slightly, but dived down upon the melee. I saw one Macchi 200 at about 100 ft. turning towards home and dived on him giving three one second bursts The first burst missed the E/A but my second and third bursts appeared to strike the Macchi but I observed no apparent results. As I was flying very low I climbed up and looking round observed an aircraft climbing after me. I thought it was an E/A and carried out evasive action but later found it was my No. 2. No further E/A appearing to be about, I flew home with my No. 2.

I was flying Northwards at 16,000 when I saw 4 Macchi flying south followed by a further formation of 8 plus. F/Lt. Pike then turned to the left and dived down in a westerly direction when a Macchi got on his tail and he took evasive action and I followed him. We then dived down to 2000 on to a Macchi which F/Lt. Pike engaged. I saw him give about 4 or 5 bursts on the Macchi but saw no visible results. I was however, about 400 yards behind him.

I, Sgt. Sutherland, was flying as Green 2 when my leader, 16,00 [sic] ft. caught sight of a number of the enemy and the two of us broke off and made diving attacks on the enemy. I picked on two aircraft and fired on them in turn. I saw some of my rounds entering the wing of the first, and aft of the cockpit of the other, but I saw no result. I continued diving past them on to four aircraft which I saw flying Northward at sea level. My leader picked on one and I took another. I fired several bursts at it from astern, and observed a few hits but with no result. A Hurricane then cut in on me and I broke off the engagement and joined my leader and returned to base with him.

Combat 47   ALLARDICE

I was White 2, and when White 1 broke away from the Squadron, at 16,000 ft., and dived, I followed him down until we sighted an E/A flying very low over the sea. My leader dived on him and broke away and I followed and gave the E/A three bursts. I did not observe any hits. I then broke off and joined White 1 again and we returned to Base and landed.

Saturday 12 July

There were four scrambles today. 'B' Flight were sent off during the dawn watch; 'A' Flight twice in their morning watch and again in the evening watch. No engagements materialised and there is 'nothing to report on the Maltese Front'.

On the last watch, the weather closed in and pilots were released earlier than usual. This was especially convenient for the Sgts who were entertaining, with the rest of their mess, the Corporals on the Station. The £10 grant for beer did not last very long and, maybe, the pilots should not be released so early next time.

Sunday 13 July

Today was quiet. There were three 'divertissements', none of which ended in an interception. Maybe the Italians were on their circuits and bumps. 'B' Flight held the fort twice and 'A' Flight once.

Most of the pilots went for a swim in the bay. They would be surprised and delighted how different they looked afterwards – some having been on the island a few months and, to the casual eye, quite sunburnt.

The landing field is still very dusty.

Monday 14 July

'A' Flight were scrambled in the morning watch against a +3. 72 miles NE. The plot moved in a further 50 miles towards Grand Harbour and then departed like the problematical sawdust from the proverbial shovel.

During the afternoon 'B' Flight sent off 12 Hurricanes to investigate +1 at 50 miles NE moving SSE and nine Hurricanes to identify a Glen Martin 50 miles NE. We must record the zest with which 'B' Flight are getting off the ground these days – it should portend good results when the opportunity occurs.

Tuesday 15 July
'B' Flight did all the flying today. They went off twice in the morning and once in the evening watch – the last effort being the best scramble since new blood was introduced into the Squadron. Within three minutes of the beloved "do you mind ..." eleven Hurricanes were well over the fence, with wheels up.

There is a story concerning the last scramble which shows the excellence of the present Control. It was rather trying at the time but Group Captain Hancock may tell it to his son thus.

"Forasmuch as our dearly beloved Controller, baptized Joe, exhorted me and my followers thus:

'Thou shalt destroy them that abhor peace and will not suffer righteousness.

Get ye above them, for wickedness is in their dwellings: the deceitful men shall not live, but death come hastily upon them.

Thou shalt bruise them with small rods of iron: and break them in pieces like a potter's vessel: this in the waters of the Gem.

For they [word unreadable] waiting secretly at a distance from the meek of 50 miles: a host of six, girding their loins about them.

Hear me: go forward and on high for they approacheth.

Are ye now persuaded that those sons of Macchi are now at a place Sing-I Sing-low [Sing Sing: code name for Grand Harbour]: then seek thy glory and have not compassion on them: for they are weak in flight'.

And after a space of a minute and a half Joe spoke again saying unto me:

'Thou shalt not get them: O let my mouth be filled with praise for their chariots: they proceedeth north at a distance of fifteen miles: they do not tarry by the wayside ...'"

Interruption by Awful Son – "But Pop, I sure guess that means they beat it at 600 mph yes sir".

OK OK we know, we know – but that's Joe's story.

(moral: don't drink gin and lime)

Wednesday 16 July
At about 6.30 this morning F/Lt Hancock led 10 Hurricanes on an offensive fighter sweep over Sicily. Lately, our two flights have been near and over the coast there quite persistently, but this morning 'B' Flight pulled their fingers out and flew from a point about 15 miles North inland

for 30 odd miles or so on a westerly course at about 10,000 ft. In spite of this 'come and get it' attitude no opposition was encountered – neither ground defences nor E/A obliging with a party.

'A' Flight scrambled nine Hurricanes against a +20 69 miles N during their morning watch. Although +6 came within 10 miles NE of Sing Sing they were not vectored to make an interception and the plot went out north.

Other scrambles were ordered and subsequently cancelled at fairly wearisome intervals during the remaining watches.

F/Lt Pike and P/O Oliver representing the riff-RAF attended army manoeuvres this morning and are now up-to-the-minute experts on all army matters. As a side line they now offer to sell detailed authoritative information concerning performances of tanks, gun positions, strategic victorious withdrawals etc. for 500 Bear Brand or, alternatively, one Player [cigarette].

By the way, it was 105° in the shade today.

Thursday 17 July

There were five abortive scrambles today. Everyone was working well in the top line, – but the only real news is that P/O Veitch, our most beautifully dressed and elegant pilot, also the most heavily armed, has gone to rest camp for a week. This allusion to individual sartorial splendour naturally excludes the Sgts who have, of course, money to spare and spend on dress.

Friday 18 July

'A' Flight successfully defended the Gem today, taking off twice in their morning watch. The E/A did not get as far as the island and no contact was established.

There is a rumour going round the Flight-Hut that six electricians working day and night in a darkened room on a most complicated hush-hush job have gone on strike since they can't get a supply of invisible rays. Apparently this is essential for harnessing energy from the sun to drive ... P/O Thompson is very secretive about it all ... we must wait.

Saturday 19 July

Ta Kali went up on the one and only daylight raid today. The night raids were on as usual.

'B' Technicians – P/Os Thompson and Winton played with bits of plywood; a few holes, a pot of paint and muttered obscenely about the strike during the 'B' Flight watches today.

Sunday 20 July

Sgt Wren had a practice flight with Sgt Vardy leading in 'A' Flight's morning watch. This is the first time he has flown as a member of our Squadron, since coming to the island and immediately going down with 'dog' ['*Malta dog*': *a form of dysentery peculiar to the island*] and then 'fly' [*sand fly fever*].

'A' Flight sent up 11 Hurricanes during their evening watch against +3. 75 miles North. However they were out of luck, the plot faded, and they landed just prior to dusk.

The respective merits of the two Flight boards provides and promotes sufficient discussion to prove that men and/or pilots can be illogically loyal to any-bloody-thing.

Monday 21 July

Our aircraft went up five times today without result – which is tear-making. During the morning, when 'B' Flight were on readiness, Italians passed right over the island and could not be caught up as the fighters were scrambled too late.

It is wearying to think what COULD have happened today – and on other similar days – given better support and the present somewhat monochromatic reviews of our fighting efforts cannot reflect the eagerness with which both flights take the air. So, line illac lacrimae, and the promise to strike hard when chance comes our way.

One Inspector-General honoured the camp with a visit today and may mention the two Flight boards to A. Sinclaire.

Tuesday 22 July

There were ½ doz. scrambles today, 'A' Flight going up on four occasions and 'B' Flight on two. The trip which showed the greatest promise was in the morning watch when 'A' Flight were on duty. The plot grew up to +25 5 miles North before going out, but no contact was made.

We hear that P/O Gray and Sgt Hodson are leaving us shortly. Both are very popular and experienced members of the Squadron and will be missed when they do leave the Gem.

Wednesday 23 July

With the convoy approaching the island everyone anticipated action during the day. Such action as did materialise was confined to 'B' Flight's two scrambles in the morning watch. The nearest plot was +1 55 miles E which was rather an anti-climax after looking forward to 'big eats'.

P/O Gray and Algy left us this morning for UK and grey-haired mothers. When anyone leaves a Service Unit it is usual to mouth platitudes about 'sterling work and worth' etc. – in both cases these would be sincere and we wish them a safe return and all the best in their future activities.

Thursday 24 July

The convoy came in today. The Navy have accomplished another job in Mare Nostrum that the owners tried to prevent, and lost a dozen aircraft, E boat and probably a submarine in their efforts to do so. The Navy lost a destroyer coming through, which was cheap for such an undertaking and only one cargo boat showed signs of wear and tear. The latter came into Grand Harbour under her own power and looked good enough for another 20 yrs' work in the Duce's private pond.

'A' Flight put a protective arm round the convoy twice in the morning, – once when it was thought that the Fulmar boys were E/A.

'185' were busy throughout the day and six scrambles (four by 'A' Flight and two by 'B' Flight) underlined the fact that the Italians are also aware of our good news but are not yet prepared to take our toffee-apples from us.

A clipping from The Times of Malta *is attached:*

> The enemy air forces were unable to prevent the difficult operation being brought to a successful conclusion, and the long series of heavy air attacks resulted in the destruction of a minimum of 12 enemy aircraft, with at least four others damaged and probably destroyed."

Friday 25 July

Unwisely unable to restrain their curiosity about our affairs the enemy decided to send over a BR 20 with an S.79 accompanied by thirty fighters.

'B' Flight decided they should not take any photographs back with them, as the accompanying reports show. F/Lt Hancock led the Squadron into the attack and was as furious as his naturally tolerant nature allows him to be when his cannon seized up after firing a few shells. His language revealed a closer study and more thorough understanding of the baser [sic] thoughts than we have imagined. That his Flight has benefited from the CO's and his preparations and enthusiasm is obvious since the two recco machines were destroyed.

P/O (Professor) Thompson and Sgt Forth have been credited with the S.79 and the other pilots share the BR 20. P/O Barnwell also attacked the S.79, after the Professor and his no. 2 had been in with cannon and machine gun respectively.

Ta Kali crowd were up at the same time and shot down three of the Macchis, also having the odd shot at one of the bombers.

'B' Flight were up again in the evening watch against a +12 65 miles NE which became +6. 40 miles NE and then went home.

On the right:
Situation report
issued from
HQ. Malta Times
26:7:41

This morning July 25. – Two reconnaissance aircraft and a large number of fighters came over. Our fighters engaged the enemy and in the ensuing combats shot down both the reconnaissance aircraft and three of the enemy fighters. One fighter as everyone knows, crashed in Valetta, the pilot baling out but was killed. One Italian pilot was picked up alive by our rescue service. There were no other enemy survivors from the raiders which crashed into the sea.

All our fighters landed unscathed from all these operations.

Below:
Journalese at its
worst – typical
extract from report
that ran to several
columns. Malta
Times 26:7:41

THE most spectacular of all the air combats witnessed in Malta's skies occurred yesterday morning when soon after the wailing of the siren, the drone of aircraft was followed by the discharge of the guns and the faint puffs of exploding shells high up in the empyrean blue of a hot July morning.
After very little anti-aircraft firing, a less familiar note was audible: the sharp, although faint, rat-a-tat of machine-gunning. Then did the shouting and the clapping, and the cheering and the waving intensify as even the poorest eyes could make out an aeroplane emitting the tell-tale trail of smoke. Larger and larger appeared the white smoke trail until at its head the descending 'plane could be clearly discerned – heading straight down upon Malta's capital city whose streets were athrong with cheering spectators.

<u>Pilots' lines covering engagement with
one BR 20; one S.79 and
30 Macchis ... Friday July 25th.</u>

Report of Sgt ALDERSON   Black II   Combat 51

At about 26,000 ft. I observed 1 B.R. 20 approaching from the West, and approx. 6 Hurricanes dived to attack from above me. I waited to allow them to complete their attack and then dived on the bomber which by this time was almost immediately below me. I fired 50 rounds from each gun at point blank range and observed hits in the fuselage. I carried on my dive straight past its tail and broke away.

Report of P/O BAILEY.

I was flying Black I [sic]. and made three attacks on Recco.

left it with starboard engine smoking and wheels down. Several other Hurricanes made attacks.

Report of P/O BARNWELL

I did a front quarter attack followed by a stern attack I saw pieces flying off and had to break over for fear of collision, and in the subsequent turn I spun. I believe this A/C might have had twin tails. After my spin I attacked what I thought was the same A/C, but it may have been another. I did four attacks and ran out of ammunition. This second A/C was definitely an S.M. 79, coloured mottled dark and light green with three yellow engines. Two attacks on the beam and two stern attacks. It had been previously damaged, the A/C [sic: U/C – undercarriage] was down and starboard motor seemed to be giving white smoke.

After running out of ammunition I followed close beside as there was no return fire, also did some dummy attacks. After about five minutes I saw flames behind starboard engine nacelle.

The A/C was continually losing height turning each way. It continued to fly for some time with the small fire on the starboard wing, and then turned back towards the Island, shortly after which the A/C exploded and crashed into the sea. I saw one parachute fall into the sea and continued to orbit the wreckage for some time with white one. I then flew back to the Island – course Z 47° M, at 180 AS1 [sic: presumably ASI – air speed indicator] for about 7 minutes which brought me over Kalafrana. I am almost certain that this A/C had three yellow engines, but do not remember noticing the tail.

Report of Sgt BRANSON.   Combat 59

I was flying Green 1 and made three attacks on the Br. 20. As there was no return fire experienced I was able to make a steady attack closing to 50 yards when I broke away, my No. 2 confirms that the starboard engine was left smoking. I carried out two more attacks using all my ammunition and then returned to base. When I left it, it was smoking and diving towards the sea.

Report of Sgt ELLIS. 25/7

Combat 51	I opened fire at about 200 yards astern closing to 50 feet. I broke away and made to [sic] beam attacks, and then one final beam attack, upon this attack white smoke came from the starboard engine, my ammunition was then finished. There were two other Hurricanes making a beam attack just as I was caught in the slip stream, which turned me upon my back.

Report of Sgt FORTH Combat 58

I was flying No. 2 to P/O Thompson, who engaged Recco over Sing Sing. I followed astern and saw my No. 1 open fire, pieces came away from the Recco, though the rear gunner continued to fire. When P/O Thompson broke away I opened fire at 200 yds. More pieces came away from the Recco and I believe my first burst put the rear gun or gunner out of action, because though he opened fire at me, for the remainder of my first attack there was no counter fire. Having broken away I climbed into the sun, and found the Recco at 16000 feet with about 3 fighters. I delivered a second attack from beam going to ½ astern, breaking away at about 150 yds when dived at by a fighter. During the flight I saw an aircraft dive vertically, but did not see it hit the sea. On my return I saw a large white splash mark about 6 miles NE Sing Sing.

Report of Sgt NURSE

My number 1, Sgt. Branson, broke away and I followed him down. I sighted the enemy and started firing at a range of 350 yards, and gave a 3–4 burst, I did not observe any hits. I then climbed and delivered a three-quarter attack, and noticed the undercarriage was down, and again gave a 3–4 second burst, hits being observed on fuselage. After breaking away, I climbed again and started to attack, opening fire from about 200 yards, and closing in to 75 yards I noticed all my bullets entering the fuselage and starboard wing. I broke away very sharply, and when I noticed the enemy again, he was too far away to catch, but was being pursued by 3 Hurricanes. I noticed smoke coming from his port engine.

Report of Sgt REAM.

I followed it out to sea, and tried to get into position for a head on attack. I failed to do this however, as several Hurricanes were attacking, from astern and quarter, so I carried out a beam attack and saw him pass through my tracer. I broke away and, as three or four other Hurricanes were attacking, I started looking for something else, and failing to see any more enemy aircraft, I turned for home, as I was about 40 miles out to sea. On the way back I saw a cloud of smoke above the water and some wreckage beneath about 25 miles East of the Island.

Report of P/O THOMPSON.

Flying as Blue 1. I was detached from the Squadron at 5000′ and ordered to climb fast, with my No 2 (Sgt. Forth). I gained height and reached 28,000′ when E/A were reported 20 miles away over Sing Sing at 26,000′. I saw S.79 with three or four fighters and attacked S.79 from astern closing rapidly to 100 yards firing three bursts from cannon. I saw large pieces fall off starboard side and red flashes where the explosive shells hit also the starboard engine begin to smoke and the undercarriage fall down. I broke away and returned to Base the guns having stopped firing. P/O Barnwell later saw this aircraft explode and crash into sea.

Report of P/O WOODSEND.

General Report:-   I was flying White 2 to P/O. Winton at 26,000 feet when "B" Flight attacked out of sun. I followed a cannon Hurricane (P/O. Winton) into the "Recco" which was followed by Macchis. Gave it a 6 second Squirt. There was no return fire. Saw 4 other Hurricanes deliver attack simultaneously. No apparent result. Return to base.

Having been tasked once again with subjugating Malta, the Italians proceeded with an audacious plan whereby they would simultaneously strike at the submarine base at Marsamxett Harbour and the recently arrived 'Substance' convoy in neighbouring Grand Harbour. Following the withdrawal of the Luftwaffe, *there had been a noticeable decrease in the number of raids. The islanders were therefore amazed when, during the night of 25–26 July, the Italian Navy's elite* La Decima Flottiglia MAS *deployed two* SLC *'human torpedoes' and nine* MTM *explosive motor boats north of Grand Harbour. Unfortunately for the Italians they were detected while still twenty miles short of their target. Furthermore, once the attack was underway, the SLCs failed to achieve their objectives, which included the destruction of an anti-torpedo net across the harbour mouth. The task was taken over by one of the* MTMs. *At 04:45 hours it hit the mole bridge of the breakwater and detonated, causing the west span to collapse which effectively blocked the entrance. The attack now turned into a rout for the Italians. As searchlights illuminated the scene, the shore defences opened fire, sending tracer rounds ricocheting off the sea into the night sky. The Italians were in a hopeless situation made all the worse when Hurricanes took off at dawn to attack the survivors as they tried to withdraw back to Sicily. Fifteen Italians were killed in the raid, and eighteen captured.*

Saturday 26 July

The latent talent in 'B' Flight found further expression today in the destruction of 1 Macchi and 4 torpedo boats.

On the left:
extract from editorial, "Times of Malta" [*reproduced below*].

FIRST SEA ATTACK ON MALTA
BRILLIANT VICTORY FOR DEFENDERS

IMPREGNABLE MALTA

The gunners of the coastal defence batteries have for long been eagerly awaiting their chance. It came last Saturday morning, when the enemy attempted their first attack on Malta by sea. E-boats and lighter torpedo carrying craft–M.A.A.R.'s–were used: the suicidal bravery of the enemy was only equalled by the accurate fire of our gunners. There was splendid cooperation between the land defences and the R.A.F., who themselves accounted for several of the attacking craft. Thousands of civilians on the bastions of Valetta and in Sliema along Tower Road and Ghar-id-Dud, watched the "suicide squadron" make their reckless futile dash towards the Grand Harbour to meet their doom before they could come within accurate striking distance of their objective.

Nevertheless the Rome radio and press, with an effrontery which throws even Goebbels' biggest lie into the shade, continue to boast

> about "the rape of Malta", which they say will go down in history as one of the most remarkable exploits of this war!

On the right

Official Italian communiqué [*also from* The Times of Malta, *reproduced below*].

ITALIAN VERSION
(Reuter's Service)
ROME, July 27.

Italy's E-boat raid on Malta was made after the news had been received that the remaining ships of the British convoy, attacked for three days and nights in the Mediterranean, had taken refuge there, says the "Voce d'Italia", which adds:

"The presence of the convoy was detected on Friday. Immediately the Italian Navy decided to attack with these tiny but powerful craft on which the designers have worked in silence for many years–one of the most precious secrets of the Italian war machine. The men chosen for the attack knew that retreat was impossible–they must either be killed or taken prisoner. None flinched before his task, despite the formidable nature of the British defences. The violation of Malta will go down in history as one of the most remarkable exploits of this war."

Bottom left.

Real 'gen' [*below, from* The Times of Malta].

---

17 E-Boats Sunk
OFFICIAL COMMUNIQUE
(Reuter's Service)
LONDON, July 27.

Further information concerning the attack on Valetta harbour, Malta early on Saturday morning is now available. A joint Admiralty and War Office and Air Ministry communiqué says:

"Shortly before 5 a.m. local time E-boats appeared off the harbour

---

entrance, and the fixed defences manned by the military garrison immediately engaged them. One E-boat was hit and blew up, while four more were destroyed by gunfire. It then appeared that the E-boats were acting as a cover for smaller torpedo-carrying craft, which attempted to break into the harbour. These were heavily engaged by gunfire from the shore defences, eight being blown up or sunk. None succeeded in entering the harbour.

"R.A.F. fighters pursued the remaining E-boats, while they were attempting to extricate themselves, sinking four more and damaging others. The British fighters then encountered enemy aircraft endeavouring to give air support to the retreating enemy E-boats. Three enemy aircraft were shot down into the sea, while one R.A.F. fighter was lost, but the pilot saved.

"Reports so far received indicate that the assault on the harbour was attempted by eight small torpedo-carrying craft, all of which were destroyed. The view that none of the assaulting force survived is confirmed by a Special Italian communiqué issued on Saturday night. This merely referred to explosions seen by escorting forces from a distance to seaward".

Before dawn the forts guarding Grand Harbour were vigorously repelling enemy 'E' Boat attacks – described by some as gallant and by others as stupid.

To condense our record of the episode, which is really worth more than a diary scribble, we have given the pilots' lines and a few of the less hysterical flag-wagging Press reports.

P/O Winton's adventures, however, must be mentioned. Thirty miles or so out to sea, he was surprised by a Macchi and received such damage to his plane that the fan stopped. Using his speed to gain height he was able to reach 700 ft and then baled out, both parachute and dinghy doing all the things a kind-hearted MO likes them to do.

For the next few hours he sunbathed; played with a friendly turtle, wondered who would have his motor cycle, and then spotted a stationary torpedo boat. He paddled the dinghy with his hands and, finding progress slow, towed it and swam towards the boat.

By climbing up the side he was able to peer into it and was confronted by eight very much dead Italians. Apparently cannon are not suitable presents for playful infants.

Taking possession of the boat was thus quite easy and he waited, – he couldn't start it – flying the flag at half mast since he didn't know which side would rescue him. An army rescue boat did a circuit round him – almost six hours after he had baled out on an empty stomach – and thinking he was an Italian, also that there was a .5 machine gun handy on the boat, left him to cool his heels for a time.

Before they could return a Swordfish with floats dropped in to pay him a visit and gave him, and the flag, a lift home where he again took possession of his motor-cycle.

The mob from Ta Kali shot down two Macchis – a Sgt-pilot got both of them – during the show. They also damaged a few boats.

'B' Flight had two more scrambles, one in their dawn watch and the second in the afternoon.

In the evening watch F/Lt Jeffries and Sgt Vardy were ordered to sink P/O Winton's torpedo boat and, after half an hour, during which Control struggled with the mysteries of variation and elevation, were given a course to steer. They went about as far as Sicily – Sgt Jolly leading the fighter cover – and on their return saw the boat being towed into Grand Harbour by a trawler.

'Pilots' lines' follow.

Report of <u>P/O Bailey</u>   26/7/41

> I took off with Black 2 at 0545 as one section. On passing over Sing-Sing I saw bofor fire at sea level, I dived down and there were two large explosions. Two patches of oil appeared and on further examination four survivors were counted in water. I reported to Banjo and circled. About twenty minutes later vectored on to 2 M.T.Bs. about 4 miles 060° Sing-Sing. I attacked with machine gun fire and one started turning in small circles and suddenly exploded leaving a large oil patch and wreckage. I attacked the other and this also went into a small circle after attack. Being out of ammunition I returned to Sing-Sing. In company with another Hurricane I returned to spot M.T.B. was stationary and weaving [sic] white flag near oil patch (Confirmation by Peanut 72).

Report of <u>P/O Barnwell</u>

> I was flying Yellow one. I followed Red section into the attack and saw F/Lt. Hancock's bullets striking all around the

first boat which immediately swung to the left and slowed up. I attacked and saw my bullets strike, no return fire. I broke left and made another attack on the other boat. Just after this attack I saw a Macchi firing on a Hurricane from above. I broke up and managed to get behind the Macchi. I observed my fire striking in the fuselage and starboard wing. I then saw a Macchi behind me followed by a Hurricane. I broke left and was attacked by a third Macchi on the beam. He broke away and did not continue his attack. I then saw the first Macchi heading North at sea level smoking profusely (black exhaust smoke). I managed to catch him and he took no evasive action until I was 200 yards away, when he did a medium turn to the left. I saw my bullets again striking his right wing and then ran out of ammunition and was forced to break off. On the return flight I saw the first boat was sunk and the second was proceeding slowly, being attacked by about three Hurricanes. I was joined shortly after this by P/O. Thompson and returned to base.

Report of <u>Sgt Forth</u>　　　　　　　　Combat √

I was flying No. 2 to P/O. Thompson who broke away to make his attack. I got into position and made attacks on the two M.T.B.s, which had both come to a stand still when I left for base.

Report of <u>F/Lt Hancock.</u>　　　　Combat √　　　　26 [7]

I was ordered off at 0550 leading six aircraft. After climbing to 10,000 ft over Malta I steered out to sea over sector 030° About fifteen miles out I saw two M.T.B's travelling north very fast. I received instructions to engage. I flew across to the west and turned, diving down to a few hundred feet. I opened fire on the nearest M.T.B. at about 800 yards, closing to 100 yards. I gave four bursts, my first falling short and the others striking the M.T.B. I then broke upwards and to starboard. Circling, I saw both M.T.B's engaged by the other Hurricanes. The port M.T.B. turned left and stopped. The starboard continued and was still being engaged when I last saw it. No return fire experienced.

I was flying No. 2 to Yellow Section Leader, P/O Barnwell, when at 10,000 ft. I sighted two M.T.Bs travelling line abreast. I followed my leader down and did a diving beam attack on the rear M.T.B. which was turning round very slowly. I broke away and did an astern attack on the front M.T.B. without visible effect. I turned and came in on a front attack on the same boat, and broke way again. The first M.T.B. was stationary with a small boat behind it. Just before I again attacked the front M.T.B., which was still travelling fast and weaving, I saw an aircraft, which I took to be a Hurricane dived [sic] vertically into the sea. I did a beam attack on the front boat and saw a flame from the starboard.

I broke away and after circling, followed two Hurricanes and used up all my ammunition, the boat stopping and catching fire.

above report. Sgt Lillywhite

Report below. The Professor

I was flying Blue 1. The Squadron patrolled at 10,000 ft. We went out to sea and saw 2 M.T.B's going N.E. very fast. The Squadron attacked. I remained at 18,00 [sic] ft. for a few minutes and saw a Macchi 200 attacking a Hurricane. I dived on the Macchi from astern and fired from 50–100ˣ. I then broke away and attacked M.T.B. my incendiary causing fire in the rear of the boat. I saw the Macchi again and fired again from astern causing smoke and pieces to fall off. The Macchi was seen to go into the sea by Sgt. Westcote [sic]. I fired the remainder of my ammo. into M.T.B. I saw one M.T.B. sinking and the other was seen by Sgt. Lillywhite to be on fire.

I was flying No. 2 to Red 1. F/Lt. Hancock, and at 10,000 feet sighted 2 M.T.Bs. I followed Red 1 down and while we were diving the T.Bs. broke up. We took the rear one and I closed to 50 yards after Red 1 had attacked and saw the gun on the launch hanging vertically. After the first attack I did a steep climbing turn and upon reaching 1500 feet I saw a Hurricane (P/O. Thompson) attack a Macchi. The tracers entered the cockpit of this machine and I saw a red glow from the cockpit. The Macchi turned over on its back and dived into the sea. I made another attack on the M.T.B. which had now stopped and seemed to be sinking slowly. I climbed up after this attack and had to return to my base, owing to high radiator temperature.

above report Sgt Westcott.

Sunday 27 July

With reports that a hospital ship was stooging about, presumably looking for a survivor to give an eye-witness report on yesterday's incident, F/Lt Jeffries sent P/O Allardice and Sgt Jolly during the dawn watch to find out if it was towing an E-Boat or so – or any reasonable excuse for attacking it.

Sgt Jolly was going alone at first but it was thought that confirmation *[?]* of his report would be quite nice if the HB proved awkward – especially if it shot him down!

They found the ship innocent of any aggressive tendencies and allowed it to carry on with its good work (probably laying more mines than that)

F/Lt Hancock led a completely successful excursion 50 miles on a vector of 135°. The dénouement, officially, was the destruction of two SM 79s by himself and the professor. For this unofficial record – which does not suffer from the anomaly of an apparently ignorant IO *[intelligence officer]* – it would perhaps be truer to say that Sgt Forth can claim half the professor's lesson to the Vagina *[sic]* Aeronautica.

No doubt, and this seriously, with another plane or two down P/O Thompson will be recommended for suitable recognition of his good work [not the IFF for devotion to Dug-Out suggested for to be filled in after demobilisation] since he has now about seven to his credit. *[Inserted in the above space: F/Lt Tommy Saxton]*

'B' Flight finished the day with a further three scrambles, which came to nothing, and we may say 'thank you' for their guardianship of the Gem during the last three days and their able defence of the Right to be Free.

On the facing page:

Pilots' lines covering engagement.
Sunday July 27th.

P/O Bailey   27 [7]

I was Blk 1. and weaving and sighted two E/A about 8000′ below Squadron. I informed leader. Squadron turned and I made first attack from beam – no effect seen. Other Hurricanes attacked and one S.79 pulled up and burst into flames. I made second attack from beam, saw red flash. may have been rear gun – other Hurricanes attacked and E/A blew up in flames. Submarine sighted just before "Tally Ho *[enemy sighted]*!"

Sgt Cousens.

General report:-   I was Red two, flying with F/Lt. Hancock when we encountered two S.M. 79s. flying below us at about 4,000 ft. My leader attacked on the beam going into astern attack. I followed him in line astern. I opened fire at about three hundred yards, and gave him about four seconds burst. His port engine was already on fire and his starboard engine now caught fire. As I pulled out the enemy aircraft went straight up climbing head [sic] and then went straight into the sea. I climbed up and did a beam attack on the port side of the second aircraft firing my ammunition, it hit forward of the wing with no visible effect.

F/Lt Hancock   Combat C

General report:-   I was ordered off leading Lygon Squadron on a sector [sic: vector] of 135°. About 45 miles [out] P/O. Bailey called to say he had sighted two aircraft I followed leading the Squadron Section astern. P/O. Bailey delivered quarter attack from port. I lead [sic] in astern of two S79s in formation and engaged the starboard machine from 300 yds closing to 50 yds. All cannon fired and large piece broke off and the port engine burst into flames. I broke away to starboard being struck in the starboard wing by a few bullets. The S79 then climbed and stall turned diving into the sea in flames. Sgt. Cousens Red 2. followed after me delivering an attack before the aircraft plunged into the sea.

Sgt Forth.

I was flying No. 2 to P/O. Thompson, and stayed with him during the engagement. I saw one S.M. 79 fall into the sea in flames. P/O/. and myself attacked the second bomber, I flying in No. 3 position and I saw my second long burst entering the enemy aircraft. P/O. Thompson and I broke away together as the 79 burst into flames, to fall into the sea a second later.

The Professor.

I was flying Blue 1. P/O. Bailey the weaver saw the 2 aircraft first and the Squadron attacked in line astern, P/O Bailey leading. I led the attack on the second machine closing to 100^x firing with four cannons. The machine blew up when I broke away.

The engagement was over in about 15 secs and many pilots in the flight did not have a chance to use their guns.

Monday 28 July

We are all aware of the absolutely grand work which is being done by the Blenheims, Wellingtons, Swordfish, Glen Martins – by the way we can suggest an excellent trip and passengers for a most serviceable Sunderland – operating from Luqua [sic: Luqa] and do not refer to them since we only jot down the good and bad fortunes of 185.

An exception must be made today as, this afternoon, the Beaufighters destroyed over 30 planes, and unfortunate odds and sods who got in the way, on various now untidy aerodromes in Sicily. We provided a high fighter cover for this show which was carried through without loss.

Maybe the Italians won't have the belly for intensive offensive action over here for a time.

On their first trip in the dawn watch 'B' Flight did not shoot down a Glen Martin which they intercepted. Things are looking up.

Tuesday 29 July

There was one scramble today when 'A' Flight sent up ten Hurricanes against +6. 55 miles NE. The plot failed before any engagement could be arranged. Incidentally, we must record that control have been a little better lately – but not much.

[Word unreadable] of our notes referring to the best dressed pilot. We did not mean to start a competition and no prizes are offered. However, S/Ldr Mould now displays a nifty pair of bare ankles set off with regulation shoes. The vulgar – unhappily they form the majority – are whispering that it is merely a question of laundry difficulties.

Wednesday 30 July

A peaceful day. One scramble with no interception and 'nothing to report'.

At the risk of the diary being uplifted to the status of a Tailor's journal we must make another reference to dress – this time to F/Lt Jeffries gent new natty suiting. Today the pilots were putting on their sun glasses whence he hove to and shone near them.

It is rumoured from 'B' Flight that the Professor and his team of scientists will shortly inflict their latest effort on a wondering world.

Thursday 31 July

During the morning watch the CO led 'B' Flight against a +9. 67 miles north. The "raiders" went home after coming in as +6. 40 miles north.

'B' Flight unveiled their latest hush-hush invention this evening – 'twas an original dinky-cute line board and reveals good craftsmanship on the part of Sgt Forth and P/O Thompson.

Friday 1 August to Thursday 7 August

A daily record of the first seven days this month would be wasting paper – unless used afterwards as shaving paper. Neither Mr Browning and his seven sisters nor Mr Cannon and his three friends spoke a word.

On the 3rd and 5th Aug. there was no flying at all, while the sole trip on the 1st was a practice flight by 'A' Flight. In all, during this period, 'A' Flight were scrambled four times and 'B' Flight six times. No engagements took place.

Notes:-

On Friday P/Os Winton and Barnwell left us, with Sgt Branson, to join the new fighter squadron. This squadron will, in future, do all the night fighting over the island. The first time the new squadron went into action P/O Barnwell shot down two enemy bombers into the sea. Most of us witnessed this splendid show – the two crashed in flames – and, while regretting the loss by posting such keen types, are very pleased with the early success.

Also on Friday F/O Murch had his first scramble with 185, in addition to a 45 mins. ack-ack [anti-aircraft] cooperation. He is joining F/Lt Hancock's gaggle.

A convoy of very fast naval units came in on Saturday from Gib [Gibraltar], carrying over 700 ground staff and we hope, without much chance, to get our fair share.

Monday might have provided an interception when +3 came within three miles of St Paul's Bay. 'B' Flight had hardly been vectored into the same hemisphere when the +3 did a smart right-about turn for home.

On the facing page there appears a **GRAPH OF AXIS AIR ACTIVITY AGAINST MALTA – JUNE TO JULY 1941** *with the following caption:*

THIRTEENTH MONTH – From June 11 until July 10, there were 58 "alerts" sounded in Malta. 24 people were killed by enemy action during this period mostly at Hamrun and Casal Pawla, and of these 1 man was over 65 years of age and 6 were children. During the same period 46 people were injured, including 1 man and 1 woman over 65 years of age and 18 children, and of these 8 died later, bringing the total of the dead to 32, including 10 children. three people were killed and five were injured by the explosion of two land mines.

Underneath, the diarist has written:

Cutting taken from the Times of Malta August 4th. We were a night-fighter squadron for the first ⅔rds of the graph. F/Lt Hancock got a probable ~~Ju 88~~ He 111 during that time. There have been 700/800 raids since Italy entered the war some 12 months ago. There doesn't seem to be any gen [?] on the camp.

The entries continue:

On Thursday 7th P/O Reeves had his first try-out with us. He was knocked down some three months ago while flying with 261 from Ta Kali and, after recovering from the incident – 109s were so ubiquitous! – has been employed down the Mine. We wish him and F/O Murch every success.

During the week the Fulmars, operating from here, have been over Sicily most nights and have undoubtedly caused the enemy to ease up on the violation business. (see duff gen July 26th)

Thus the past week's official air activities have been quiet as far as we are concerned and there is little to record – this isn't a scandal sheet on private lives etc –; any pilot who wishes to digress on any news that has been inadvertently omitted may do so on the opposite page. This is a standing invitation so long as the paragraph is initialled.

Friday August 8th to Thursday August 13th *[sic]*
It is regretted that owing to other duties Sgt Burton was unable to write up the diary for this week.

The only event worth recording is that on the 10th 'A' Flt chased some bandits back to Sicily. P/O Oliver's machine packed up and he bailed out, landing in the water about 30 miles from Malta. Lt Ayres *[sic: Lieutenant D.E.C. Eyres, Fleet Air Arm]* of the Rescue Service picked him up exactly ½ hr later – a magnificent performance.

An Appreciation:-

I would like to note that the present diarist, one, Sgt Burton, is about to leave us, consequently, he has handed his "onerous" duties over to me. The reader will no doubt notice the change in style.

Sgt Burton's humour, is unique, spontaneous and pungent, making this diary a joy to read.

Apart from his qualities as a writer "Stanley" is a stout fellow, a founder member of 185 and one of the best, but for his accident two months ago, which affected his eyesight, he would be doing readiness with us now, no doubt relieving the tedium of the monotonous watches.

"Stanley" would be embarrassed by lavish praise, so I will just say:- "Thank you for everything and good luck".

Tommy *[Pilot Officer Peter D. Thompson]*.
for 185.

Wednesday 13 August
A day of inactivity as far as we are concerned. – No scrambles.

"Readiness" resolves itself into a series of public house games, at which certain officers relieve unsuspecting Sergeant-Pilots of any surplus cash they may have.

We hear that Sgt Burton ("Butch" or "Stanley" to his intimates) will shortly be leaving us for that "green and pleasant land". As a result of a "hangar" episode he is now seeing double; or is it too many gin and limes; and is going home for treatment – so he says. More anon re "Stanley".

Thursday 14 August

'A' Flt kicked off at dawn but nothing happened until 08.45 when Sgt Jolly led four aircraft towards two float planes, but the R/T packed up and no contact was made, the float planes were friendly anyway, so what the hell!!

Mid morn:- The CO went off with 8 lads from 'B' Flt to shoot down the odd six or so <u>BUT</u> as <u>SOMEONE</u> left his transmitter <u>ON</u>, the ice-creamers got away with it. Jeff had a flip in the P.M. for the mythical +1 which was orbiting way up N – no result.

The CO took 'B' Flt up again in the evening, but only for the purpose of dispersal[;] +6 were over the Island just after the take off. 'B' Flt adjoined for shandies at 20.15.

Friday 15 August

Just one of those days! The serviceability at Comiso must be as good as ours?!! Merlin XXs are so temperamental and refuse to be pushed. Fast climbing and high temperatures continue to increase unserviceability – we have five on the line today. The Squadron had their photograph taken.

Affixed to the facing page above the caption "A slight Italian exaggeration" is the following excerpt from the RAF Daily Intelligence Summary, No. 57, dated 17 August 1941.

14.   <u>ITALIAN RADIO</u>. It may be of interest to record the following description by Rome Radio of the night bombing of MALTA on the night 11/12 August. It is as well to recall that on that particular night 9 raiders were over of which <u>two</u> were definitely destroyed. A small fire was started in a warehouse at Marsa causing little damage otherwise there was no further damage and no casualties.

"The naval and air bases of MALTA have been made the object of another very heavy attack by the Fascist air force. Formations of bombers and dive-bombers brought themselves wave after wave over the more important military objectives of the Island. A veritable shower of bombs was rained down on Mqabba [Luqa] aerodrome. Aerodrome buildings and other establishments, stores and aircraft dispersed on the airfield were hit by medium and heavy calibre bombs and hundreds of grenades which caused vast destruction and fires. The attack on the naval base of VALLETTA was extremely effective. Loud explosions were heard and huge fires visible from a great distance were started. The fires served as beacons for later waves of aircraft and facilitated the location of objectives. Serious damage was caused to harbour installations and to the dry-docks. Anti-aircraft and fighter opposition supported by the wide employment of searchlights did not prevent the crews of our planes from carrying out one of the most heavy attacks that the Island has experienced in the last few months.

Saturday 16 August

"O' dreary morn, will your end never come" must have been the prayer offered up by 'A' Flt on the dawn watch.

'B' Flt were luckier, having two 1 section scrambles for that ghostly +1 which appears then fades with monotonous regularity.

Jeff in sheer desperation for something to do in the P.M. took 'A' Flt to have a look at the opposition on their own ground, but the Italians kept very much to ground and nothing happened worthy of record.

F/L Hancock took up 6 A/C in the evening for a +12 which came over the Island but owing to being scrambled late no contact was made, but it was a very close thing.

Sunday 17 August

The dawn watch as usual! with 'B' Flt in the chair. During the day the occasional 1 section scramble for that +1.!!

Some kind person presented us with some jig-saw puzzles and sundry other fireside comforts, these were pounced upon with great eagerness, but they only proved a momentary diversion as they were finished in a very short time. The CO is agitating for a day's release, to improve the serviceability, which now stands at four, but will we get it? Will we hell!!!

Monday 18 August

Three flips today, consisting of two scrambles for +1s., which of course faded, and a gross exhibition of hour hogging, reputed to be a patrol over two submarines; the CO is now saying he is hard worked, having done more flying than anyone else this month.

We regret to announce that F/L Jeffries aided by F/L Pike, was seen to remove his nether garments in the Sgts Mess, later in the evening, whether under great stress or provocation or whether it was just a nudist party, is not known; but "apparently" a good time was had by all.

Note:- the serviceability has now increased to 12, a grand show on the part of the ground staff.

Tuesday 19 August

Nothing happened in the Dawn Watch but later in the morning F/L

Jeffries was scrambled with six others to chase a +6 which were 40 miles N. Not receiving any other instructions Jeff went up in a flat out climb, but he was completely ignored by "Banjo". The Italians passed over the Island at 23.000´ when Jeff was at 18.000´ and consequently no contact was made. On landing every one was chagrined to hear that they had been scrambled 15 mins late and then only for the purpose of dispersal, so the climb up was an unnecessary waste of flying time and engine hours, preservation of which is so essential to the serviceability.

It makes you think!!!

In the afternoon P/O Thompson and Sgt Sutherland went to look at a +3. 60 miles E but it was only a friendly MTB.

In the evening Sgts Hayes and Hunton were vectored on to a plot 60 miles E[;] the plots coincided for about 5 mins but nothing was seen. Another day over.

Wednesday 20 August

Enemy Activity for the day 20.8.41. NIL. – so runs the daily summary.
Activity at 185 dispersal. NIL.

Thursday 21 August

The dawn-watchers were rudely interrupted at 6 o'clock, they were scrambled for a +3 25 miles N but lo and behold, as they took off, 3 Macchis flew across the aerodrome at 200´ firing into space and hitting precisely nothing, however P/O Bailey leading P/O Reeves and Sgt Westcott happened to be directly underneath them and the Bofors which were pooping off madly seemed to be shooting at our three Hurricanes and only by the Grace of God did they escape being hit.

10 mins later 3 more Macchis attempted the same thing with net result NIL, but kindly look on the opposite page and see what "really" happened, according to the Italians.

On the facing page is an excerpt from the RAF Daily Intelligence Summary, No. 63 (sic: No. 64), dated 24 August 1941.

NOTE: It is hardly necessary to recall that the low flying attack carried out by the ITALIANS and reported in D.I.S., dated 21st. AUGUST, caused neither damage or casualties. TWO MACCHI 200's were hit by BOFORS. The following is the version of the story broadcast by ROME RADIO –

" A particularly audacious action was carried out over MALTA. In "the early hours of yesterday (THURSDAY) an ITALIAN Fighter "formation escorted by another formation of Fighters flew over "MALTA and from a very low level machine gunned the highly

"equipped air base of HAL FAR, while another formation crossed
"the sky for indirect reasons over the Island. The daring attack of
"our fighters although met with a most intense anti-aircraft fire
"was crowned with success. Two large twin-engine bombers were
"set on fire and destroyed, while another two bombers and two
"single engine planes were hit and rendered unserviceable.
"Furthermore several other aircraft to the South-East of the
"aerodrome were hit and, judging by the flames, they sustained
"extensive damage. Enemy's A.A. batteries were likewise attacked
"with armaments available on board our aircraft. British fighters
"flying over Malta did not engage our planes all of which
"returned regularly to their respective bases."

Later in the morning S/L Mould took off with six others to investigate a +3, he finally chased them all the way home, but all in vain, on landing he was torn off an official strip for being over Sicily without permission. What a life!!!

There were a few more 1 section scrambles during the day, and in the afternoon a continuous convoy patrol was carried out – no fun at all.

It is as well to note that while some members of the squadron seem to have joined the temperance society, the drinking capacities of others seem in no way impaired by the heat.

Friday 22 August

F/L Hancock led 10 A/C from 'B' Flt after a +6 which faded very shortly after he became airborne. P/O Thompson force landed on the aerodrome after ½ hour.

There were 4 1 section scrambles in the evening for that blasted +1. nothing else to report.

Another uninspiring day.

The "vicious" round of swimming by day and drinking by night is becoming as monotonous as the everlasting watches.

Saturday 23 August

Once again no activity, but the very welcome news arrived this afternoon [that] S/Ldr Mould has received the bar to his DFC.

A newspaper cutting is attached:

Actg. Sqdn. Ldr. P. W. O. Mould, D.F.C., 185 Sq. This officer has led the squadron on 62 daylight sorties since last May. He has also carried out seven night sorties. Under his leadership the unit has destroyed eight, probably destroyed 14, and damaged seven hostile aircraft.

> Sqdn. Ldr. Mould has destroyed one and
> damaged two. By his example and courage he has
> contributed largely to the high standard of
> operational efficiency and moral *[sic]* of the
> squadron.

His four months leadership of the squadron is summed up by the wording of the signal which was, "– – – for courage and determination and highly successful leadership – – –" but as anyone who has read this diary or has been with him since the foundation of the squadron will see, these words do not cover all that he has meant to those who have worked with him.

Everyone offers their sincere congratulations on his well deserved award.

Sunday 24 August

One scramble and one scramble only. 1 section for a +1 which was a PRU Hurricane anyway – So what!!!

The Italians respect the Sabbath apparently, even if the Germans don't.

Messrs Sutherland, Ellis, and Co Ltd have procured a boat – of sorts – they hope to use it for a quick getaway in case of invasion, – it is hoped they can swim.

Monday 25 August

F/Lt Pike took 'A' Flt up in the morning for a +3, but apart from a pleasant hour's flying nothing occurred.

P/O Thompson took 'B' Flt up in the afternoon for another +3, but nothing happened and they landed in time for tea.

Tuesday 26 August

Nothing for the dawn watchers.

3 one section scrambles in the morning for 'B' Flt for the odd +1. doing circuits and bumps at Comiso. 'A' Flt did nothing in the afternoon except play poker but hard working 'B' Flt were scrambled for +3 40 miles N – however when airborne they were told to patrol a ship about 40 miles west of the Island. On landing they were told that 126 Squadron, our neighbours at Ta' Quali *[sic]* had waded into about 15 Macchis and destroyed 3 for the loss of 1.

"Butch" Burton caught a boat going homewards this evening, he takes with him our best wishes and lots of mail.

In the evening the S-Ps *[sergeant pilots]* threw a party for the "Orficers" *[sic]* – the party got underway *[at]* about 8.30 when 'B' Flt came off watch – the standard of entertainment was very high *[and]* the programme included such famous acts as Cousens & Cousens – Raconteurs – Jokes – various. Alderson & Bates – Tap Dancers Caruso Walmsley – Soloist –

Songs – clean and otherwise Ream, Wren & Ream – at the Guitar and Organ and with Sgt Horsey as ringmaster?!!!

Several of the audience were overcome – by the heat – and various striptease acts added a bit of spice to the proceedings.

Sgt Sutherland was very efficient as a filler-upper of empty glasses.

Wednesday 27 August

No activity at all, perhaps it was just as well because sundry pilots were perhaps not quite feeling as fit as usual.

Thursday 28 August

One one section scramble for something that might have been something but wasn't.

A Blenheim got lost in the afternoon and 'our Jeff' went to look for it?

Complete and utter boredom for the twenty odd pilots who did not fly.

In the evening the CO's two Flight comms and the two stooges, threw a party for their friends – the AOC was present. (?) Hosts of other people were seen to be there and imbibing tonic water, the notables including the nobs from Ta' Qali – Lashings of spirit and the corresponding headaches in the morning.

Friday 29 August

In spite of headaches, nausea etc., F/L Jeffries pushed off in the morning with 8 others after +6 which mercifully faded as he approached.

In the afternoon S/L Mould repeated the dose for "+1" – which faded.

It seems so unfair – odds of 10 to 1 – in OUR favour.

Jeff went up again in the evening for a +9 which was 40 miles N and eventually crossed the Island – being late off the ground (NB no fault of his) Jeff decided to call it a day and just tootled around at a few thousand feet waiting for the all clear to go.

– After all, what's the use – – – !!! –

Congratulations are in order for Messrs Bailey and Thompson who are now Flying- Officers – and about time too.

Saturday 30 August

Nothing happened until the evening when 4 aircraft with Pat Hancock leading went out to help some Wellingtons who were being attacked, the E/A sheered off at our approach and no engagement took place.

However some damage was suffered by F/O Murch, when his No 2, Sgt Cousens, knocked his empennage for a burton, L.C. [Murch] was unhurt and made a good landing complaining that he could not make his elevators work.

It is understood that Sgt Cousens apologised to F/O Murch; no doubt the CO had a few words with the aforementioned Sgt Cousens. – We leave the two participants sucking inky fingers and glaring at sheets of paper headed:-

Sir,

I have the honour to report – – – – –

Sunday 31 August

There was one 'do' in the morning for a plus one up north the gallant Jolly leading three others – but of [sic] no avail.

Messrs Murch and Forth got together to produce or design a squadron crest, and a very creditable effort it was.

We hope shortly to produce of [sic] copy for insertion in this diary, together with photographs of the squadron and 'B' Flt Line board.

(Dear Lord, send me something to write about next month!).

T.

Monday 1 September

2. "one sections" for the dawn-watchers. 'B' Flt had one scramble in the morning watch, for a +12, which came within 24 miles of the Island and then b—— off at high speed.

In the afternoon one section scramble – nothing happened.

The Gladiator which arrived from Kalafrana a few days ago, became serviceable, and to the chagrin of the FAA (the previous owners) the RAF in the person of the CO put it through its paces. F/L Jeffries tried to emulate the CO but after a short time he (landed) arrived back at the aerodrome. [*The Gladiator was N5520, formerly of the Fighter Flight. The partly restored aircraft is now on display in Malta's National War Museum.*]

Tuesday 2 September

Once again the Gladiator took the air and F/L Hancock. 50 mins. later, after frustrating all the attempts of 'B' Flt pilots to sleep, Pat managed to regain control and much to his surprise he was able to step out of the machine on to terra firma. The Harbour-Master was not amused and Pat was awarded seven days CH (confined to Hurricanes).

'A' Flt were scrambled twice during the day but nothing happened.

Wednesday 3 September

'B' Flt went up in the morning for a +6, the "plots"? of which coincided with ours for some considerable time, causing a great deal of "rubber necking", but in actual fact the 'bandits' were about 30 miles removed from us and consequently no contact.

F/O Thompson <u>flew</u> the Gladiator!!

Thursday 4 September
Nothing for 'B' Flight in the dawn watch. 'A' Flt were scrambled in the morning for a +24 – CO leading.

Jeff saw one lone aeroplane and thought it was a Hurricane but on closer examination, it proved to be a Macchi so Jeff and Oliver did their stuff in no small way and although Jeff was only credited with a 'probable', 52 cannon shells delivered at 25 yds range rather leads one to believe that one little Macchi did <u>not</u> get home, Jeff was then the object of affection of 4 more Macchis, but believing discretion to be the better part of valour, he decided it was time for his morning cup of tea and promptly removed himself from the locality.

The remainder of the squadron was vectored out to sea but owing to a slight discrepancy on the 'plots', a mere 20 miles" [sic] no further contact was made.

A lone Macchi plucked up enough courage to have a look at the aerodrome from a low altitude, the Bofors opened up, but claimed no hits.

Just before lunch, one section was sent off to look for a dinghy containing one Italian they did not see him, but it was later reported that he had been picked up and he has since given quite a lot of information.

L.C. was sent off to investigate a boat but 'twas only a local whaler!!

During the morning's engagement 126 Sqdn shot down 5 with no loss to themselves – a very fine effort.

In the afternoon 249 Sqdn intercepted some Macchis and shot down 3, but losing 2 themselves. The fight, according to S/Ldr Barton, was very tough going and in all probability it was during this fight that Lt Romagnoli, one of Italy's crack pilots, was shot down.

Pat Hancock was U/S [unserviceable] for the day having [been] imbibing freely of the cup that cheers on the previous evening.

Friday 5 September
During the morning the CO and Sgt Hayes went up to find survivors of a Cant 1007 which had been shot down during the night bits of wreckage were seen and these were later collected.

The bloke wot did it – P/O Barnwell is to be congratulated on his magnificent effort, he has now four confirmed destroyed at night over Malta, such an achievement will not be long unrecognised and a suitable recommendation made.

Later in the morning a dinghy was seen being paddled frantically towards the Island, when investigated, five Italians, very much alive, were picked up by the rescue launch, they were survivors from the Cant.

The only other activity was in the morning when 'B' Flt went up 10.00 for a +9 which did not come in.

Saturday 6 September

'B' Flt in the dawn watch were vectored on to a +3, but no height could be given and eventually, when the bandit was seen, only <u>one</u> by the way, a slight discrepancy in height, a mere 10000´, made all the difference to a successful interception.

Chubby Eliot has actually left the Island!!

Any interference with his departure was prevented by Pat and L.C. acting as close escort. An attempt by Pat to stow away on the Sunderland was thwarted and he is now planning to borrow the Heinkel *[special operations He 115 floatplane of the Government Intelligence Section]* which, we are told, can make the trip to UK.

Among those who came to see the Sunderland off were, the Governor and the AOC. Chubby was quite flattered, but it 'twas *[sic]* later seen that their presence was not associated with the departure of a former 'A' Flight commander, of 185 but with the presence of a most distinguished member of a sister service.

Sunday 7 September

No operational flying today, in fact so little flying has been done recently, that quite a lot of practice flying is being carried out in order to keep our hands in.

After a diversion to a raid, 4 a/c of 'B' Flt carried out practice formation attacks. 'A' Flt followed suit in the afternoon and 'B' Flt rounded off the day with still more practice attacks.

At dispersal time an unfortunate accident occurred when Sgt Forth decided that he could taxi one A/C and push another at the same time, with disastrous results, and now 'Lil' is bemoaning the loss of his rear portion and the airscrew of O has lost most of its cooling properties.

8 September

<u>Black Monday. September 8th.</u>

Another dull day. 'A' Flt getting all the flying, 1 section scramble and a couple of air tests.

We heard this morning that our stay on the Island is to be increased to twelve months in spite of the fact that we had been given to understand that the tour of duty for those who came out in April was six months.

This action shows typical lack of understanding on the part of those who order these things and who obviously fail to realise what it means to be an operational fighter pilot on Malta.

The people who have been here for five months or more and who were eagerly looking forward to going home in a few weeks time must regard the whole affair as a definite breach of faith.

This action gives truth to the rumour that the dockyard is refitting several ships with padded (cells) cabins. It is also believed that among the comforts for their prospective passengers are many domino sets and a goat.

We were later somewhat lifted from the slough of despond by the news that more Hurricanes are arriving tomorrow.

Tuesday 9 September

'A' Flt were scrambled late in the dawn watch, thus enabling 'B' Flt to eat their breakfasts at leisure. The plot of +6 faded.

'B' Flt had one one section scramble – plot faded.

'A' Flt up again late in the P.M. watch so that 'B' Flt were again able to eat in peace and comfort, – this synchronisation of scrambles with taking over times shows remarkable foresight on the part of ops [operations] B.

Fourteen new Hurricanes arrived today but they all landed at Ta Kali, they were all Mark IIBs and rumour has it that still more are arriving and we hope that we get our share.

The Squadron embarks on a round of social diversities.

This afternoon Messrs Bailey, Reeves, Oliver and Allardice were escorted to the Governor's party at the Palace where they were able to enjoy swimming, tennis, and no doubt they drank tea in large quantities.

In the evening the CO and Jeff went to a party thrown by the Anglo–Maltese Union. The AOC was presented with a shield commemorating and acknowledging the services rendered by the RAF in the defence of Malta.

Jeff and the CO thought that the liquid refreshments provided was quite good but they had to drink large quantities of same before it was appreciated.

Wednesday 10 September

2. aircraft from 'A' Flt did a practice interception in the morning. 'B' Flt had the only scramble for the day. In the afternoon they went up for a +6 102 miles north – steering north. As the Hurricane is not capable of doing 700 mph there was no interception.

The CO has been feeling pretty ill for about a fortnight and has at last been persuaded to go off flying for a few days, what he really needs, together with several others, is to go off the Island, that is the only cure.

Thursday 11 September

Some practice flying and a practice interception in the morning, and 1 section scramble for +9 80 miles N which faded. In the afternoon another two one section scrambles for 2 Blenheims and a PIU [sic: presumably PRU] Hurricane.

F/L Pike and F/O Thompson return from rest camp looking very fit.

Sgt Branson, ex-185, now in the MNFU [Malta Night Fighter Unit], did some low flying along the Sliema front, for the benefit of a girl friend, unfortunately the AOC was also an interested spectator and decided that Branson could do some more low flying – along the banks of the River Nile.

Apart from the injustice of the punishment, it puts ideas into people's heads – if you want to get off the Island – low fly along the Sliema front!!!

Friday 12 September

'B' Flt were scrambled within two minutes of coming to readiness on the dawn watch they were up for nearly one and a half hours chasing a +3 which wandered up and down the coast of Sicily but did not come in. 'B' Flt again up in the afternoon for another +3. F/O Thompson went up to guide a Wellington home which was lost.

Sad news – Pat Hancock, hearing that he would have to remain on the Island for another six months decided to apply for posting to ME *[Middle East]* with a view to going into Training Command in Rhodesia.

Pat has a particularly good record – he was in France in 1940, came home for the London blitz and just when things were quietening down at home, he was posted to Malta just in time for the German blitz. And so after doing eighteen months continual readiness he decided that he had had it.

As 'B' Flt Commander he was very popular – his efficiency beyond question and it is with sincere regret that we see him go.

It is interesting to note that out of the 24 founder members there are only 7 left.

Another disappointment – the Gladiator, in which we had visions of doing practice flying, is now to be used only for Met trips and only half-a-dozen or so of us are to be allowed to fly it.

P/O Barnwell's (Barny) splendid achievements in the MNFU have been recognised in the immediate award of the DFC everyone offers their sincere congratulations.

Saturday 13 September

'B' Flt had 1 section scramble and a squadron scramble this morning for a +8 84 miles away which did not come in.

'A' Flt did a practice calibration flight and some other practice flying in the afternoon.

During the morning 8 long range Hurricanes arrived from HMS Ark Royal, we hope to keep them all, but what a hope.

L.C. went to a party in the evening given by the Anglo–Maltese Union – no comments.

Sunday 14 September

For the first time in weeks the Sabbath was interrupted.

1 one section scramble in the morning for a PIU *[sic]* Hurricane.

In the afternoon a +1 appeared on the board and F/O Thompson and

Sgt Nurse patrolled for some time over St Paul's Bay, he [sic] was relieved by F/O Murch and Sgt Westcott but the bandit did not come in.

'A' Flight had two scrambles in the evening for plots which did not materialise.

A strange disease has bitten the people at dispersal, cries of "Four Hearts" in a loud voice, followed by a whisper of "Little Slam in Clubs" are to be heard whenever 'B' Flight are at readiness.

Good news – Two of the new Hurricane Mark IIBs are being fitted with bomb racks and it is the intention of the AOC for Hurricanes to dive bomb bits of Sicily – Here is the offensive spirit in no small way.

Monday 15 September

Some practice flying and a few 1 section scrambles which came to nought.

In the evening the majority of the officers went over to Ta Kali for a party and most of them got "very nicely thank you!!" It is worthy of record that the CO drank nothing but lemonade the whole evening.

Pikey also got the better of an argument with a Takalite, and presented him with a beautiful black eye.

We are now allowed 24 Hurricanes on our establishment.

Tuesday 16 September

There was a lot of practice flying today – no less than 20 pilots had a flip, there was also a couple of 1 section scrambles but no plot was given.

Sgt Branson goes on to ME in a Sunderland – we wish him lots of luck.

Four new pilots arrived today P/O Lintern and Sgts Eastman, Comfort and Steele we hope they will be happy with us and enjoy great success in the Squadron.

Wednesday 17 September

1 scramble for Sgts Sutherland and Eastman and some practice flying.

A chappie came down from the Met Office and gave the Met pilots a short lecture on what to do. Met flights will be done at dawn and they will start tomorrow.

Pat Hancock left us this evening and went on to Egypt in a Sunderland, he was given a great send off, practically the whole of 'B' Flight foregathered at Kalafrana and wished him luck to the accompaniment of pops and gurglings from champagne bottles, it is a small comfort to know that Pat went on to the Sunderland feet first.

F/L Pike takes over 'B' Flight and we wish him the best of luck in his new Command.

A slight rearrangement of flights was necessary. P/O Lintern and Sgt Comfort go to 'A' Flight as well as F/O Murch as Jeff's No 2. P/O Allardice and Sgts Steele and Eastman come into 'B' Flight.

On the opposite page is the Squadron photo and overleaf the 'B' Flight line boards. *[A copy of the squadron photograph can be seen in the plate section of this publication.]*

Thursday 18 September

The CO did the first Met Flight. One scramble for 'A' Flight in the morning for a +3 over Sicily which developed into +12. 50 miles N but did not come in closer.

The CO carried out a test on a Hurricane fitted with bomb racks and he found it to be OK so in the afternoon the CO[,] Pikey, Gay Bailey and Tommy carried out some dive bombing practices on Filfla with 8 x 20 lbs bombs. A fair degree of accuracy was obtained and it was decided that dive bombing bits of Sicily would probably do them a power of no good. We hope to get cracking very shortly.

The Royal Tank Corps visited us this morning and everyone was impressed by the 3 – 25 tonners they brought with them. The CO tried his hand on one of the tanks and nearly wrote off the ambulance, we, in our turn showed off our Hurricanes, but a request by one of the Tank Corps to try <u>his</u> hand had to be politely refused.

'B' Flight pilots are still bitten by Bridge's Disease.

Friday 19 September

F/O Thompson did the Met Flight this morning.

There was a one section scramble for 'B' Flt in the morning and a squadron scramble for 'A' Flt in the afternoon.

'B' Flight in the evening had a 3 section scramble.

Jeff and L.C. did some more practice bombing in the morning and the CO and Tommy followed suit in the evening, this time it was done from a greater height, but even then a remarkable degree of accuracy was obtained. The results of all these practices are to be combined in order to be able to formulate the best method of bombing from Hurricanes.

P/O Reeves leaves us for a week's sojourn at St Paul's Bay.

Saturday 20 September

Jeff did the Met Flight.

'A' Flight had a plus 3 to chase in the morning *[although]* in actual fact they were scrambled late and then for dispersal only – but nobody told us?

In the evening, Shep (Sgt Sheppard) led two others for a +1 – up North – but of *[sic]* no avail[;] meanwhile P/O Veitch defended the aerodrome.

Later in the evening several officers led by the CO went into Valetta on the pretext of wanting to buy some hairpins, surprisingly enough, after the odd "quickie", it was decided to pay Sliema a visit, and when the party returned – in the early hours of the morning – they still had not got any hairpins –

The CO happened to look in on the AOC while he was in town and was delighted to hear that the AOC approved heartily of dive bombing – we may expect the fun to start any day now.

Sunday 21 September
Pikey had the privilege (?) of doing the Met Flight – (I wonder if the Met Pilots will be so keen when the weather deteriorates. [cloud 500´–50.000´])
Only 1 section scramble the whole day when P/O Veitch patrolled Sing-Sing as an answer to some "activity up north". Jolly and Vardy did some bombing practice.

Monday 22 September
L.C. – Met Flight.
Every diarist should make some note about the weather – the azure sky remains unmarked except for some odd cloud which sneaks hurriedly across the "empyrean blue", the sun is still there too.
2. 1 section scrambles for 'B' Flight and a squadron scramble for 'A' Flight led by L.C. the plot was +3 – 25 miles N.
On landing, Sgt Comfort thought he was a steam engine and tried to stop against some buffers – the buffers in this case being the corners of the hangar – however little damage was done to the aircraft or the hangar so everyone is happy.

Tuesday 23 September
The CO had his second go at the Met Flight – this duty comes round much too quickly.
'B' Flight had all the flying today 1 section and the Squadron up in the morning but nothing developed.
Gay Bailey had a shot at flying the Gladiator as a practice before doing the Met Flight tomorrow.

Wednesday 24 September
Gay almost did the Met Flight but had to return owing to engine trouble after 40 mins.
9 A/C up – Jeff leading for +2. 47 miles N plot did not develop.
P.M. – A most hectic afternoon – there were 4 1 section scrambles – Sgt Sutherland leading in 3 and Sgt Lillywhite 1.
'A' Flight did some practice flying in the evening, they also had a 1 section scramble for a Blenheim.
Now for the funniest story yet:- Time:- 'B' Flight in the afternoon watch.
'Phone rings – "Scramble one section – Beaufighter being attacked".
Sgts Sutherland and Ellis dash off.
1 min. later.
'Phone rings – Cancel scramble – Beaufighter <u>was</u> attacked at 10.45 a.m.

300 miles away. – Rings off.

Thursday 25 September
Tommy. – Met Flight. –

11 aircraft – Jeff in the van – "beat up" Hal Far in a "Pansy" (?) squadron formation.

Only one operational flight – for P/O Allardice and Sgt Eastman.

Sgts Jolly and Sheppard went to Sliema this morning and returned in the afternoon with a wireless set for use in dispersal, this addition to the pilots' "comforts" is very welcome.

We are very sorry to hear the Sgts Wren, Swire, Horsey and Comfort have been posted to ME [and] we wish them all the luck in the world.

Sgts Nurse and Ream go to 'A' Flight to replace those posted.

Rumour has it that Pat Hancock has arrived safely in Rhodesia.

Friday 26 September
Gay Bailey – Met Flight.

There were four one section scrambles and 2 Squadron scrambles throughout the day but there were no interceptions and consequently nothing to report.

In the early evening the signal came for Sgts Horsey, Swire[,] Comfort and Wren to report to Luqa as they were leaving that evening in a Wellington for ME BUT they were not to be found until after exhaustive enquiries had been made in the "low" haunts of Valetta, they finally arrived back at Hal Far – only to find that the whole thing was off – the crew of the Wellington having caught Malta Dog – or something –

Their arrival back at Hal Far, however coincided with another signal, this time for F/Lt Jeffries awarding him the DFC [so] everyone then adjoined to the Sergeants Mess to celebrate.

If ever a man earned the DFC, Jeff has; he has been leading 'A' Flight practically since the formation of the Squadron, and leading it most successfully. In England he was a Flight-Commander of 232 Squadron for some considerable time, before that he operated from and over France, and on one occasion had to walk back to his base, he now has six confirmed victories to his credit, as well as many other probables and damaged. In the early days of the Squadron when things were not going so well for us, Jeff, more the [sic] anybody else kept us going by his constant cheerfulness and almost continual wisecracking. – Good luck Jeff and here's to the next one.

Saturday 27 September
Jeff – Met Flight.

A convoy consisting of 8 merchantmen with a large Naval escort came in today and we had to patrol over convoy, doing so 1 section at a time. On their way here the convoy was attacked by a large number of aircraft *[and]* one ship was damaged and subsequently had to *[be]* sunk by our own ships, but in reply the escort vessels shot down no fewer than sixteen enemy aircraft.

The CO announced this afternoon that we are to make our first bombing raid tomorrow – the target to be Comiso Aerodrome in Southern Sicily the attacking force to consist of six "bombers" and six fighters as escort; everyone got together to discuss ways and means, and when we were released an hour earlier, everyone was more than a bit excited in anticipation of tomorrow's "do".

Later in the evening nearly everyone went to the Sgts Mess to drink to our own success.

Sunday 28 September

L.C. did the Met Flight.

I think today's activities can be best explained by Duff gen.

'B' Flight – CO leading kicked off at dawn with the following effort:-

Extracts follow from the RAF Daily Intelligence Summary, No. 100, dated 29 September 1941.

13.　　HURRICANES. SIX Hurricane (Fighters) SIX Hurricane (Bombers) of No. 185 Squadron despatched to attack COMISO AERODROME. Pilots of the former were: F/O. THOMPSON, P/O. ALLARDICE, Sgt. STEELE, Sgt. EASTMAN, Sgt. ELLIS and Sgt. SUTHERLAND. Pilots of the Bombers were: S/Ldr. MOULD, F/Lt. PIKE, P/O. BAILEY, P/O. WOODSEND, Sgt. ALDERSON and Sgt. LILLYWHITE. The Bombers approached the target from the EAST at 9,000 feet 07.15 hours, dived down to 7,500 feet on the Main Northern dispersal area and Officers' Mess. Total 1,860 lbs. (40 lbs. G.P. and 25 lbs. incendiary) burst in target area. TWO aircraft were seen to be on fire in N.W. & N. corners by the Fighters and other aircraft certainly damaged. OFFICERS' MESS appeared also to be well shaken. The enemy aircraft were clustered in their pens. Light and medium A.A. opposition, intense 4–5,000 feet barrage. NO enemy Fighters. ONE Macchi 200 seen near COMISO at 12,000 feet, made off Northward at full speed. ONE aircraft (P/O. WOODSEND) came down in the sea 10 miles off NORTH point of GOZO. Pilot was later rescued.

As soon as 'B' Flight had landed and refuelled 'A' Flight – CO leading again went back and handed out another dose as follows:-

---

14.　　HURRICANES. TWELVE Hurricanes – No. 185 Squadron, took off at 09.30 hours to attack COMISO AERODROME. SIX of them (TWO sections of THREE) S/Ldr. MOULD – (Leader), P/O. LINTERN, Sgt. SHEPHARD [sic]; F/Lt. JEFFRIES, – (Leader), P/O. VIETCH [sic] and Sgt. VARDY. Each aircraft 6 x 40 lbs. G.P. and 2 x 25 lbs. incendiaries. The remaining SIX aircraft – F/O. MURCH, P/O. OLIVER, Sgt. HAYES, Sgt. NURSE, Sgt. JOLLY and Sgt. HUNTON acted as Fighter Escort. They approached <u>COMISO AERODROME</u> from the EAST at 17–18,000 feet, dived and released from 10–12,000 feet at 10.05 hours. Bombs seen to burst in N.W. and N.E. dispersal areas and amongst Administration buildings SOUTH of HANGARS. TWO small fires seen in dispersal area. P/O. VIETCH machine-gunned one large building S.W. of COMISO AERODROME and a car on the road. One bomb that hung up in F/Lt. JEFFRIES aircraft dropped when aircraft was over KALAFRANA area, reason unknown. No opposition. ALL aircraft landed safely.

When everyone landed, it was voted a good idea to knock off for lunch; afterwards 'B' Flight with Pikey leading this time had another smack with very much the same result:-

15.　　<u>HURRICANES</u>. SIX Hurricane (Bombers) and SIX Hurricane (Fighters) of No. 185 Squadron were despatched at 14.00 hours to attack <u>COMISO AERODROME</u>. Pilots of Fighters were: P/O. BAILEY, P/O. REEVES, Sgt. LILLYWHITE, Sgt. WESTCOTT, P/O. ALLARDYCE [sic] and Sgt. ALDERSON.

Sgt. ALDERSON returned at 14.05 hours with engine trouble. The aircraft were over the target at 14.35 hours. The first section of Bombers – F/Lt. PIKE – (Leader), Sgt. SUTHERLAND and Sgt. EASTMAN bombed the HANGARS and other BUILDINGS on the SOUTH EAST side of the AERODROME. Hits were observed on HANGARS. The second section – F/O. THOMPSON, Sgt. ELLIS and Sgt. COUSENES [sic] bombed the OFFICERS' MESS and QUARTERS on the NORTH WEST side of the AERODROME. Direct hits and near misses were observed. Bombing was carried out from 12,000–13,000 feet. About SIX craters were seen in the CENTRE of the AERODROME. These are thought to be the result of the TWO previous sorties. No opposition of any kind was encountered. Weather and visibility were both very good. ALL aircraft returned.

<u>GENERAL NOTE:</u>　　　The total weight of bombs dropped by the THREE SORTIES was 5,140 lbs. and it is estimated that 90 percent of these fell in the target area.

A few other happenings:-

Woody in the first show on his way home decided that travelling in an aeroplane that might blow up *[at]* any moment was not his idea of fun he indicated this feeling to the CO by a well known gesture before making a rapid if undignified exit from his aeroplane, He was seen to make a safe landing in the water; unfortunately, and this seriously, his exact position was not made known and it was not till 5½ hours later that he was picked up by the rescue launch "Clive"; in the course of the search 2 Swordfish, 1 Gladiator, 2 Hurricanes, 1 Fulmar 1 Cruiser, 1 Destroyer, 2 Motor boats <u>AND</u> the Rescue Launch took part.

When the 'Clive' first spotted him Woody appeared to them as if suspended in mid air, this effect was due to fact that he was jumping up in his dinghy and then falling into the water.

When the CO went down to collect him, Woody was asleep; he returned to Hal Far dressed in Naval tunic, with last war's medals, and *[wearing]* grey flannels, but apparently none the worse for his adventure.

Jeff on his way home from the second show had one bomb hang up and try what he might he could not get rid of it so he decided to land with it still attached but the bomb apparently had a mind of its own and as Jeff approached the circuit, the bomb fell off and landed on Malta, fortunately (or otherwise) it did no damage. *except kill a goat*

<u>*Sgt Ellis please note*</u> *[Addendum by unidentified writer shown in italics.]*

Apart from the AA opposition on the first raid no other opposition was encountered. However, after the third raid had finished a plot of +20 appeared on the board, orbiting Comiso. This patrol was maintained until dusk, but the Italians were just a wee bit slow on the uptake.

Facing page:

```
HAL FAR
HQ MED NR12


GR65          TO HAL FAR (FOR O.C. 185 SQDN)
              FROM A.O.C.
OPS715 29/9 PLEASE ACCEPT MY WARMEST CONGRATULATIONS ON YOUR
MAGNIFICENT PERFORMANCE YESTERDAY IN BOMBING COMISO
AERODROME. THERE IS NOT THE SLIGHTEST DOUBT THAT THE BOMBING OF THE
AERODROME KEPT ENEMY FIGHTERS AND RECONNAISSANCE AIRCRAFT FROM
COMING OVER HERE AND WATCHING THE CONVOY AND PERHAPS ATTACKING IT
WHEN APPROACHING THE GRAND HARBOUR . MAGNIFICENT EFFORT AND YOUR
SQDN MAY WELL BE PROUD OF IT = = = = = = = = = = = = = =1435 LT

MRM      VA      R 1637 LT WN B1        Q1
```

The above signal was received from the AOC this evening – It is very much appreciated by the squadron and encouraging to note that our little effort was recognised.

Monday 29 September

As a slight reward for our effort of yesterday the whole squadron was released, bar one, Yours truly was dragged out of bed to do the wretched Met Flight.

As everyone, bar none, had had the odd drink or two the night before, the day off was very much appreciated.

While attacking Cómiso on 30 September, 185 Squadron encountered for the first time the new Macchi C.202s. Powered by the same model Daimler Benz DB601 engine as the latest Messerschmitt Bf 109F, the Folgore *was considerably more powerful than the Hurricane as 185 Squadron quickly discovered.*

Tuesday 30 September

Twice in the morning 'A' Flight were scrambled *[with]* L.C. leading in a search for the crew of a Blenheim which had force landed in the sea during the night.

Later in the morning Tommy led 'B' Flight for a +3 which vanished, the Flight was kept airborne as a cover patrol for some Beaufighters. The CO did the Met Flight.

In the afternoon 'A' Flight did another successful bombing raid on Comiso. See Duff gen below:-

Excerpt from the RAF Daily Intelligence Summary, No. 102, dated 1 October 1941:

11.   HURRICANES. ELEVEN HURRICANES – NO. 185 Squadron took off at 13.55 hours to attack COMISO AERODROME. FIVE of them – (S/Ldr. MOULD – Leader), Sgt. JOLLY, F/O. MURCH, P/O. OLIVER & P/O. LINTERN), carried 6 x 40 lbs. G.P. and 2 x 25 lb. incendiaries. The remaining SIX aircraft – (F/Lt. JEFFRIES – Leader, Sgt. SHEPHERD *[sic]*, Sgt. VARDY, Sgt. KNOGHT *[sic]*, P/O. VEITCH & Sgt. HAYES), acted as Fighter Escort. They crossed the SICILIAN COAST WEST of SCALAMBRI at 19,000 feet and after circling the target approached it from the NORTH EAST at 13,000 feet, dived and released bombs 9–10,000 feet at 14.05 hours. Bombs seen to burst N.W. & N.E. of OFFICERS' MESS. ONE stick EAST of the NORTH WEST dispersal area, ONE stick in CENTRE of the AERODROME and the FIFTH in front of the HANGARS. NO A.A. was encountered, but THREE MACCHI 200'S were observed N.W. of AERODROME at 7,000 feet but did not engage.

> 9/10ths cloud over target at 12,000 feet. ONE aircraft – (P/O. LINTERN) failed to return.

P/O Lintern did not return so Jeff led four other Hurricanes to escort one Fulmar in an effort to locate him. When 10 miles from [the] Sicilian coast a Float plane was observed. Immediately afterwards the boys were engaged by some Macchis with inline engines [Macchi 202], a new job but not so good as the Hurricane.

Pilots' line shoots now follow:-

Jeff. – Claimed one probable

> I, Red one, was leading a formation escorting I Fulmar to try to locate P/O Lintern. We approached the Sicilian coast at 2000 ft. When about I0 miles off the coast I sighted I Float-plane. Black I, Sgt Jolly, went to investigate We were engaged by 5 enemy fighters, I fired several bursts at close range at enemy fighters. I then concentrated on one a/c. He tried every evasive action but my machine was more manoeuvrable and had a better performance. I broke off the engagement over the Sicilian coast and returned with the Fulmar. I last saw the enemy a/c going down at 800 ft with smoke and bits trailing behind.

P/O Veitch. Claimed one damaged.

> <u>General Report:-</u>   I yellow I, was operating on a Search patrol looking for P/O Lintern about I0 miles south of Sicily, when 2 Macchi 200 came down and engaged. We were flying at about I000 ft. I made four attacks and saw my tracer enter the fuselage and tail unit. I am claiming this as damaged.
>
> These enemy A/C had <u>inline engines</u> with a fuselage similar to a Macchi 200 and they might quite possibly have been Macchi's with an inline engine.
>
> No enemy aircraft were shot down. I had no difficulty in out-climbing them.

Sgt Jolly. Claimed one damaged

> As black, I was approaching the coast of Sicily when I saw a seaplane moving south just above the water. I called up red 1, and gave him the position receiving no reply, I dived down towards the seaplane, when a fighter crossed in front of me I got a short burst, when he did a roll and dived down I followed it around and got in four bursts at close range.

71

> My bullets entered the fighter but he broke off the engagement and went inland. I then lost him.

Sgt Ream. No claims.

> As yellow 2 I was approaching the Sicilian coast, when I saw a Macchi diving down across my nose, with a Hurricane on its tail. I lost sight of it beneath my wing, and did a steep climbing turn to the left.
>
> I again saw the Macchi approaching me in a dive, slightly below me. I put my nose down and did a head on attack but saw no results as he disappeared beneath my nose I did another climbing turn, and saw 2 Macchi's about 2000 feet above me. I looked round the sky for others but saw none and finding myself alone I returned to base.

The original operation to find P/O Lintern was unsuccessful, but it is hoped, in face of the fact that the Italian rescue boat was in the vicinity, P/O Lintern is now a prisoner-of-war. *[Pilot Officer Donald W. Lintern was, in fact, killed.]*

Although Lintern was only with us a short time he had already proved himself to be a capable and resourceful leader, and his loss is very much felt.

September proved to be quite an eventful month, apart from the loss of P/O Lintern operations of the Squadron can be viewed as quite satisfactory.

There had been a noticeable decline in Italian aerial activity over Malta during August and September. For the first time, Malta's forces were able to meet the enemy on an equal footing with the Navy delivering, between July and September, seven Swordfish and twenty-two Hurricanes in addition to thousands of tons of supplies. The Italians did what they could to disrupt operations, but of some sixty-seven vessels making up the convoys 'Substance', in July, and 'Halberd', in September, just two ships had been sunk and four damaged.

Wednesday 1 October

There were two squadron scrambles this morning.

It is with a deep sense of loss that I have to record the death our CO affectionately known to everyone as "Boy" Mould; the following is a short account of what happened or at least what we think must have happened:

The CO was leading 'A' Flight in a scramble after a +2, these he spotted and proceeded to give chase, as they were above him he was compelled to lose speed in order to gain height. A further plot of +9 then appeared, which apparently he did not hear about owing to RT failure, and just when he was unfavourably placed, – he had followed the +2 out of *[the]* sun, the formation was "jumped" by about a dozen Macchis and Falcos *[FIAT CR 42]*. F/O Murch was hit in the wing – severals *[sic]* other in an attempt to turn to engage spun off – the situation was hopeless and our pilots broke off the engagement and returned to base – with one exception – the CO, immediately the rescue services were put into operation – two MBs a Float-fish and three Hurricanes led by P/O Veitch, went to search in the area in which the CO was presumed to have crashed – a patch of oil was reported 25 miles on a bearing of 030° – As time went on and still no further definite news arrived, the grave faces of the pilots at dispersal reflected the general feeling, that little hope could be held for the CO's rescue. Another 3 Hurricanes led by myself went out later in the afternoon but nothing was seen. At about 4 o'clock Controller phoned up Jeff and reported that Lt Eyres of the Rescue Service had seen the patch of oil with fluorescence in the middle of it, and so much against everyone's will, the following conclusion was reached – The CO had been killed.

Everyone joins in offering their deepest sympathies to the CO's wife. The tragedy of his death is beyond real expression, he was the most courageous, popular and beloved CO – we count it a privilege and an honour to have *[been]* associated with him.

The following, apparently cut from The Times of Malta, *appears in the page preceding the above entry. Two ×s are written at the start and end of the fourth verse.*

With proud thanksgiving, a mother for her
children,
England mourns for her dead across the sea.
Flesh of her flesh they were, spirit of her spirit,
Fallen, in the cause of the free.

Solemn the drums thrill: Death august and royal
Sings sorrow up into immortal spheres.
There is music in the midst of desolation
And a glory that shines upon our tears.

They went with songs to the battle, they were
young,
Straight of limb, true of eye, steady and aglow.
They were staunch to the end against odds
uncounted,
They fell with their faces to the foe.
×
They shall grow not old, as we that are left grow
old:
Age shall not weary them, nor the years
condemn.

At the going down of the sun and in the morning
We will remember them.   ×

They mingle not with their laughing comrades
again;
They sit no more at familiar tables of home;
They have no lot in our labour of the day-time:
They sleep beyond England's foam.

But where our desires are and our hopes
profound.
Felt as a well-spring that is hidden from sight,
To the innermost heart of their own land they
are known
As the stars are known to the Night;

As the stars that shall be bright when we are
dust
Moving in the marches upon the heavenly plain,
As the stars that are starry in the time of our
darkness,
To the end, to the end, they remain.

Thursday 2 October

F/O Thompson had one scramble after a chummy A/C.

The Squadron was released at 13.00. result – parties in Valetta.

Friday 3 October

The Squadron came to readiness at 13.00 hours this afternoon. 'A' Flight keeping continuous watch until 13.00 hours tomorrow when 'B' Flight take over for 24 hours under the new system – the Squadron comes to "readiness" for 48 hours and then is released for 24 hours. This arrangement is meeting with considerable rejoicing – but it's only the beginning of the month.

At long last, after months of promises we have VHF [*very high frequency wireless*] – 'A' Flight tried it out this morning and voted it a great success, [*at*] any rate it is a great improvement of [*sic*] the old TR 90 and will greatly facilitate flying in bad weather.

Our new CO arrived today – S/L Lefevre – who was a Flight-fuhrer [*sic*] in 126. With him came F/O Ambrose – we wish them both the best of luck.

Saturday 4 October

Another catastrophe – this morning P/Os Veitch and Allardice went up on a one section scramble – 30 mins later a Hurricane was seen to come out of the clouds, which were down to fifteen hundred feet, in a TV dive and go into the sea about ½ mile off-shore, 5 mins later P/O Allardice landed and told us the following story, he was up at 25.000´ when he suddenly felt groggy, the next thing he remembers is pulling out of a dive at 500´, the trouble was oxygen, and therefore we must conclude that the same thing happened to Veitch, only, unhappily he was unable to pull out in time.

Veitch was rather a queer personality, and we are all very sorry about his death, which was so avoidable. Oxygen trouble is a thing which can and must be remedied.

Veitch was a man – very quiet and did not mix with the Squadron, he was a very capable pilot and his loss can be ill spared.

'B' Flight took over at one o'clock and had 3. 1 section scrambles but no fun. The Squadron is now released at 18.00, owing to the fact that the time has been put back one hour.

Sunday 5 October

'B' Flight had a 1 section scramble during which Tommy achieved "remarkable" height of 33.000´ but all to no purpose.

The Squadron was released for 24 hours at 13.00.

Monday 6 October

'A' Flight came to readiness at 13.00 hours – during the A.M. there was 1 section scramble and a lot of Air Tests but nothing else.

Tuesday 7 October

A Sunderland in Kala [Kalafrana] Bay, and Luqa were effectively patrolled by Sgt Jolly and F/Lt Jeffries respectively – later on in the morning Jeff had another scramble for a +3 up north but nothing happened.

S/L Lefevre left us this morning to return to Ta Kali – S/L Pike now takes over command of the Squadron – this is what should have happened in the first place – the way things happen in the Air Force is still a mystery.

L.C. takes over 'B' Flight, and we wish both him and our new CO the very best of luck and the greatest success.

F/O Bailey goes to 'A' Flight to act as Jeff's "stooge".

In view of the many recent changes which have taken place in the squadron a revised list of Flights appears opposite [see below].

S/L S.A.D. Pike.

'A' Flight.		'B' Flight	
F/L C.G. St D. Jeffries	※	F/L L.C. Murch	×
F/O G.G. Bailey	※	F/O P.D. Thompson	×
P/O Allardice	×	P/O Reeves	×
P/O Oliver		P/O Woodsend.	※
Sgts Jolly	×	Sgts:- Ellis	

„	Sheppard	×	„	Eastman	
„	Vardy.	×	„	Cousens	×
„	Knight	※	„	Forth	×
„	Nurse		„	Lillywhite	
„	Bates		„	Steele	
„	Hunton		„	Sutherland	
„	Hayes	×	„	Alderson	
„	Ream.		„	Westcott.	

Wednesday 8 October

F/O Thompson led 'B' Flight on a scramble which nearly gave everybody heart failure, as the Squadron was climbing for height – the plot of the bandits was given as "25.000 ft to port". This put them as 2000´ above us and into sun – this plot was followed by frantic warnings from Controller, "Look out Mustang – bandits just behind you – Collapse of Mustang Squadron.

NB All A/c returned safely.

The Squadron was released at 13.00.

Thursday 9 October

'A' Flight came to readiness at 13.00 but apart from a "Hectic" Bridge session, they had a dull afternoon.

Next morning they had one scramble when S/L Pike led them after a +6. but nothing developed.

The Gladiator was put u/s enabling sundry hard worked pilots to sleep on in peace.

Friday 10 October

1 scramble for +3 one of which passed over the Island at enormous altitude; for some time past the Regia Aeronautica have developed a habit of sending 1 PRU Macchi over at a great height, the plot comes in so fast that we do not get sufficient warning, but we are still expected to climb to 30.000´ in about 10 minutes?!

'B' Flight took over at 13.00, no flying took place in the afternoon.

The Gladiator is still u/s, but this morning both Messrs Jeffries and Thompson were dragged out of bed to no purpose.

Saturday 11 October

A dull morning – no flying.

Squadron released at 13.00.

Sunday 12 October
'A' Flight to readiness at 13.00 hrs.

S/L Pike led them on a scramble for 3+ which receded after orbiting for about ½ hr.
F/O Thompson did the Met Flight.

Monday 13 October
Two more stooges have been pressed into service for the Met Flights, one – Sgt Jolly did it this morning, the other Sgt Vardy – has yet to be initiated.

F/O Bailey led in two scrambles this morning – but no interceptions.

The Hurricane originally a short range interceptor-fighter has since been converted in [sic]
1. Medium Bomber
2. Recco – long range.
The latest idea and/or inspiration is to make the long suffering Hurricane a Long Range Fighter the idea being to add two external long range petrol tanks – then make equally long suffering pilots fly them for a long time, during which time they are expected to shoot down Italian transport A/C – rather long odds – but still??!!

'B' Flight came to readiness at 13.00 but apart from a practice flight – no other flying.

Tuesday 14 October
Just as 'B' Flight were coming to readiness – about 05.30 – the Regia Aeronautica delivered a half hearted low level attack on Luqa.
The MNFU were up at the time and P/O Barnwell apparently caught up with the Macchis.
At about six o'clock F/O Thompson and two others – P/O Woodsend and Sgt Sutherland were scrambled for a plot of +3 which was obviously the high cover for the low level attackers, the plot came in but was not contacted owing to some confusion in the plots.
On landing it was learnt the [sic] "Barny" had baled out and was in the water just off Grand Harbour. – Sgts Lillywhite and Eastman were immediately sent off on search, they were relieved by P/O Reeves and Sgt Forth – later in the morning F/L Murch and Sgt Forth escorting some Swordfish in the search, spent over one and a half hours, in the vicinity, but in every case nothing was seen and it was concluded that P/O Barnwell had been killed.
Barny was a loveable character, barely nineteen, his short career in the

Air Force was marked with brilliant success, he was awarded the DFC a short time ago for shooting down four aircraft at night, he had a positive craving for action, taking every opportunity to, as he so aptly put it, "to have a crack at the Huns".

Barny comes from an air-minded family, his father, designer of several famous aircraft was killed in a flying accident three years ago and both his brothers killed in action whilst flying in the Royal Air Force, Barny at least added further honour to an already distinguished family, Barny is a type we can ill afford to lose, and his death is very much felt by his many friends.

There were two other scrambles but no contact made – 13.00 – Squadron released for 24 hrs.

Wednesday 15 October
Jeff did the Met Flight.

'A' Flight came to readiness at 13.00 hrs. F/O Bailey led two sections for a cover patrol for two long range Hurricanes from Ta Kali.

Thursday 16 October
Sgt Vardy was initiated into the Met Flight this morning.

'A' Flight had two scrambles and three patrols this morning.

'B' Flight had one scramble.

In spite of the fact that the pilots have more time off under the new system of watches, the amount of flying done this month far exceeds that done last month, this is mainly due to the fact that our friends in Sicily are getting rather "uppish".

This afternoon S/L Pike and Sgt Jolly took off in the long range Hurricanes to do an offensive patrol over Lampedusa, they returned three hours later, having made no contact. It was noticed that on return they showed a marked preference for soft cushions? The CO reiterated his opinion that the whole thing was a "bloody waste of time".

Friday 17 October
During the morning 'B' Flight was led by the CO on two scrambles and also a cover patrol for six Blenheims in an attack on Catania. Fighters were seen to take off from an aerodrome near Cape Passero but nothing else was seen and no contact made.

Jeff and Sgt Vardy set off to do an offensive patrol but had to return after ten minutes because Sgt Vardy had engine trouble.

The whole of the Officers Mess was invited by the Sgts Mess to a party in the evening. Apparently it was a farewell party, but it was not quite clear as to who was leaving, anyway, it was a good party.

Saturday 18 October

Jeff and Vardy set off again on an offensive patrol, but returned two and a half hours later having seen lots of water and cloud but no enemy aircraft.

'A' Flight had two scrambles after coming to standby at one o'clock.

Sunday 19 October

'A' Flight had two scrambles in the morning and 'B' Flight had one in the afternoon, the weather deteriorated towards evening and nothing further happened.

Monday 20 October

While L.C. was doing the Met Flight Sgts Ellis and Alderson were sent up on practice combat and proceeded to shoot L.C. down??

L.C. and Sgt Lillywhite took off at 11.45 to patrol Lampedusa. After patrolling for about an hour they sighted 6 SM 81s just below them, what happened and the result can be seen by reading the combat reports.

L.C. had atrocious luck when his windscreen oiled up and he was unable to make an effective attack.

Sgt Lillywhite nearly had heart failure when, on landing, it was pointed out that the bullet which had cut his trimming gear had passed through his hood, missing him by a mere couple of inches – phew!!

There were two other scrambles in the morning but nothing happened.

Combat cuts follow:

F/L Murch:-

I was flying on patrol 30 miles south of Lampedusa with Sgt Lileywhite [sic] as No, 2. I had reached patrol line at 1230 and at 1310 Sgt Lilleywhite called my attention to six S.M.81 passing below us heading North. Our height was about 2000 feet and that of E/A was about 50 feet I turned to port and dived down on to the formation. I found that I could not see through the windscreen so I passed behind the formation hoping to draw their fire while Sgt Lilleywhite attacked a straggler from the starboard quarter astern. Fire was opened from the formation when he was at about 300 yards range and continued until he had broken away and was returning to base. The E/A which was attacked at first trailed smoke which later stopped. It was losing speed and height. It eventually hit the sea and exploded with no hope of survivors. The rest of the formation continued on course for Lampedusa. I fired a very short haphazard burst while behind the formation but as I could not see the aircraft no results were observed. I then returned to Base with Sgt Lileywhite and landed at 1400 hrs.

Sgt Lillywhite:-

I was flying No, 2 to F/Lt Murch on his right. We were patrolling at 2000 feet West to East 30 miles due south of Lampedusa when I sighted 6 enemy aircraft immediately below us. They were flying very low in a broken Vic formation towards Lampedusa. I called upon [sic] the R/T and we turned to port and began to dive on to the E/A. I closed in and opened fire from quarter astern at 300 yards and observed hits in the fuselage and engine. I closed to 25 yards firing another burst and seeing a flame and smoke on the port side. I had to break away violently and as I did so I hit the slipstream of the next E/A in front. There was a flash and a puff of smoke and I saw petrol coming out of my starboard long range tank and at the same time I found that the trimming gear was out of action. Set course for Base both hands on stick.

Tuesday 21 October
'A' Flight on at 13.00 and had 1 scramble.

Sgt Forth has produced an original flying times log – entitled Hog Log – it emphasises – perhaps too much – the amount of hogging done by 'B' Flight, it is hoped that pilots do not regard flying as, "just so many hours", and consequently just fly with the idea of beating the other fellow.

Wednesday 22 October
'A' and 'B' Flights had two scrambles each during the day.

F/O Bailey and Sgt Sheppard went off to do the offensive patrol but returned an hour later doing a steady 250 mph, it appears that 3 CR 42s had arranged a little reception party for them Gay Bailey decided that it was not the time and place to do affiliation exercises with the Regia Aeronautica, and so taking advantage of cloud cover he high tailed [it] for home. We offer him congratulations on successfully avoiding contact with the enemy.

NB. The offensive patrol was cancelled for four days – sighs of relief from at least <u>two</u> members of 'B' Flight.

Alongside the above entry GB – *evidently Flying Officer G.G. 'Gay' Bailey – has added:* Libel action pending.

Thursday 23 October
'B' Flight had one scramble. Squadron released at 13.00.

([*Word unreadable*] of my remarks on the 13th inst. re the long suffering Hurricane, it has since come to my ears that plans are afloat to convert the Hurricane into a Heavy Bomber, this, I imagine, will be done by removing the undercarriage, slinging on a 4000 lbs bomb and launching us into the air with a catapult!!! – Foo.)

Friday 24 October
'A' Flight had two scrambles, but for what purpose?

(In the writing of this diary it will be observed that I have confused people by using First and Third person (apart from other grammatical errors!!) and so I intend to, at the risk of severe censure, always use first person i.e. addressing F/O Thompson as "I".)

Saturday 25 October
During the morning 'A' Flight were scrambled with Gay Bailey leading for a plot of 18+ which developed to 25+. 4 Bombers probably BR 20s or Cant 1007s crossed the coast with a high cover of about 20 Macchis. 'A' Flight attacked the Bombers from astern – results of attack can be seen by reading the accompanying line shoots. Bombs were dropped on 700 tons of kerosene, which comprised the whole of the Islands supplies for civilians. (Somebody is going to get cold this winter.)

Sgt Knight did not return from the engagement and in the subsequent search which lasted all afternoon no trace of him could be found. It is assumed that he was jumped by the fighter cover.

Sgt Knight showed great promise as a fighter pilot, he was deservedly popular with everyone, and it is with sincere regret that I have to record his death.

It has been impressed on pilots that they must maintain "pair" forma-tion under all circumstances. No 2s have been told to keep with their No 1s. This also applies conversely. No 1s must keep with their No 2s. It so often happens that the No 1 has the superior machine, and if he goes "balls out" his No 2 cannot keep up. It therefore behoves the leader of the section to maintain a speed which enables his No 2 to hold formation comfortably.

Sgt Knight, flying a heavy cannon machine was probably left behind with the disastrous results that we all know.

Combat cuts follow:

> I was Mustang Red 1. When approaching Kalafrana from the S. East at 25,000′ I saw ack-ack bursts and then 4 Enemy Bombers, the enemy aircraft were leading [sic] towards us at about 20,000′. We dived for a head-on attack [but] E/A turned and went out to sea [and] we caught them about 6 miles N.E. of Grand Harbour. I opened fire on E/A. on the left [and] fired one burst at 400 yds and closed firing broke to the left and re-engaged and fired all my ammo. Enemy fighters were circling

above all the time. I noticed strikes on the s'board engine. I was hit by .5 bullet in fuselage.

(Sgd.) G.G. Bailey, F/O.

I was flying as red II in Mustang formation. I saw 4 B.R.20's about 4 miles in front. When within range I fired 4 three-second bursts at the left hand bomber obtaining a few hits on port wing and engine:- range 300–200 yds.

I then saw a Macchi about 300 yds to STBD and 600 feet above diving at me so I broke off the engagement.

(Sgd.) R.M. Oliver P/O.

I was Blue 2, when approaching Kalafrana from S.E., when I saw 4 enemy aircraft. We went in to attack. I was the fifth aircraft to attack. I opened fire from 300 yds. astern, my bullets entering the fuselage. I opened fire again from 200 yards giving a 6 second burst, and observed strikes on the fuselage and port engine. I closed in again, firing until my ammunition ran out and again observed my bullets entering the port engine and wing root. I broke away at 50 yards, and I think I stopped the port engine.

(Sgd.) W.F. Nurse, Sgt.

I was flying yellow I, I saw enemy bombers with fighters above. I engaged bomber on left from astern and opened fire from about 200 feet to point blank range when my guns stopped – something flew past me when I was about 100 feet away.

(Sgd.) T.H. Bates, Sgt.

> I was flying as Yellow II with Sgt. Bates as Yellow I when at 24,000′ I saw on my starboard side about 5 miles away 4 enemy bombers. Immediately Red I turned and began to dive to attack. I followed my number 1 who went into [sic] attack one of the bombers. I was about 300 yds. behind him when an enemy all black fighter with in line engine came up to attack Sgt. Bates and crossed over my sight. I fired, and got on its tail firing continually until I saw three Macchis attacking from above when I broke off firing, as I turned toward the other fighters and fired but ran out of ammunition. The first Macchi I attacked was leaving a thin trail of smoke when I broke off and came back.
>
> (Sgd.) C.S. Hunton, Sgt.

> I was Blue I Flying on leader's left when I sighted 4 Bombers as our formation went into [sic] attack.
>
> I dropped back a little to watch for the fighter escort, and went in and gave the port side bomber a short burst. Then I saw a Macchi diving down on my tail, so I turned and took evasive action. When I straightened out I lost sight of the formation, and returned to Base which I orbited till plot faded.
>
> (Sgd.) T.E.J. Ream, Sgt.

Sunday 26 October
S/L Pike led 'B' Flight on one scramble in the morning. Squadron released at 13.00.

In the evening all the people who have been here six months fore-gathered in Valetta for the purpose of celebrating their survival.

P/O Woodsend deputised for Jeff who was feeling very ropy.

Later in the evening, after having had dinner, Woody felt rather out of things and wanted to leave, this request was of course refused and in the ensuing fun and games Woody locked himself in a small room and then proceeded to climb out of the window on to what he thought was a balcony, unfortunately it wasn't, and he fell the odd 50′ before coming to rest on the concrete floor. After some delay he was carted off to Imtarfa *[90th British General Hospital, Mtarfa]* where he is likely to remain for some time.

Woody sustained a badly broken pelvis and some superficial cuts, he was however very lucky to get away with his life.

Monday 27 October

Apart from Vardy doing the Met Flight no other flying was done today.

Jeff left us today for Ta Kali preparatory to his proceeding to Middle East; to say anything about Jeff would be rather pointless. I can only repeat my remarks made on the 26th September, and add that with his going the old 185 goes also. Everyone wishes him the very best of luck and wish that he achieves his desire – ferrying Bombays.

Tuesday 28 October

S/L Pike and Sgt Sutherland went to have a look at Sicily with a view to hotting up the train service, but had to return owing to good weather.

We are awaiting replacements which we so badly need.

Two photographs, not reproduced here, are included in the diary: on the facing page, a portrait of Squadron Leader P.W.O. Mould, DFC and Bar and, overleaf, a portrait of Squadron Leader S.A.D. Pike.

Wednesday 29 October

One scramble for 'B' Flight when L.C. led 6 others after a +1. nothing developed.

Jeff returned this evening for a farewell party which was given in the Sgts Mess later, it was thought a good idea to paint the pigs (which are being fattened up for Xmas). The pigs were duly painted.

Thursday 30 October

The Harbour-Master objected to Silverside and much to Jeff's chagrin he was compelled to clean the pigs.

S/L Pike and Sgt Jolly went to have a look at Pantelleria but were not impressed and returned without seeing any E/A.

Friday 31 October
Gay Bailey took 'A' Flight up on a practice which developed into a scramble which developed into 18+ which developed into nothing.

October has proved to be a disastrous month both as regards pilots and machines and the least said about it the better.

Saturday 1 November
Sgt Sutherland joined the happy band of Met Pilots this morning.
'B' Flight did a practice "bullshit" formation but it was interrupted by a 3+. as the cloud was 10/10ths over the Island the raid did not develop.
Sgt Eastman and myself sent to Sicily in the p.m. We attacked a train, but my four cannons did not fire. Eastman however successfully sprayed the engine, using twelve machine guns. – Squadron off at 13.00 hrs.

Sunday 2 November
Gladiator u/s.
'A' Flight to readiness at 13.00 hrs. P/O Allardice and myself did a long range patrol over Pantelleria, in the afternoon. The patrol developed into a round trip of Sicily we shot up a wireless station (?) on the way home and landed at dusk.
Sgt Vardy has been incarcerated in M'tarfa, having developed a nasty dose of jaundice.
Sgt Vardy is now the oldest inhabitant and it is hoped he will be going home soon. *[Pencilled addendum follows]* – (This is not meant spitefully).
[signed] PD Thompson

Monday 3 November
F/O Bailey did his stuff in the Glad. The CO and Sgt Hayes "intruded" on Sicily and successfully interrupted the train service.
Sgts Jolly and Bates went on a search for a Blenheim crew, they were relieved by Sgt Sheppard and Hayes, but in neither case did they see anything.
'B' Flight came to readiness at 13.00. The peaceful afternoon was only disturbed once, when reports *[were received]* from the "Hole" about a parachutist which had descended just off Filfla. Sgt Westcott went to have a look, but as the weather closed down shortly afterwards he had to be recalled, and the Squadron was released ½ hr earlier than usual.

Tuesday 4 November
Sgts Jolly and Ellis proved to be a successful combination when they visited Sicily together this morning. Jolly put a train out of action with a few well-placed cannon shells and afterwards attacked a factory. Ellis, after shooting up the train, amused himself by following the railway line

and shooting up every signal box on the way, obviously a one track mind.

These raids on Sicily, are great fun and appear to be achieving their object [sic].

The CO led 3 others, (including Joe Hall who had come out for a day's rest?) on a scramble. The clouds were 10/10ths at 1500´ and as nothing developed they pancaked [returned and landed] after 10 mins.

The Squadron was put to 30 mins availability at 13.00 but were brought back to readiness an hour later because of the bad state of serviceability at Takali. As the weather was pretty well operationally u/s bringing us to readiness was just a waste of taxiing hours – however during the p.m. Alderson and self went to look for a lost Hurricane, which was about 10 miles North of the Island – visibility was pretty duff.

Wednesday 5 November

No flying apart from practice. We were treated to a grand display of fireworks this evening when the A/A guns engaged some enemy raiders, they brought one down – a Ju 87.

Thursday 6 November

The CO and P/O Oliver went over to Sicily and shot up a factory and the CO P/O Allardice led 3 others as a cover patrol [sic]

F/O Bailey led a scramble for a +6 which came within 10 miles of the coast before receding.

Sgt Sheppard joins the happy band of Met pilots. L.C. joins the happy band at M'tarfa.

Friday 7 November

'B' Flight led by myself were scrambled for a 18+ which developed into a 40+, we had plenty of time to gain height, but the raid turned round after coming to within 20 mls of the Island. – (Some people complained of the cold.)

F/O Bailey and P/O Reeves did a long range patrol over Lampedusa but nothing was seen owing to cloud being 10/10ths at 2000´.

'A' Flight at 30 mins at 13.00.

Saturday 8 November

I did the Met Flight and at the same time saw Jeff off from Takali.

'A' Flight at readiness at 13.00. 4 A/C for a +1 were scrambled followed by 6 A/C for a +3 but nothing developed.

Sunday 9 November

F/O Bailey and P/O Oliver, flying long range Hurricanes, went out to patrol Force "K" which was returning home after attacking an enemy convoy.

Gay Bailey did not return, and for some considerable time nothing was known as to the reasons why, until later in the morning Joe Hall phoned me up and said that he had interviewed Captain Agnew of the "Aurora" who told him that Force "K" had been attacked by torpedo bombers. F/O Bailey was seen to deliver attacks upon both the E/A, and then go straight into the sea from about 200′, his aircraft caught fire when it hit the water.

P/O Allardice and Sgt Bates went out to search for about 60 miles off but nothing was seen. As little hope could be held for Gay Bailey the search was abandoned. The way in which Gay Bailey met his death is very debatable, but it is assumed that he was shot down by the rear gunners of the E/A.

Gay was one of the founder members of the Squadron and his loss is deeply felt by everyone, particularly by the people who have known him over 7 months – somehow one never thought that Gay would buy it, he seemed to be one of those people who always came back.

Gay was very popular and one of our most capable pilots, his loss to the Squadron is irreplaceable.

S/L Pike led one scramble this morning for a +3, but nothing came in.
'B' Flight took over at 13.00 but had a quiet afternoon.

Joe Hall is to be congratulated upon receiving his second stripe, he is doing sterling work down in the "Hole", and though he himself would like to come back to the Squadron he appreciates the fact that he is doing more important work as controller.

Force 'K' this morning, attacked an Italian convoy, and sank nine ships and left the other one on fire, two escorting destroyers were also destroyed.

Monday 10 November
I led 'B' Flight on one scramble for a 3+ up north but nothing came in.
'B' Flight at 30 mins at 13.00. No other flying.

Tuesday 11 November
F/L Hall and Sgt Sutherland did a patrol this morning in hopes of catching the recco. The recco came in, but Joe Hall did not have sufficient height.
'A' Flight came to readiness at 13.00 but did not fly.

Wednesday 12 November
During the night a Wimpy [Wellington] crashed near the Island. Sgts Nurse and Bates went out to have a look for any survivors but saw nothing – During the same night 4 Swordfish of 830 Squadron failed to return. 126 and 249 attacked Gela. W/Cmdr Brown and Sgt Simpson did not return.

During the p.m. 33 *[sic]* long-range Hurricanes arrived ex-Gibraltar they comprised 605 and 242 Squadrons. They all landed extremely well including one chap who landed with his undercarriage up. *[Pencilled in red on the facing page:* intentionally*]*

On 12 November thirty-seven Hurricanes and pilots of 242 and 605 Squadrons had taken off for Malta from the decks of Argus *and* Ark Royal. *All but three arrived. The following day HMS* Ark Royal *was sunk by the German submarine U-81. The previous month the carrier had also delivered a Swordfish and eleven Albacore torpedo bombers. Information about potential targets for the island's strike force was frequently obtained through the interception of enemy messages confirmed by reconnaissance sorties flown by men such as Flying Officer Adrian Warburton, who was operational from the very early days of the battle. Their role was vital to the offensive operations of the Royal Air Force, the Fleet Air Arm and the Royal Navy, whose efforts were having a telling effect on Italo–German supply lines to North Africa. Axis land bases also continued to be prone to attack wherever they came within range of Malta's aircraft.*

Thursday 13 November
P/O Reeves and Sgt Cousens followed by Sgts Forth and Westcott did standing patrols to catch the recco NBG.
One scramble of 1+ – weather bad 'A' Flight at 30 mins at 13.00.

Friday 14 November
'A' Flight at readiness, one practice flight.
Sgt Ellis, when rather pixilated this evening, decided to cool his rather fevered brow in Sliema Creek, however after entering the water he lost all sense of direction and was "unable" to move in case he went out of his depth.
For about half-an-hour he pondered upon the subjects of a watery grave but was finally "rescued" by Sgt Alderson, who tells me his attention was drawn, by very feeble cries of help.

Saturday 15 November
'B' Flight at readiness at 13.00. In the afternoon there was low cloud and rain so the CO decided to do a little "rhubarb" Sgt Alderson and myself carrying bombs (8 x 20 lbs) and Sgts Ellis and Lillywhite (4 cannon and 12 MG) went along to shoot up the railway line.
Messrs Hall, Jolly, Westcott and Cousens provided fighter cover.
The weather was pretty duff but we arrived over Sicily according to schedule.
Ellis and Lillywhite went in to shoot up the railway line, while Alderson and I proceeded to drop the odd bomb on Noto Station. I was attacked by

a Macchi (which I did not see till afterwards) but suffered no damage. Some Pongo [i.e. army] marksman put one bullet through my engine cowling!! Having dropped our bombs and securing several hits, we went rapidly homewards, warming up some signal boxes on the way. Ellis caught the wrong train, but managed at [sic] shoot up a "pier" (Lil had a few quiet words with Ellis on their return home).

In view of the weather quite a successful do.

There was no further flying, as the weather closed down and it started to rain!!

Sunday 16 November
Raining all day. 'B' Flight at readiness till 11.30 and then released. Several aircraft were "bogged" when dispersed.

(General adjournment to Valetta.)

Monday 17 November
'B' Flight called to readiness from 30 mins, owing to the fact that the aerodrome at Ta Kali was U/S.

'B' Flight did one practice flight just before it started to rain again.

'A' Flight to readiness at 13.00.

Tuesday 18 November
'A' Flight had one scramble but to no effect.

'B' Flight to readiness at 13.00 no activity weather still very dull.

Wednesday 19 November
'B' Flight had two scrambles of 1 hour each but nothing resulted from either of them.

F/L Hall was about to take off on a practice interception exercise, but the Hal Far gremlins (under command of Sgt Forth) thought otherwise, they pushed his undercarriage up just before he was airborne, this resulted in the aircraft coming to an abrupt halt, while the airscrew ceased to rotate.

'A' Flight were put to 30 mins at 13.00.

Thursday 20 November
'A' Flight at readiness at 13.00. 4 A/C were scrambled for a +1 the CO leading the plot did not come in.

(In the evening Sgt Forth was overheard saying, to a fair member of the opposite sex, "Of course, now that I am chief controller of Gremlins on Malta!!")

Friday 21 November

Rather a busy day, S/L Pike started the ball rolling when he led 'A' Flight for a +3. The raid came in at dawn. Some Macchis (?) shot up Hal Far and Ta Kali doing hardly any damage.

'A' Flight jumped one part of the of the [sic] high cover at about 12.000´, and a general dog-fight ensued, during the fight 5 more Macchis (?) joined in making the odds 10–7 (in their favour).

The pilots' individual line shoots are on the opposite page [see below]. Although 'A' Flight did not claim any definitely destroyed, it is a safe bet to say that some little Macchi (?) pilots did not have any breakfast this morning.

The fight was watched from the ground with great interest. The Italians were seen to do some amazing evasive manoeuvres, including rolls off the top and bunting!!

Sgt Nurse was attacked by an enemy "Hurricane" (fitted with .5s) and received considerable damage to his ailerons on port petrol tank. Nurse landed OK.

The Italians on this particular occasion showed considerable initiative, they split up into two formations, one formation acting as "stooges" and the other as jumpers – they might have met with more success but for the skill of our pilots and the handling qualities of the old Hurricane!!!

During the morning a PRU Hurricane II piloted by W/Cmdr Dowland o/c 69 Squdn was shot down 30 miles North of St Paul's Bay. We sent out 2 sections on search and the Winko [sic: Wingco] was spotted by P/O Oliver, and afterwards picked up by the Float-fish piloted by S/L Hurle-Hobbs.

In the afternoon we did a convoy patrol. I took Sgt Horricks up with me and did a spot of practice flying.

Sgt Horricks although a recent addition to the Squadron, has been on the Island for two months having been incarcerated in M'tarfa for "sandfly" and "dog".

We wish him the very best of luck and great success in the Squadron.

Horricks and I were relieved on the convoy patrol by Sgts Forth and Alderson.

At about 17.00 4 A/C P/O Reeves and Sgts Lillywhite, Steele and Cousens, were scrambled for a 3+ and 2+.

Thirty minutes later they were unavoidably mixed up with about 18 Macchis (?) after having first been vectored on to them the plot having been only a 6+, and then when it was seen that the 6+ was a 17+, they were told to come home, but it is probable that the Italians kept our 4 A/C in view the whole time and jumped us, just as we were coming back to the Island. Tony Reeves, who was leading had to turn into them, and a general dog-fight took place, just north of St Paul's Bay.

Sgt Cousens failed to return, he was last seen breaking away to port and downwards.

The MNFU and several [of] 249 did an extensive search, over that area, and discovered an oil patch which was investigated by the high speed launch, but nothing [else] was seen.

The search was resumed in the morning without success.

Dicky Cousens, when he came to 185 had a lot to learn in the way of flying and discipline, after a short time, however, he settled down and became one of our most efficient and conscientious pilots. He was well liked and popular with everybody, and we are all very sorry that he has gone.

Combat cuts follow:

I was leading squadron at 15,000′ over Zonkor [sic: Zonqor] Point when I saw 5 Macchi 202's going south. I dived to attack and gave numerous bursts at enemy without any visual damage. I was never outmanoeuvred by enemy in spite of the aerobatic display put up. Our formation was fired on by heavy anti aircraft. On the original attack I pulled up before attacking as I thought the enemy were Hurricane [sic] they had Red noses and a white roundel, rest of fuselage all black. Evasive tactics consisted of aerobatics of all sorts and particularly diving and zooming. I followed one Macchi 202 at sea level but was losing ground.

Red Leader.   (Sgd.) S.A.D. Pike, S/Ldr.

I was flying in Mustang formation when I sighted 5 Macchi 202's below us and to the left. The squadron dived to attack and I dropped back slightly being uncertain of the identity of the Macchi's. I then identified a black Macchi 202 and gave it two 3-second bursts with no visible results. I was then attacked twice by Macchis and took evasive action. I then attacked another Macchi giving it a 4-second burst. apparently scoring hits but with no effect. While returning to base I was attacked by a Macchi at 1,000′, I took evasive action and the Macchi broke off the attack.

(Sgd.) R.M. Oliver, P/O.

The Squadron was at 16,000 feet East of Zonkor Point when I saw the C.O. dive down to Port. There were five fighters about 2,000′ below us. We went down in rough line astern and I chased the second Machine from the starboard side. They turned as we came down on them and I tried to cut across his turn but could not catch him. He then did very violent evasive action including a "roll off the top". I got on his tail briefly in a spiral dive and gave him a short burst. I then lost him diving seaward with a Hurricane on his tail. I then climbed to join a dog fight going on above me, but the Machines disappeared to the North. I could see no other aircraft, I was told by GONDAR [*fighter control*] to orbit Filfla and shortly afterwards to land.

Enemy Aircraft was black with white band round tail of fuselage.

(Sgd.) P.M. Allardice, P/O.

I was flying Red. II to S/Ldr. Pike when we saw several Macchi's going E we dived to attack, we then climbed again, I saw two machines above and behind diving down, I turned, they then opened fire, I pulled up and as they passed I followed them down giving two bursts before they were out of range again, another machine attacked from above [*and*] I turned quickly but could not catch him. I returned to base 0745.

White ring round the tail, painted all black.

(Sgd.) R.V.F. Ellis, Sgt.

I was flying as Green 2 in Mustang formation when the Squadron jumped 5 enemy aircraft flying below and a dog fight developed. I attacked one Macchi and gave him a reasonably long burst and my bullets entered the fuselage but it did not seem to be damaged. Before I could deliver another attack a Hurricane cut me out and at the same time red tracer came spurting past both sides of the cockpit. I tried all evasive tactics but did not shake the enemy aircraft off until I was very low. I climbed once again but was immediately warned by R/T that a Macchi was attacking from rear. I took evasive action and got on its tail but as it was above and making for Sicily I was unable to climb and catch it. I then came home.

Enemy Aircraft were all black with a whitish roundel just on front of tail plane with in line engines.

(Sgd.) C.S. Hunton, Sgt.

I was flying white II with Sgt. Nurse. We jumped 5 aircraft [*and*] I followed one down and out towards Sicily, but could not catch it. A

Macchi attacked me from behind *[and]* I took avoiding action and came back towards Malta with the Macchi on my tail but not firing, then I saw it turn back towards Sicily. I got one burst at it as it turned but again could not catch it.

(Sgd.) Bates, Sgt.

I was white 1, and followed the leader down. One Macchi pulled up in front of me and I gave him a long burst from 200–150 yards and I saw my bullets appear to enter the fuselage. He rolled over and went down, presumably evasive tactics. I was later attacked by another machine which I thought was a Hurricane and sustained hits in the tail and wings.

(Sgd.) W.F. Nurse, Sgt.

———— *"* ————

(The afternoon show.)

I was flying as Blue 1 leading 3 other aircraft and after we had been airborne about half an hour we intercepted 2 formations of Macchi's 202's. 6 at 15,000´ and 6 at 18,000´, our height was between the 2 enemy formations, we engaged the higher formation and a general dog fight took place.

I fired 2 long bursts at different Macchi's, but did not observe any results.

(Sgd.) Reeves P/O.

Saturday 22 November
Two scrambles for 'B' Flight in the morning but no interceptions, Sgt Horricks having *[sic]* his first operational scramble.
'B' Flight at 30 mins at 13.00.
Sgts Hayes and Vardy return to the fold but both have 10 days sick leave!!
Flight-Lieutenant Thompson takes over 'A' Flight at the end of the month when L.C. comes back from sick leave!!

Sunday 23 November
2 sections were brought to readiness in the morning and had one scramble for a 1+ which did not come in.

'A' Flight at readiness at 13.00 but they had a quiet afternoon.

Monday 24 November
Nothing in the morning for 'A' Flight. 'B' Flight came to readiness at 13.00 and during the watch they had a visit from General Recall accompanied by his aide-de-camp General Panic. We were sent off in sections to search for some mythical 'E' Boats, about 40 of them – nothing was seen!!!

Tuesday 25 November
'B' Flight had one scramble just before lunch – this disagreed with our digestion so we quickly landed again, (apart from the food question there was 10/10ths cloud).
Sgts Sheppard and Hunton came to readiness in the afternoon.
The 2 A/C were scrambled for a +2. Shortly after they were airborne, the heavens opened and the rain fell down. Shep and Hunton landed at Ta Kali quite safely, but one long range Hurricane of 242 Squadron landed very neatly across the Kala Road, after going through a brick wall.

Wednesday 26 November
It rained so much during the night that the CO put the aerodrome U/S. Everybody adjourned to Valetta, where they succeeded in getting quite merry – (no trouble at all!).

Thursday 27 November
Apart from the Met Flight there was no other flying today. 'B' Flight came to readiness at one o'clock but they had a quiet afternoon.

Friday 28 November
L.C. becomes serviceable again, he did the Met Flight this morning.
I came to readiness with 'B' Flight for the last time. There was a one section scramble in the morning for the elusive +1.
At one o'clock 'B' Flight at 30 mins with the exception of Sgts Lillywhite and Horricks who remained at readiness – they had one scramble.
Sgts Vardy and Hayes are also AIB again – they both had a practice flip this afternoon to get their hand in again.
About half a dozen of us went down to Birzebbuga to have a look at a GL *[gun-laying]* set, we were very interested even if we did not understand anything about it.

Saturday 29 November
Sgts Eastman and Steele came to readiness in the morning – they went up on a GL exercise which turned into a scramble!!
'A' Flight came to readiness at 13.00. We went up to do some practice

attacks *[and]* a plot came on the board, which we chased for about an hour, but were not successful owing to the fact that all the three plotting devices, the RDF *[radio direction finding]* GL and GCI *[ground controlled interception]* broke down.

Sunday 30 November

'A' Flight to readiness at dawn – they had an abortive one section scramble.

L.C. came to readiness with 'B' Flight whom he led round the sky on a practice flight. He, later in the day, led two sections after a +2, 20 miles west of the Island. L.C. did not intercept owing to being scrambled too late.

S/L Pike and Sgt Jolly went to look at Lampedusa again, but they returned early owing to bad weather – no cloud at all.

November:-

This month on the whole can be regarded as a mediocre one, we lost two good pilots, but on the other hand, when we came up against superior odds, on two occasions, we acquitted ourselves very well. This augers very well for future dates with the Regia Aeronautica.

In November Generalfeldmarschall *Albert Kesselring, commanding* Luftflotte 2 *in Russia, had been designated Commander-in-Chief South. With the onset of winter the Germans began to transfer aircraft from the Eastern Front and elsewhere to Sicily. It was the beginning of the end for the Hurricane's short-lived reign over Malta. In December the* Regia Aeronautica *was replaced in day operations over the island by* General der Flieger *Bruno Loerzer's* II Fliegerkorps. *German raids began on a relatively small scale, increasing in intensity towards the end of the month, with daylight bomber sorties heavily escorted by Messerschmitt Bf 109Fs.*

Monday 1 December

'B' Flight at readiness in the morning. Sgts Vardy and Hayes, at readiness in the afternoon, almost had a scramble!! but it started to rain again and they were released at about 4.30.

Sgt Hunton, when taxiing, tried to emulate a rabbit, when he started burrowing in a hole that was at least 10 feet deep.

Tuesday 2 December

Two A/C from 'A' Flight at readiness Sgts Sheppard and Nurse – they had one scramble.

'A' Flight at readiness at 13.00 nothing doing owing to duff weather.

Wednesday 3 December

It has rained all night and the aerodrome is well and truly U/S. Net result – Squadron released. Nothing to report that a good dose of ENOs [*presumably Eno's Liver Salts*] can't cure.

Thursday 4 December

Nothing to report – that phrase contains the news for the day. Aerodrome still U/S.

'B' Flight came to 30 mins at 13.00 but were released shortly afterwards.

Friday 5 December

L.C. did the Met Flight. 'B' Flight brought one section to readiness. They had one scramble.

'A' Flight came to readiness at 13.00 and had one one section scramble at about tea time.

The MNFU operated from here tonight in the hopes of catching the Ju 88s which have been intruding for the last three nights.

Rumour has it that the Luftwaffe has re-established OTUs [*operational training units*] in Sicily (watch out for fireworks!!!)

Saturday 6 December

'A' Flight at readiness at dawn – A Wimpy had been reported lost during the night – Sgts Jolly and Hunton were sent to look for survivors – the position given was 5 miles SW of Cape Scalambri!!! – Nothing was seen. Sgts Ream and Nurse went to relieve in the search but had to return owing to a bad rainstorm in "Mid Channel". In the meantime there was a one section scramble for a +1 – 35 miles north – nothing happened.

'B' Flight at readiness at 13.00 but they had a quiet P.M.

Sunday 7 December

'B' Flight at readiness at dawn and 'A' Flight at 30 mins availability at 13.00 but apart from the Met Flight and a couple of air tests there was no other flying and nothing to report.

Monday 8 December

'A' Flight at 30 mins at dawn and at readiness at 13.00. 2 one section scrambles and no other flying – weather very dull. One Ju 88 intruded rather well last night dropping bombs on the aerodrome and barrack blocks. Fortunately only one casualty.

Tuesday 9 December

'A' Flight at readiness at dawn and no scrambles.

'B' Flight came to readiness at 13.00 and the CO led them on an offensive patrol over Sicily – no opposition and no contacts.

Wednesday 10 December

'B' Flight on at dawn. 2 sections were ordered off to patrol destroyers, but were shortly afterwards pancaked.

Later in the morning L.C. led 'B' Flt after a +3 which faded, the scramble then developed into a patrol over Sicily, without any opposition. Sgt Johnny Alderson's glycol tank blew up (i.e. the tank of the aeroplane that Alderson was awaiting), but he successfully force landed on the aerodrome, slightly wet around his trews, but apparently none the worse for his "adventure" – he is to be congratulated on bringing his aircraft safely home – Jolly fine show.

One section of 'B' Flight came to readiness at 13.00 and had three scrambles – but all to no purpose.

Thursday 11 December

2 scrambles for one section at readiness. 'A' Flight at readiness at 13.00 hrs. One "squadron" scramble (the first this month for 'A' Flt.)

As a direct result of the recent bad weather, the serviceability has improved.

As many as 10 A/C and sometimes more can be seen on the line almost any day!!

Friday 12 December

'A' Flight at readiness.

126 Squadron were detailed to bomb Comiso. We put up 11 A/C as high cover. We followed 126 right over the target – no opposition apart from some heavy A/A which was accurate for height but some way astern.

'B' Flight did some practice hogging in the P.M.

Saturday 13 December

'B' Flight on at dawn and 'A' Flt at 30 mins in the afternoon. A very quiet day and one without incident.

Sunday 14 December

'A' Flight at 30 mins at dawn, the one section at readiness had two scrambles.

'A' Flight at readiness at 13.00. 4 A/C went out as a cover patrol for some Blenheims coming ex-Gib. 4 more A/C were scrambled to intercept the first four (the interceptors were apparently shot down!!).

Monday 15 December

'A' Flight on at dawn one section scramble.

"L.C." Murch is leaving us, he suddenly decided to see a bit more of the world. Previous to coming to us L.C. had just finished a six months enforced stay in hospital after having been shot down in the "Battle of Britain". Since he has been with us he has never really felt truly fit, spending quite some time in M'tarfa, he therefore followed the wisest course when he applied for posting. He proved to be popular in the Squadron, *[and]* made a very keen and efficient Flight-commander, everyone is truly sorry to see him go.

F/O R.M. Lloyd arrived today ex-Gib, presumably to take over 'B' Flight. He aviated in a Hurricane for the first time today – we wish him the very best of luck and every success in his new appointment.

Tuesday 16 December
One practice formation flight, one section scramble.

Sgt Hayes and myself did a long range patrol to Kuriat, but sighted nothing apart from a Blenheim over Lampedusa, we nearly attacked it before we recognised it, the Blenheim however opened fire on us as we were breaking away.

While L.C. was up doing a calibration flight in the Gladiator, a signal came posting him to ME tonight on a Wimpy. L.C. was duly seen off in the correct manner, we wish him lots of luck in his new job, whatever that may be.

Wednesday 17 December
Several one section scrambles and air tests. The CO and P/O Reeves did a long range patrol, but they were recalled owing to bad weather over the Island, the CO was very irked as the weather out west was perfect.

In the evening the Officers Mess invited the Sgts Mess over to have the odd noggin – Net results – complete shambles and partial destruction of the OM furniture. "Bottoms up" was frequently heard, both during the evening and after the party.

In spite of headaches in the morning the party was voted a success.

Thursday 18 December
'A' Flight's early morning slumbers were rudely interrupted by a scramble. Force K was being attacked 70 miles south of the Island, by the time we reached the convoy, however, all the fun was over, so we patrolled the convoy before return. P/O Allardice led P/O Oliver and Sgts Hayes and Nurse to continue the patrol. While they were doing so the convoy was attacked by BR 20s and Ju 88s. Our boys had a smack at the BR 20s with results as shown on the adjoining line shoots.

No other flying today.

No 'line shoots' are attached. The squadron ORB includes only brief details:

1105 4 aircraft P/O Allardice leading Convoy patrol over Force "K"

*which was attacked by 3 BR 20's P/O Allardice and P/O Oliver claim
2 BR 20's damaged.*

The RAF Daily Intelligence Summary is slightly more descriptive:

*Three BR. 20's. flying at 500 feet were sighted at 1115 hrs. Three
Hurricanes attacked firing all guns until all their ammunition had run
out. Hits were obtained on Two aircraft and oil was seen to be coming
from one of them. The enemy aircraft returned the fire, One Hurricane
being hit in the rudder. The enemy aircraft then made off in a South-
Easterly direction.*

Friday 19 December

The CO led 'B' Flight 11 strong to cover patrol a convoy, while they
were doing so, a strong force of Me 109Fs, and Macchi 202s did a sweep
over the Island. 249 and 126 were "jumped".

Night bombing, recently, is being carried out by the Luftwaffe.

The Huns' return to Sicily presages a pretty warm time for us in Malta.

Sgt Bates and myself came to readiness at 13.00, we had three scrambles.
On the first one, we successfully intercepted an Albacore "bandit" which
we refrained from shooting down. We also chased a Ju 88 back to Sicily
but could not catch him.

Sgts Lillywhite and Ream are to be congratulated on being promoted to
Temporary Flight-Sergeants. Lillywhite gets quite irate at being called
"Chiefy".

Saturday 20 December

Sgts Jolly and Hunton were scrambled for a 1+ but as it developed into
a 15+ they were pancaked. 'A' Flight were called to readiness and soon
afterwards scrambled. Takali engaged but we did not make contact.

Sgt Sutherland and P/O Reeves did a long range patrol, but while they
were away it rained enough to put the aerodrome U/S so they were
ordered to land at Takali where Sutherland thoughtfully put our one and
only long range Hurricane on its nose.

Sunday 21 December

'A' Flight scrambled for a 25+ and ordered to patrol Luqa. No contact
made. We were scrambled again for a 30+ and joined up with 249. When
we were at 17,000'–18,000' we met 6 Me 109Fs head on. I chased two of
them up to 25.000' but could not catch them, the Squadron joined up again
and we started to come down. Sgt Hayes did not return, and it is assumed
he was jumped on the way down.

With the Huns about losses are to be expected, but it is with deep regret
that I have to record the death of "Shaky-do" Brian Hayes, a sound and

efficient pilot, but perhaps not quite experienced enough. He is a great loss to the Squadron and will be particularly missed.

The CO took 'B' Flight up in the afternoon for a 25+ but did not make contact.

Two more one section scrambles rounded off an extremely busy but profitless day.

Monday 22 December

Two scrambles for 'B' Flt in the morning for a 6+ and a 15+, but both these raids were fighter sweeps and as the policy at the moment is to patrol below cloud, they did not make contact.

'A' Flt also had two scrambles but successfully avoided contact with the enemy.

I don't think people are quite so keen on hogging nowadays!!!

Tuesday 23 December

One scramble for 'A' Flt in the morning and one for 'B' Flt in the afternoon [and] on both occasions a few Ju 88s came over heavily escorted by Me 109Fs. The Luftwaffe seems to have completely taken over this theatre of war. The Regia Aeronautica [is] taking a back seat.

The Takalites have recently suffered heavy losses at the Luftwaffe's hands.

The predominant feature of every raid is the heavy fighter escort, comprised of Me 109Fs. These have had in every case, so far the advantage of height and consequently, speed.

24 December
Wednesday Xmas Eve.

'B' Flight patrolled a convoy in the morning, they also had a scramble for a 1+ which faded.

'A' Flight had two scrambles in the afternoon, the first for a 12+ which did not come in the second raid of 18+ developed, we formed a wing (12 A/C in all) with Wombat (126) with Mustang leading. We patrolled at 8000′ and for 10 mins 4 109s followed us around about 3000′ above us, but they did not attack. (A moral victory!!)

25 December
Thursday Xmas Day.

'A' Flight at readiness had a scramble for a 3+ which mercifully faded. 'A' Flight then showed their appreciation of the Officers v Sergeants football match then in progress, by bombing the bums with bog-bumff.

Other Xmas Day festivities included the presentation to Jimmy Forth of the one and only German Gremlin in captivity, said Gremlin being brought here under close escort by Sgt Sutherland. Chief of Gremlins Forth showed his appreciation in the manner usual to Gremlins.

Sgt Alderson was seen to run around the Dispersal Hut indecently clothed.

'B' Flt at readiness in the afternoon showed great signs of ring twitch when the blower whistled only to be followed by the cheering words "Merry Xmas". "Moral???" Mental?? and Physical (?) collapse of 'B' Flt.

The Squadron foregathered in the Dispersal Hut in the evening and spent a very pleasant three hours sitting round the Yule log (stove in Maltese) yarning and telling feelthy [sic], drinking sherry, thoughtfully provided by the CO and eating cake, which had belonged to Brian Hayes, altogether, a most successful day.

Facing page:

Sgt Johnny Alderson takes over Sqdn Diary from "Tommy" as from 26/12/41

26 December
<u>Friday Boxing Day.</u>

After allowing the squadron a raid-free Christmas day, in which to pursue our nefarious activities the wicked Germans didn't seem prepared to allow us to suffer our hangovers in peace.

B Flight tried out a new formation in the morning and owing to various reasons there were only six aircraft still airborne when they were ordered to patrol above cloud to meet a plot coming in at a phenomenal height. Said six aircraft showed admirable celerity in returning to base before the plot arrived.

"A" Flight at readiness in the afternoon rather wisely survived for the evening's celebrations by patrolling below cloud when plots of 32 and 52 came over the island bombing Luqua [sic] and Valletta.

In the evening various individual parties were held all over the camp. Jolly held an "at home" in his room where chicken and champagne were consumed in vast quantities, much to the disgust of those who arrived too late to take an active part.

Saturday 27 December
This morning the Luftwaffe returned to the fray three times. "A" Flight were airborne on each occasion and saw 109s above them which did not attack. The squadron formation with 109s above could show Hendon a few things these days. The idea seems to be to entice solitary 109s down

by appearing as one aircraft.

Our friends the Ack-ack tried their hands at shooting down enemy aircraft for a change this morning and got an 88.

This afternoon "B" Flight flew around a couple of times looking for 109s but luckily didn't see any.

While we were enjoying the station concert party's show in the evening we learnt that the MNFU had just shot down another 88 in flames.

Sunday 28 December

There were two one section scrambles for "B" Flight this morning hunting the elusive 88 but nothing was seen.

In the afternoon the visual controller sent "A" Flight above cloud and they were promptly jumped by Tal [sic] Kali which resulted in Hurricanes pouring out of the clouds in all directions.

This evening an 88 had lots of fun machine-gunning the aerodrome. He came a little too low for his health however and the bofors warmed his pants very efficiently causing him to crash on the edge of the 'drome.

Monday 29 December

To-day was one of the worst days we have yet experienced. In the morning "A" Flight and two sections of 242 Squadron were shambled rather than scrambled to meet a 23+.

They were just about to pick off some 88s diving on Luqua [sic] when 6 109s decided to do some picking off for themselves and jumped the squadron.

In the ensuing panic F/LT Andrews and P/O Blanchard of 242 collided, the latter being lost, while Jolly and Vardy had their pants warmed by the odd electric light bulb but managed to get down safely. Tommy bagged one of the offending 109s and made an excellent landing on one wheel – a very good show.

The squadron was then ordered to land as quickly as possible. Two 109s seemed to think we weren't landing quick enough so they shot us up as we were coming in. They got three aircraft which were luckily already on the ground and caused bags of panic to people in the middle of the drome who were making noises like pieces of rock. P/O Oliver in a power dive from 8000 ft looked like catching them but when they saw him they opened their throttles and he seemed to be going the other way.

During the afternoon "B" Flight were scrambled for a 15+ and broke up owing to a "duck" being given by one of the other squadrons. The CO and F/O Lloyd jumped five 109s at sea level but the 109s passed them on their way down and started jumping them. Nevertheless F/O Lloyd shot one down and *[the]* CO had the odd squirt at the three that attacked him.

I am sorry to have to record that during this scramble Jimmy Forth crashed on the aerodrome and was killed. Jimmy was a very keen and efficient pilot and had done some excellent work for the squadron with his exceptional powers as an artist. He was one of our most popular members and the loss of Jimmy the Gremlin was felt very deeply by everyone.

Altogether a very good day for the Germans who destroyed sixteen Wellingtons and destroyed or badly damaged nine Hurricanes for the loss of 2 109s.

Tuesday 30 December

After an uneventful scramble for "B" Flight the squadron was released because only one aircraft was serviceable. General pilgrimage to Valletta.

Wednesday 31 December

We were released all day to-day owing to unserviceability.

The CO received the accompanying signal couched in far from official terms to-day and spent an amusing half-hour trying to extract a confession from various people. We came to the conclusion that the offender was the CO himself but it afterwards appeared that the signal was an example of the Wingco's low humour.

```
    HAL FAR
Q MED NR X27              IMPORTANT    NOTWT

    GR23                 TO    RAF STATION HAL FAR
                         FROM HQ RAF MED
OPS924 30/12 FORWARD NAME OF MUSTANG PILOT WHO USED FOLLOWING
LANGUAGE OVER R/T YESTERDAY SOUTH OF HAL FAR YOU SHITS ASSHOLES
ASSHOLES = = = = = = 1700+

CLW    VA       R1745  LT    ES    VA    OFF
```

The diary is continued by Sergeant J.R. Sutherland.

Review of the Year.

Since the squadron was formed, first on 30th April as "C" Flt of 261 Sqdn, and then officially as 185 Sqdn, on 12th May, it has done remarkably well and helped to write another page in the history of the "Gem of the Med".

Up to the end of the year, the Squadron has accounted for <u>18</u> destroyed, 7 probables and 21 damaged enemy aircraft, and four "E-boats" destroyed. For a little variety, we have done the odd spot of dive-bombing with Comiso as the target, when at least 4 aircraft were set on fire. Railway engines and stations in Sicily are also our meat, though one member of the

Squadron much prefers signal boxes to engines.

Our losses have been fairly light in number, though severe in value. Most tragic and lamented of all was the loss of our most popular CO, S/LDR "Boy" Mould, DFC and bar who was shot down by Macchi 202s. 10 other pilots have been either killed in action or posted as missing, while one other is believed [to be a] prisoner of war. Numerous pilots have had to bail out at odd times, but have returned to fly again.

Since S/LDR Mould's death, we have had two more COs, first, S/LDR Lefevre, and then S/LDR Pike, who started with us as an auxiliary F/LT in "A" FLT, then became Flight Commander of "B" Flt, before taking over the command of the Squadron. As Flight Commanders in "A" Flt we have had F/LT Eliot, F/LT Jeffries and now F/LT Thompson, and in "B" Flt, F/LT Westmacott, F/LT Hancock, F/LT Pike, F/LT Murch, and now F/LT Lloyd.

At present the only members who were in the Squadron when it started and are still in it are F/LT "Tommy" and Sgt Jolly. There are two other "originals" still on the island but no longer with the Squadron, namely P/O Joe Hall, now F/LT and kingpin Controller, and F/LT Westmacott, now S/LDR i/c that brilliant unit the MNFU. The "oldest inhabitant" is Sgt Vardy, although he has not been with us during all of his stay on the "Gem", as he came to us from 261 on 5th May.

Easily the most memorable occasion in the Squadron's history have [sic] been the "E-boat do", the bombing of Comiso, and the several drunken orgies in the Sergeants Mess, with Jeff and Pikey in the chair(s). There have been three separate phases in the "Air War over Malta" since the Squadron's formation. The first phase was the Luftwaffe's attacks up till June, then the quiet period when the pickings were to be had, i.e. the Regia Aeronautica's spasmodic attacks (?) during the summer and autumn, and now we have entered the third stage with the Luftwaffe's return to Sicily. Let's hope that we will soon be able to treat the Luftwaffe with the same carefree manner that we showed when Macchi 200s were 10 a penny.

1942

During the following two months of January and February, F/Lt Thompson had very little time to attend to the writing of the diary as the Squadron was in a rather unsettled state. He also spent a short time in hospital and on his return to the Squadron was awaiting positing to the Middle East and had therefore, I should think, little inclination for diary writing.

I have therefore agreed to take over the diary where he left off, and, to make up lost ground I will only summarise the events which happened in January and February.

I intend to carry on Tommy's example of using the first person.

J.R. Sutherland.

January.

S/LDR Pike left us on the 1st, to go East. He was escorted to Luqa by P/Os Allardice and Oliver, and Sgts Steele[,] Nurse, Ellis, Bates, Alderson and myself. We were indeed sorry to see him go as he has proved to be one of the most popular members of the Squadron since he joined it on 27th June. He was at first an auxiliary F/LT in "A" Flt, then, when F/LT Hancock left us, "Pikey" took over "B" Flt, before becoming CO. We all wish him the very best of luck wherever he may go.

On the 2nd we were led by our new CO S/LDR McGregor who comes to us from Ta Kali. He opened his innings with us by leading "B" Flt after some 88s, but owing to their speed, only he and Sgt Steele managed to get long range squirts at them. In the meantime I tackled a 109 and another tackled me so I gave one a headache and the other gave me a sore leg containing some cannon shell splinters. I got a probable for the first 109.

An 88 was shot down by "B" Flt on the 3rd, Sgt Horricks doing the spade work. All the crew bailed out over the island. Sgt Westcott was making a noise like a 109 so the Bofors shot him down and he had to bail out over Kalafrana, unhurt. P/O Reeves observed a 109 fly up close alongside of him and obligingly blow up – Ack Ack again.

On the 4th Sgt Vardy's machine was somewhat dilapidated after the attentions of a 109, but he landed it safely. A few "guests" from 605 Sqdn were flying with our boys at the time, and one of them had a short "poop" at a 109 but claims nothing – P/O Beckett.

The 5th was quiet owing to the weather, and the night 5th/6th was the first raid free night for 40 nights. The 6th was again quiet through bad weather. On the 7th there were a few alerts but nothing came in until the evening when the weather cleared a bit. On the 8th, the Squadron came back on the line again in spite of a high cross wind, as there was a convoy expected in.

On the evening of the 9th we had a party in the Dispersal hut. We had champagne and beer to wash down sausages and eggs fried by "Tommy" ably assisted by a few "keen types". During the course of a hilarious evening we amused ourselves by putting Verey cartridges in the stove, and shooting at a bottle placed on a window ledge, with a .38 revolver.

The period 10th–13th was uneventful (?) apart from air raids. On the 13th P/O Tony Reeves and F/Sgt Ream were taken off Ops pending posting to the Middle East for a rest.

On the 14th, Force "K" was coming in, so the Hun started the day with a raid on that before breakfast.

On the 15th and 16th the aerodrome was U/S so there was no "dicing with death" on these two days. P/O Reeves and F/Sgt Ream went to Ta Kali and Luqa respectively on the 15th as they were to fly long range jobs out East.

The Squadron came back on the line at dawn on the 17th, and I was among the happy (?) band, it being my first time on Readiness for 14 days. We did not fly however. On the 18th we took over at midday from 605 at Luqa where the planes had been taken the previous evening. All the Ta Kali boys were there also, so quite a formidable display of Hurricanes was to be seen.

At dawn on the 19th, W/Comm "Ragbags" led some of the "Ta Kali-ites" on a bombing raid on Comiso to provide a diversion for an incoming convoy, over which there were Hurricanes patrolling all the morning. Needless to say the 88s were also patrolling the convoy, and several of our pilots were greatly impressed by the head on view of an 88 seen from fairly close range. The same evening, back at Hal Far, two Swordfish arrived from Benghazi and before landing demonstrated the correct method of putting a building between attacker and attacked, when two 109s jumped them as they were about to land.

On the 20th the drome was again U/S so there were no aircraft on the line till the afternoon, during which F/LT Lloyd took a long range "poop" at a 109 but claimed nothing.

On the 21st the Squadron was again "stood down", and at 30 minutes availability on the 22nd, and 23rd.

W/Comm Rabagliati was leading when the Squadron came back on the line at midday on the 24th. During a scramble, two Cant Z1007s were intercepted and fired at by "Ragbags" and S/LDR McGregor but no claims were made. Sgt Horricks intercepted an 88 and had a smack at it. Later it was confirmed as destroyed by the German R/T.

The 25th was a bad day for the Squadron. "Tommy" was leading a mixture of 185 and 605 when they were jumped by 109s with the result that there was [sic] Hurricanes going in all directions – mostly down. Tommy damaged an 88 but was shot up by 109s so he had to bail out at 200 feet. He was slightly wounded in one arm so was hauled off to Mtarfa. Sgt Eastman's kite was badly shot up but he landed at Ta Kali unhurt. 2 of 249 bailed out and are OK also one of 242's pilots. A 126 pilot is missing, and two of 249's machines had to crash-land.

On the 26th at midday, only 2 of us came on Readiness, Sgt Eastman and myself, owing to the bad state of the drome, and then were put back to 30 minutes, before being released about teatime. There were a few more machines on Readiness on the 27th but there was little or no flying.

The squadron was released on the 28th due to aircraft unserviceability and the same on the 29th and 30th. F/Sgt Ream is to stay with the Squadron now, and I expect he will be Permanent Met Pilot. The 31st Jan was also a "Released day".

February.

The Squadron came on at midday on the 1st but nothing happened. Tommy has been awarded a well-earned DFC so we all offer him our sincere congratulations, and hope that a bar will soon follow.

We had several 88s bombing the drome again on the 2nd, setting one machine on fire and damaging several others. The 3rd was quiet owing to bad weather.

Some of the Squadron were on at dawn this morning, but nothing worthy of note happened. In the afternoon when we were released we had one very long alert of nearly 4 hours. Some of the Ta Kali boys were jumped by 109s and 3 of them shot down. When the rescue launch went out to pick a pilot up it was also attacked and 3 of the crew killed.

Most of 605 officers and sergeants and some of the 185 officers have evacuated to Marsa Shlok [sic: Marsaxlokk], but the 185 sergeants prefer to suffer in comfort.

On the 5th, 4 of our 109 friends were "doing the mile" (Delimara to Filfla to the uninitiated) and decided that our tame Heinkel 115 was too conspicuous, so they attacked it in Kala Bay, setting it on fire, at its moorings.

Sgt Jolly tipped the "Gladiator" over on its back when returning from the Met trip on the 6th. He mumbled something about an inverted approach, but we mumbled "Bomb holes". In the afternoon, the 109s did a standing patrol at 15,000 feet over our doorstep. Later in the day, the hangars were polished off by 3 88s.

On the 7th a 109 was shot down from 20 odd feet by a Bofors gun just as he was opening fire on the drome. An aircraft doesn't usually fly very well with no tail left so he went straight in. 6 of us came on readiness at midday but when we were released at dusk only one kite was left serviceable. All the rest had been holed by shrapnel from bombs. One of the raids was particularly hectic as the 3 88s came out of the sun with little or no warning.

The morning of the 8th was spent taxiing U/S aircraft, with none on the line.

We went over to Ta Kali at noon on the 9th to operate from there. There was one scramble during which nothing happened.

Back to Ta Kali at dawn on the 10th with 605, who are flying with us (or were we flying with them?).

On the 11th the Squadron was released and the same on the 12th.

Friday 13th was a real Black Friday as there were continual air raids all day. From 09.30 till 18.30 there were three breaks between raids, totalling less than 1 hour 25 minutes. Grand Harbour got most of the bombs. Some 87s appeared during one of the later raids, but they thought too much of Grand Harbour barrage to do much damage.

The following day, 14th, was much the same, and also the 15th. On that day an 88 was brought down by the Bofors near here and another near Luqa. In the afternoon W/Comms Satchell and Rabagliati tried out two ex-4 cannon jobs minus two of their cannons – result, a 109 apiece. Our new CO arrived on the 15th, S/LDR Chaffe. He has come out to us from England to replace S/LDR McGregor who is going East for a well-earned rest.

Everyone shifted over to Rabat on the 16th as we were to operate from Ta Kali for the next week or so. Several pilots went on Readiness at midday and were scrambled shortly after. Just as the squadron was forming up over the drome it was bombed by an 88, to the great consternation of all.

During our stay in Rabat, the officers were billeted in the Officers Mess, Mdina, while the sergeants occupied the Protection Office, becoming a free peepshow for the whole population of Mdina.

Dawn on the 17th saw us on Readiness with 605 at Ta Kali. The Squadron was scrambled twice with S/LDR Chaffe leading but did not engage either time. Released at midday. In the evening Tommy invited us up to the Officers Mess Mdina for a drink as he had learnt that he would be leaving shortly. Well, we had a drink, and another and another and so it went on. It is believed that F/LTs Lloyd and Thompson were in "cahoots", and endeavouring to make every Sgt/Pilot well and truly tight. In a few cases they succeeded. Sgts Jolly and Ellis were found at 11.30 in the Cathedral Square burrowing for gremlins or something, while Sgts Vardy and Alderson had to retire early, probably due to electrical failure as they seemed well lit up. During the evening W/Comm "Ragbags" gave us an exhibition of a Zulu dance, to which S/LDR Andrews and Sgt Wilson of 605 replied with a Maori war dance. F/Sgt Fletcher of 605 did a few things of his own, or maybe they originated from the American Indians. It was a pity our own Indians, Sgts Horricks and Eastman were not there, or they might have shown us something.

None of our pilots were required on the 19th, so we spent most of the day recuperating. The 20th was wet, so once again, no pilots from 185 were on. F/LT Thompson, and Sgts Jolly and Vardy left for Kalafrana in the afternoon to await an aircraft to take them to Middle East. Sgt Sheppard is going with them, but he is already at Hal Far, as he is U/S with a cut hand. We wish them all that we wish ourselves and hope they will get the rest which they so much deserve and need.

On the 21st several of the 185 pilots and 605 pilots were called down to Ta Kali, but on arrival there they found they were not needed and so returned to Rabat.

Some new pilots have arrived from England by "Sunderland", and as they are all Spitfire pilots, several questions are being asked but no satisfactory answers are forthcoming (What is a Spitfire, anyway?).

On the 22nd, the Squadron came to Readiness at midday, with W/Comm "Ragbags" leading. Three 88s and some 109s were intercepted over Hal Far on a scramble. We jumped the 88s as they were pulling out of their dive, but only one is claimed as damaged (by self). I managed by a lucky shot to fix up a 109 who was about to tackle Sgt Westcott, who later observed his late attacker spin down minus a wing. Sgt Eastman had quite an enjoyable time as the attached newspaper clipping will show. P/O Oliver was very indignant when he landed after being attacked by a 109 as his one and only good pair of trousers were ruined by glycol. He put up an excellent performance in bringing back safely his much damaged aircraft. S/LDR Chaffe did not return, but nobody knows why. It is with sorrow that I record his death, as, though he had been with us for so short a time, we had admired him as a leader and a man, little though we knew him. He was rather quiet, though that may have been because he was still feeling his way on the island, but what he did say or do, had a very definite purpose behind it, and we were happy in having such a man as our leader.

Cutting from The Times of Malta *follows:*

AIR BATTLES OVER MALTA

Fighters – A.A. Gunners In All Day Action

SCORE:	DAMAGED 4 "JU 88's" 4 "ME 109's"	PROBABLES 1 "ME 109"	DESTROYED 1 "ME 109"

ONE OF OUR FIGHTERS MISSING

The following Situation report was issued from the Information Office yesterday February 22, 1942, at 5 p.m., covering the previous 24 hours:

R.A.F. fighters have been in action with great success during a series of determined attacks on aerodromes by large formations of enemy aircraft throughout the day.

In spite of the German air force bombers being heavily escorted by "Messerschmitts", our "Hurricanes" time and again eluded the fighters and relentlessly attacked the "JU 88's".

During these all-day combats, one "ME 109" fighter was definitely shot down, a second probably destroyed, four "JU 88's" damaged and four more fighters damaged. Many probably did not reach their bases. Only one of our fighters is missing. Anti-aircraft Artillery has been in action throughout the day.

There has been military and civilian damage, but, reports so far reveal that only eight persons were seriously injured and one slightly injured.

Written: SGT SUTHERLAND

"ME" FALLS TO GUNS OF SERGEANT PILOT

The "ME 109" was shot down by a Sergeant Pilot. He flew so close to press home his attack that he had to break off to avoid a collision. Black smoke was then pouring from the "Messerschmitt's" engine. Another pilot saw the starboard wing fall off, the fighter then spinning into the ground. The Sergeant Pilot then attacked a "JU 88", damaging it and silencing the rear-gunner.

Written: SGT EASTMAN

Another Sergeant Pilot attacked in turn two "JU 88's" and two "ME 109's". His tracer bullets ripped the fuselage of one bomber, the underneath side of the other and hit the rear gunner of the second. Bursts of tracer also hit both the fighters.

Written: "TA KALI-ITES"

This afternoon a formation of "JU 88's" were all attacked as well as the fighter escort. A Pilot Officer who attacked the centre bomber scored hits on the tail and starboard wing. He had to break off when attacked by two "ME's" but he succeeded in evading one and getting a burst into the second. Another Pilot Officer and a Sergeant Pilot were, meanwhile, dealing with the other two "JU 88's", both of which were hit. The engine of a fighter was damaged by a Squadron Leader and as he came out of the dog-fight he saw another "ME 109" which had just been attacked by a fighter Flight Lieutenant, going down on its back with white smoke streaming from its radiator.

The remainder of the article is missing. The diary continues:

The Squadron was on at dawn on the 23rd, and 8 of us went off fairly early to search for S/LDR Chaffe without, however, having any luck. Later, the Squadron escorted a Maryland away from the Island, out of the danger zone. I had to return due to engine trouble and was chased part of the way by a 109. We were scrambled again just before dinner for some 88s and 109s. Sgts Steele and Horricks both got a 109 and various others fired but made no claims. Horricks also tried his hand at his first love, 88s, without having any luck, however. (That guy, Horricks, is good!). While this was happening, I was sitting in the Ops dugout, Hal Far, having crash-landed there with a duff engine.

The Squadron was off on the 24th and 25th. F/Sgt Lillywhite is now P/O Lillywhite. Good show Lill, and good luck in your new position. We have now been given 4 new officers, all ex-Spitfire pilots, so we would like to take this opportunity of welcoming them to the Squadron and wishing them luck during their stay on the "Gem". The newcomers are F/O Lawrence, P/O Sergeant, P/O Milburn and P/O Daddo-Langlois.

On the 26th 4 of the Squadron went on with 605 – F/O Lawrence, P/O Sergeant, P/O Daddo-Langlois and myself. There was no flying, however, as the weather was duff.

The 27th saw the Squadron preparing to move back to Hal Far, which it did in the evening after much procrastination. Several pilots came over by air, bringing the machines we will use at Hal Far. On the 28th the same pilots + 1 came on at daybreak to defend the "Gem" but did very little defending as the weather was on our side – i.e. raining like nobody's business. 605 took over at midday.

Thus we come to the present, so in future the diary will carry on as before.

Malta's fighters tended to use the outdated vic or line astern formations, leaving themselves vulnerable to attack by the Luftwaffe, *whose fighter pilots had adopted the procedure of flying in pairs and fours in line abreast, with the pilots able to look inwards so as to cover as much sky as possible. In February 1942 Squadron Leader Stan Turner had arrived to take command of 249 Squadron. He quickly decided on some radical changes. It was due largely to his intervention that the RAF in Malta began to follow the example of the* Luftwaffe, *flying in pairs and in loose 'fingers four' sections.*

There was also a tendency to scramble Hurricanes too late. Another decisive tactic implemented by Turner and Malta's outstanding Operations Controller, Group Captain A.B. 'Woody' Woodhall, saw the fighters scrambled as the raids approached, thus giving Hurricanes time to gain altitude south of the island, well away from the enemy's course of attack. Then, on the word from ground control, they would dive on the intruders, gaining precious speed in the process.

In order to survive as an Allied base, the island continued to be re-supplied by sea, but there remained an urgent requirement for additional fighters. On 7 March fifteen Spitfire Mk VB (Trop)s were flown in off HMS Eagle. *At last, here was a machine with a speed to match the Messerschmitt Bf 109 and the firepower necessary to destroy the Junkers Ju 88. At about this time, 1435 Flight (formerly the Malta Night Fighter Unit) received as a welcome addition to its own Hurricanes four Beaufighters on detachment from 89 Squadron in Egypt. On the 27th Hurricane IICs of 229 Squadron were also*

112

transferred to Malta from North Africa. During March there were further changes as 242 and 605 Squadrons were absorbed by 126 and 185 Squadrons.

Soon after the arrival of the Spitfires, the Luftwaffe *devised another strategy and dispatched large formations of bombers against the island's air bases, initially in an attempt to destroy the fighters on the ground. First to be targeted was Ta' Qali, where aerial reconnaissance had revealed to the Germans the construction of what appeared to be an underground hangar. To deal with this latest development, a number of Ju 88s were armed with rocket-assisted, armour-piercing bombs with an alleged capability of penetrating up to forty-five feet of solid rock. On 20 March a powerful force, including some sixty Ju 88s, opened the new phase by attacking Ta' Qali. These efforts were wasted on what was in reality a dummy target! Although the RAF had indeed attempted to excavate a hangar in the cliff bordering the airfield's south-west perimeter, the stone had proved unsuitable for such a scheme and the project was abandoned. Instead, mock hangar doors were painted and damaged fighters left at the 'entrance' in order to lure the enemy into attacking the site.*

On 21 and 29 March Malta was reinforced with sixteen more Spitfires. In the interim, the survivors of convoy 'MW10' reached the island. One merchantman, Clan Campbell, *and an escorting destroyer, HMS* Southwold, *had been lost. The* Luftwaffe *next redirected its efforts against the harbours, thereby easing the pressure on Ta' Qali which had been rendered temporarily unserviceable after attacks on 20 March. Vessels sunk at Malta as a result of heavy raids on 26 March included the destroyer* Legion *and the submarine P39, the remaining cargo ships,* Talabot *and* Pampas, *and the Commissioned Auxiliary Supply Ship* Breconshire, *the latter a veteran of the Malta run. An oiler, RFA* Plumleaf, *was driven aground.*

Sunday 1 March
The Squadron came on Readiness at dinnertime, and operated the odd half-dozen aircraft from Luqa. No attempt was made to "harass the enemy" so the only scramble of the day was not a scramble, but a search for a "Ta Kali-ite" in the drink, the "searchers" being P/Os Oliver and Milburn. The other pilots justified their existence by ferrying the aircraft back from Luqa at dusk.

This morning two of the Ta Kali boys went "West" and one of 605 had to bail out when some 109s got the better of an argument.

Monday 2 March
Early this morning a "Sunderland" was due in, so, as some 88s were bombing Kalafrana and generally making a nuisance of themselves, four of our happy band of "keen types" were scrambled in darkness to chase the naughty 88s away from our backyard, the "keen types" being F/LT

Lloyd, P/O Oliver, and Sgts Alderson and Westcott. The 88s must have smelled the difference in the air, as they went home immediately. Our four aviators were then sent off in the direction of Sicily to look for two wandering Swordfish. They were brought back again at high speed when some 109s restarted their inquisitiveness and took off from Sicily to do something about it.

No more operational flying was done for the rest of the morning, though five other pilots flew aircraft over from Ta Kali, and Sgt Alderson air tested another.

Tuesday 3 March
The Squadron did not come on Readiness at midday, as, due to unserviceability, we have been released until the serviceability improves. Sundry pilots were impressed to fill 4 gallon "ex-100 Octane" tins with sand and place them around the aircraft dispersals to form anti-blast pens. This healthy exercise was not appreciated. Other pilots were to be seen in the Dispersal Hut sucking inky fingers and pouring [sic] over Forms 540 and 541, and this diary. The first set of workers will not believe the second set, when they are told, indignantly, that the mental fatigue brought on by clerical work is just as great as the physical fatigue brought on by pen-building.

F/Sgt Ream left us this morning for HQ Valetta. He is going on Visual Controlling from the Palace Roof until such time as he can be sent to the Middle East, to get the rest he so much requires.

Wednesday 4 March
8 a/c were on the line at dawn this morning but none took the air. The nearest approach they had to flying was a scramble which was cancelled.

Thursday 5 March
I omitted to record the departure of P/Os Daddo-Langlois and Sergeant after a very short stay with us. They left us on the day following our return from Ta Kali. 249 Sqdn was disbanded two or three weeks ago as most of its members were due for a rest. 249 has now been reformed, composed entirely of Spitfire pilots, and P/Os Daddo-Langlois and Sergeant are joining them as they came out here from Spitfire squadrons.

Two other pilots have arrived from UK to take their places, the new arrivals being Sgts Broad and Tweedale, an Australian. We wish them lots of luck and "pickings".

6 pilots came on Readiness in the afternoon and flew once, a search for a Ta Kali pilot "in the drink" off Grand Harbour. P/O Milburn had to return early as his hood blew off in the air. He apparently has no faith in windsocks – – – – !! Sgt Tweedale "took the air" once on an air test.

Friday 6 March

As we came on the line this morning, a late Ju 88 "intruder" bombed Luqa so P/O Allardice and myself took off in an attempt to catch it, but were too late. The Squadron were scrambled later in the morning for a 9+ with attendant 109 plots around it, but no contact was made as the scramble came through too late.

605 took over for the afternoon.

Saturday 7 March

Today was a big day in the history of the "Gem" for 15 Spitfire 5Bs arrived to operate from here against the "wily Hun". They arrived in the afternoon in two groups and were escorted in by the Hurricanes (What irony!) They were a beautiful sight to watch, and many people felt it was definitely an occasion for a party. They will be flown by 249 from Ta Kali.

Later, 4 machines were scrambled for a 9+ and joined up with Ta Kali, but no contact was made.

Sunday 8 March

There were 3 scrambles during the morning, the first for a "Maryland" escort, the second for a 3+ and 6+, and the third for 2 +3s. No contact was made on the second and third trips, owing to insufficient height. The Squadron was relieved at 13.00 hrs by 605.

Monday 9 March

6 pilots took over at midday from 605 and were scrambled twice with F/O Lawrence leading. The first time, a +12 came in but no contact was made. The second time however, 6 Ju 88s and about 18 Me 109s were intercepted just off Hal Far by 10 Hurricanes – 6 from Ta Kali and 4 of us. It was one of the biggest scraps yet. Sgt Steele had a day out as he shot down a 109, damaged an 88, and hit a second 109 without, however, observing any damage. Sgt Tweedale, our new "Digger" pilot, did marvellously well in the scrap, his first action out here, as he sat on the tail of an 88 and gave it all he had, from close range, in spite of the attentions of at least 3 109s. Unfortunately he was slightly injured when his kite was hit, and a small piece of cannon shell hit him on the foot. His kite was in a slightly dilapidated condition so he had to crash land. At the same time, a 109 attempted to shoot him up, but Sgt Steele, who was coming in with his wheels and flaps down, scared him off with a few rounds of .303 in his belly. Sgt Baines, our Armourer Sgt, had mounted his pet twin Brownings on top of the "Ops Dugout" and blazed off the odd 40 rounds at our friend, without however, any effect being seen.

Tuesday 10 March

The Squadron came to Readiness at dawn. 4 a/c, F/O Lawrence

leading, joined with Ta Kali for 3 Ju 88s with fighter escort. At 10,000 ft, 2 ME 109s attempted to jump us so we turned toward them. I was so ham, that I spun down, and took no further interest in the proceedings. A Spitfire shot down 1 of the 109s and Sgt Steele had a good burst at the belly of the other. Archie Steele then attacked one of three 88s over Luqa, and made him jettison his bombs, the other two making off without bombing at all. A second 109 tried to attack but Archie made a head-on attack at him, and used the rest of his ammo on him, without any apparent effect, however.

This was the first time the Spitfires had operated, and they succeeded in getting two 109s.

The same 4 pilots were again scrambled for 6 Ju 88s with fighter escort. A certain Ta Kali S/LDR who shall be nameless was leading, and suffered from Finger Trouble with the result that he successfully avoided contact with the enemy.

605 SQDN relieved us at midday.

Wednesday 11 March

4 pilots came on Readiness at 13.00 hrs and were scrambled once, F/O Lawrence leading, for a +3, 50 MILES N but made no contact. FO Lawrence later tested the cannons of our one and only cannon job, "Y".

Sgt Broad made two short practise flights, these being his first trips on the island, and also on Hurricanes. When asked his opinion of Hurricanes he replied "Very shaky".

Thursday 12 March

The Squadron was on from dawn till 13.00 hrs, but no operational flying was done. The one and only scramble of the watch was cancelled before anyone could take off. F/Sgt Hunton who is to be congratulated on getting his "crown" tested the cannons on "Y" again.

Sgt Alderson and myself, who were off duty, paid a visit to the 4 sick members of the squadron now resident in Mtarfa. F/Sgt Nurse, who was injured by a bomb in January, and suffered from shock, concussion and a broken leg, is now able to hobble about with the aid of crutches. P/O Lillywhite went in on the 28th Feb. with influenza, has since has [sic] bronchitis, pneumonia, and now pleurisy, is able to sit up and take notice. P/O Oliver had an argument between himself and a motor car – the car won, so Olly is now suffering from "conclusions". Sgt Tweedale who duffed up the 88 a few days back, and is recovering rapidly and cheerfully.

We also had a chat with 3 German POWs who are in Mtarfa and heard one or two rather interesting pieces of information. For instance, an 88 in the hands of a good pilot can be looped and rolled quite easily. The 88 pilot had flown an old "Spit" and also a 109E, and for landing and take-off, liked the "Spit" best.

Friday 13 March

The Squadron came on at 13.00 hours, the session being opened by me, with an air test. Later we were scrambled with F/O Lawrence leading and were joined by 3 Hurricanes and 4 "Spits" from Ta Kali. We sat up at 10,000 ft and waited for the 88s to come in. However the bright boys must have been tipped off, and caught a dose of cold feet, for they turned back without crossing the coast. There were several 109s about, mostly above us, but though we turned towards them several times, they definitely wouldn't play, thus giving us a decided moral victory. This is an example of what can be done when all fingers are well out, and proper formation is kept.

Saturday 14 March

The Squadron did no flying at all this morning as the "wily Hun" was rather quiet until nearly dinnertime. Owing to petrol shortage at Ta Kali, the 3 serviceable aircraft from there came over here to operate. Shortly before noon several 88s came over and bombed the drome. 1 Ta Kali kite went up in smoke, while several others were damaged by splinters.

605 took over at 13.00 hours.

In the evening, 5 sgts, myself and F/Sgt Fletcher of 605 went for a walk over to the cliffs and amused ourselves by heaving huge rocks into the sea. (??!! – we've been on the island too long!) When darkness fell, we visited an Army post and joined in a game of Tombola with remarkable success. Needless to say, the odd bottle of beer was to be seen. Several pilots did not return to base for a long time!

Sunday 15 March

At 13.00 hrs, 4 a/c came to Readiness led by P/O Allardice. The first scramble was for a +3 but no contact was made, due to bad visibility. Later there was a second scramble for a +15, which turned out to be 2 Ju 88s with fighter escort. One of the 88s was intercepted at 16,000 feet. He jettisoned when the fighters attacked and dived to sea level. The Hurries had the odd squirt but could not catch the e/a, so they started back home. Just then the 109s decided to hurry them up and chased the boys back. Bates had 4 on his tail pooping at him, but [they] did not damage him at all. Twitch was flying around, though. The rest were also fired at but no one was hit.

Monday 16 March

The Squadron was on from dawn but were not scrambled at all during the watch, as the visibility was bad, and very few raiders came in. Those sergeants who were not on Readiness spent the forenoon building anti-blast pens round the dispersals.

Tuesday 17 March

This afternoon the first scramble (4 a/c) was led by W/Comm Riley, the new Station CO. Owing to his not having flown for some time, he was rather unsteady, but realised it himself and apologised handsomely for it afterwards. We managed to intercept an 88 and a Heinkel 111 but owing to their speed, very little damage was done to either e/a. Sgts Steele and Broad had long range squirts at the 88, while only the Ta Kali boys fired at the 111, which Steele swears was a "Maryland" (?). However, according to Ops, no Marylands were airborne at the time.

The second scramble of the afternoon was led by F/LT Lawrence, whom we have to congratulate on his promotion. We were actually sent off to disperse below cloud, as it was thought that it was Hal Far's turn to be bombed. We made one circuit of the island below cloud base (2,000 ft) and watched the Ack-Ack guns firing and bombs bursting all over the island. When we were over Hal Far on our first lap, Archie Steele sighted an 88 about 4,000 ft above us and to one side, being fired at by the Bofors which hit him once in the starboard engine. Backed up by self, Archie chased the 88 about 15 miles out to sea, and succeeded in closing to firing range. He (Archie) hit him with 3 bursts, then his ammo finished [and] he returned to base, so I took over and also hit him. I made 3 attacks then turned on to a second, making a half hearted climbing attack on him, then started home. On the way back I met a 109 on his own 2,000 feet up, so I made an attack on him, and saw him turn on his back, diving towards the sea.

Later at night, F/Control confirmed the 88 so it is shared between the Bofors, Archie and myself. The 109 was given as a probable.

We have now a new Squadron Commander, S/LDR Mortimer-Rose, DFC and Bar, whom we welcome to the Squadron, and wish him the very best of luck during his stay with us. Several of us have already met him "down the Hole", where he was serving as a Fighter Controller during a period of convalescence. Little as we know him, we do know he is a thoroughly "good type" and look forward happily to serving under him.

Wednesday 18 March

There was only one scramble for the Squadron during the morning watch, and even then we were only sent off to be out of the road of bombs, as cloud base was about 1,200 ft. However, the six "bombers" turned out to be fighters which did not come in, as they stayed at 15,000 feet, 15 miles NE and orbited, so we pancaked.

Today, 605 Squadron merged with 185, so that we have now a more or less new squadron. The 605 boys, led by F/LT Stones, DFC will be "C" Flt 185, for the next few days, and then will be split up, to make up the numbers in "A" and "B" Flights.

This general reshuffle is brought about by the [im]pending departure of several pilots to the Middle East, said pilots having served 9 months on the island. These pilots will be leaving the island when 229 Sqdn arrives on the island within the next few days (we hope!), and will be going with similar "veterans" from Ta Kali, 242 and 126 Sqdns having merged in a similar fashion to ourselves, to form a new 126.

Opposite is the temporary Squadron list [*reproduced below*].

185 SQUADRON
TEMPORARY LIST OF PILOTS (18/3/42).

S/LDR MORTIMER-ROSE, DFC AND BAR.

"A" FLIGHT.

F/LT LAWRENCE.
P/O MILBURN.
F/SGT BATES.
F/SGT HUNTON
SGT BROAD
SGT ALDERSON.
SGT SUTHERLAND
SGT ROBB   (EX-605)
SGT WILSON („ „).

"B" FLIGHT.

F/LT LLOYD.
P/O LILLYWHITE (SICK).
P/O ALLARDICE
P/O OLIVER (SICK).
SGT EASTMAN
SGT ELLIS
SGT HORRICKS
SGT STEELE
SGT WESTCOTT
SGT TWEEDALE (SICK).

"C" FLIGHT.

F/LT STONES, DFC
P/O BECKETT.
P/O LESTER
P/O McKAY
P/O NOBLE
P/O ORMROD   } EX-605
P/O WIGLEY
F/SGT FLETCHER
F/SGT HOWE (SICK)
SGT FINLAY(SICK)

NON-EFFECTIVE – F/SGT NURSE.

Thursday 19 March

Yesterday (Wed.) the new "C" Flight came to Readiness at 1300 hours for the first time in 185 Sqdn. They were scrambled for a big plot, which turned out to be 7 Ju 88s and over 20 Me 109s. F/LT Stones was leading 6 of "C" Flt and 4 of Ta Kali, while 4 "Spits" were supposed to be high cover. The "Spitfires" however, disappeared after the 88s, and left the boys without any cover. Only F/Lt Stones and F/Sgt Fletcher fired at the 88s, Fletch damaging one by getting its port engine. The others engaged (or were engaged?) the 109s. P/O Ormrod fired at 3 of them, and P/O Wigley at one, while P/O "Chuck" Lester was jumped by 4 of the sods. He fired at one of them and got a probable for it, but unfortunately became non-effective when he was shot down from "nought" feet by another 109. However, when his plane hit the drink, the force of the impact threw him clear. He was picked up an hour later by the Rescue Launch and taken to Mtarfa, suffering from broken bones and two bullet wounds.

Today (Thurs) no flying has been done at all apart from air tests.

Friday 20 March

"B" Flight came to Readiness at Dawn with 8 machines, and were scrambled once for a +3 and a +6, but nothing came in. "A" Flight relieved them at 13.00 hrs, but did nothing except "hog" ferrying hours, and air tests.

Once again the Squadron has been reshuffled. F/Lt Stones, F/Sgts Bates and Hunton and Sgt Westcott go to the Palace Tower, Valetta, to do the odd spot of Visual Controlling – (shaky do!) while "C" Flight ceases to exist. Once again, a squadron list is given opposite [see below].

Also shown, as a matter of interest, is the formation which we have been using – quite successfully – for the last month or so. It will be noticed that the flanking aircraft cover each other. The most important thing is the necessity for the sections to fly well up, almost line abreast.

185 SQUADRON (20/3/42.)

S/LDR MORTIMER-ROSE, DFC AND BAR.

"A" FLIGHT	"B" FLIGHT.
F/LT LAWRENCE	F/LT LLOYD
P/O BECKETT	P/O ALLARDICE
P/O McKAY	P/O ORMROD
P/O NOBLE	P/O WIGLEY.
F/SGT FLETCHER.	P/O MILBURN.
SGT BROAD	SGT ALDERSON.
SGT ELLIS	SGT EASTMAN
SGT STEELE	SGT HORRICKS
SGT SUTHERLAND	SGT ROBB.
SGT WILSON	

SICK PILOTS NOT INCLUDED.

PRESENT FORMATION USED BY SQUADRON

RED

t_4 t_3 t_1 t_2

WHITE

t_4 t_3 t_1 t_2

YELLOW

t_2 t_1 t_3 t_4

SECTIONS SHOULD BE, AS NEAR AS POSSIBLE,
LINE ABREAST.

Saturday 21 March

"A" Flight normally would have been on watch at dawn, but owing to the absence of several Sgt/Pilots, armed with vaseline, log books, and "best blue", a mixed bunch of pilots came on watch. Just about dinner time the aforementioned sergeants returned from Valetta, looking very pleased, and muttering among themselves such things as "Where are you getting your uniform?" and "How much does a P/O get?" At approximately the same time the "mixed bunch" were scrambled for escort duties, some "Spitfires" being due in, and the CO led them out over Gozo. There they found 8 aircraft flying in vic, and the CO thinking them to be "Hudsons" thought that control must be wrong about the Spits. However, a closer inspection was made when the 8 "Hudsons" made an ugly pass at Ta Kali armed with "hafna bombes" [sic: in Maltese, hafna bombi, i.e. many bombs] and were discovered to be ME 110s, so the Squadron piled in. In the ensuing running fight, much ammo was expended on our side and more on the "other side" with the result that 4 110s went in the drink. The CO and P/O Allardice each got one, while P/O Beckett and Sgt Robb, and P/Os Ormrod and Wigley, shared the other two. The last four also got a ¼ damaged each.

There were no more scrambles for the rest of the day.

Sunday 22 March

Once again, a "mixed bunch" came on watch at Dawn, as the same sergeants had departed once more to Valetta, for a medical this time.

Led by F/Lt Lawrence, 7 of the "mixed bunch" went off for 3 Ju 88s. Only 3 pilots engaged, P/Os Allardice, and Wigley, and Sgt Robb, but I have to record with regret that P/O Allardice, who was leading, was shot down by the combined crossfire of the 88s and went straight in. He succeeded, however in damaging one of the 88s.

P/O Allardice was one of our keenest pilots, and his success yesterday had done nothing if not increase his keenness. His death is all the same to be regretted when it is recalled that he was shortly due to leave the Island for a well-earned rest.

In the afternoon 8 pilots, led by the CO went off after six 88s which, however did not come in.

As a convoy is coming in tomorrow the pilots were released early.

Once again our Squadron Diary changes hands. Ian "Jock" Sutherland has had his wish realized and he is preparing to depart for the Middle East. So I have promised to take over our "dear Dairy" [sic] and with my tongue in my cheek, will endeavour to record future events in an accurate and interesting manner.

G.E. Horricks 185.

Monday 23 March

As recorded yesterday, our Convoy's arrival was expected today. So we weary pilots departed to our respective Messes, and did indulge in considerable drinking. Just to be in good condition.

The dawn broke dull and dreary, with the Convoy just off the SE coast. Fighter Control rang up and said we were to keep a standing patrol over it. Two Hurricanes up at a time. The first pair, Sgts Sutherland and Ellis came across a Ju 88 peeking in and out of the low clouds. Ellis managed to get in a good burst and was awarded a damaged. The next pair, Sgt Eastman and myself, had just become airborne, when a Ju 88 appeared before us. We each took an engine and in the ensuing chase we stopped its stbd engine and left it in a very battered condition, and got a probable. The next pair, F/L Lawrence and Sgt Broad were even more fortunate, coming across a lovely new He 111. As it was nearly breakfast time, they decided to clear the air as soon as possible. So they shot down our nice new He 111, and returned to eat a hearty meal.

And so it continued throughout the day. Besides the aforementioned scraps, P/O Wigley and F/Sgt Fletcher damaged a Ju 88, P/Os Noble and Beckett attacked two Ju 88s and S/L Mortimer-Rose and Sgt Eastman had a long range shot at one.

The Squadron was released as planned and every one "hit the hay" tired, but happy.

Tuesday 24 March

Hal Far was today visited by 27 Ju 87s. "Stukas" to you. All that can be said of their visit is that it was "short and unsweet". They unloaded their pills on our buildings. Anybody that wants to see the results can walk around and look, because it's too sad to tell about. Our casualties were many, and our feelings were hurt. Our new CO S/L Mortimer-Rose, while deftly, defying the downpour, had both ear drums bust or broken and will not be flying for some time to come. He was the only casualty among the pilots.

The Squadron came to readiness at dawn, and kept up the standing patrol. This time however, it was over the "Breconshire", disabled, off Zonkor Point. Throughout the day, enemy activity was on a reduced scale. The Huns taking a day off to lick his wounds. The combined defences yesterday accounted for six of their – – –. – – – –! aircraft. However just before dusk he retaliated with a plus 60. P/Os Noble and Beckett, F/Sgt Fletcher and Sgt Broad were scrambled and had squirts at three Ju 88s. Everyone returned and went to bed, none the wiser.

Wednesday 25 March

Squadron came to readiness at dawn, and as the Group Capt has a new scheme for doing readiness with the aircraft dispersed in their proper points, we retired to the Dispersal Hut at the Windsock. Things were decently quiet for part of the day, but when a plot of +6 and +12 was rumoured to be on its way to Malta, it can be stated, that things definitely began to happen. Eight of us immediately became airborne and F/L Lloyd brought about a wonderful interception. There followed a terrific air battle, one of the largest Malta has seen. Hurricanes, Spits, Me 109s and Ju 87s totalling 40 aircraft. And when the sky had cleared and everyone had returned and told their tale, it could clearly be seen that the GAF [*German Air Force*], sometimes called Luftwaffe had received the dirty end of the stick. P/Os Ormrod and Wigley, between them accounted for one Ju 87, and everyone else had probables and damaged. We later learned that twelve enemy aircraft went off the plot, and we all feel certain that most of the probables never got home. However they were not seen to go in, so cannot be counted [*as*] destroyed. Everyone is quite happy, as it was our first crack at 87s. Here's to many more.

Thursday 26 March

The Squadron came to readiness at dawn, and we had with us a few of the "old soaks" from Takali. We appreciate their doing readiness with us, as at present we are quite short of pilots.

There was one scramble for 6 Ju 88s and 6 of their pals, Me 109s. Due to cloud and 109s we were unable to make a perfect interception, but some of us had shots at the 88s, who soon realized we were around. It was noticed that the 109s have painted the underside of their noses a bright yellow. So, pilots, take note. Grand Harbour was today bombed by a total of 50 Ju 88s and "Stukas". They left one of our much escorted MVs [*merchant vessels*] in flames. Of the Convoy, we thought was safely in harbour, only the "Breconshire" remains.

Friday 27 March

Squadron on readiness, but no scrambles, due to shortage of serviceable aircraft.

Last night the "Breconshire" was bombed and set on fire. This morning it rolled over on its side and sunk [*sic*] in Kalafrana Bay. She was the last of the convoy.

There were two scrambles in the afternoon for the arriving 229 Squadron. They all (10) arrived safely from the Middle East, in brand new, cannon Hurricanes. There was much cheering by 185. As they will probably be operating in conjunction with us, we all wish them the best of luck. (They'll need it). As most of their pilots have run up against the Jerries in the desert, they should prove very valuable in the defence of the Island.

Three Me 109s dropped bombs on our Windsock dispersal today, and killed two of the runway crew, and slightly damaged an aircraft.

Saturday 28 March

There were several scrambles today in 9/10 cloud for single Ju 88s dropping bombs on nothing in particular. Owing to the cloud there were no interceptions.

Sunday 29 March

There were only two scrambles during the day for single 88s. The cloud is still about 9/10ths.

The CO has found a pastime for pilots doing readiness. To keep us from becoming bored we stagger out and fill sandbags (hundreds of 'em). By so doing, we are not required to do same on our days off. So we still get our day off and get our quota of "diggings for Victory" done too??

Sgt Eastman and myself are [*word unreadable*] the line before dawn to escort a Catalina in. Here comes the mail. Hope. Hope.

Monday 30 March

The weather is still u/s so the escort job didn't come off. There was no flying to-day at all. What a lovely thing 10/10ths is.

The Squadron has moved back to our old dispersal hut. 229 are going to start operating within a few days, and are going to use the windsock dispersal. All 185's serviceable aircraft are dispersed on Safi strip so we still do readiness with the aircraft properly dispersed.

Tuesday 31 March

The weather is still the same. 9/10ths with rain. However Sgts Steele and Broad were scrambled after some Ju 88s hiding in the clouds. While flying at cloud base 4 Me 109s suddenly appeared behind them. Steele, it appears was a bit slow in turning, and one of the Me 109s shot him down. Broad had a quick squirt at one of the 109s but observed no results. Sgt Steele's death came as a great blow to the Squadron. He was one of the most skilful and keenest pilots on the Island. He can be ill spared during these hard times. Steele was just getting into [his] stride, having destroyed two Me 109s as well as having some probables and damaged to his credit.

I knew Archie Steele in private life, and I know everyone agrees with me when I say he was a damn good fellow.

Shortly after Steele and Broad encountered the 109s, a Mosquito, in fact the only one on the Island appeared over Halfar with two Me 109s on its tail. The results were disastrous. With one engine on fire, the Mosquito crash landed on our drome and was burned to a cinder. The crew of two, fortunately escaped unhurt.

The weather cleared considerably during the day and when a plus 55 appeared at dusk, it was decided that our night operational pilots, namely, P/Os Wigley, Ormrod, Milburn and Sgt Eastman, would take the air and do battle, landing at Takali. And so they did. Everyone waded in and got their feet wet. With the results that they probably destroyed one Ju 88 and damaged a second. They all landed OK.

While the entertainment was at its height, P/O Ormrod looked like a Ju 87, or so the Searchlights and Bofors thought. For he was illuminated and duly fired upon by those worthy people. However, the Bofors are quite harmless so there was nothing to worry about. When Mr Ormrod landed he was seen to be walking bomb happily about the field with a dazed and dazzled look upon his face mumbling something about wanting to know where the light switch was, because somebody had turned the lights out on him.

So ended a fairly eventful day. Our drome is now u/s, as a good share of the 55 Ju 88s dropped their bombs on it. It was too smooth anyway.

Wednesday 1 April

Crews worked all night on the drome and had the runway serviceable for this morning. We also had 16 aircraft on the line. Good show on the ground crews' part. About mid-morning a plot of +60 appeared and forty Ju 88s and "Stukas" bombed Halfar, and in between the bombs Me 109s machine gunned the drome and 'planes. Despite F/L Lloyd's persistent pleads [sic], fighter control would not scramble us. It was indeed a foolish move on their part, for after the raid, of our 16 serviceable aircraft, only two could take the air. Two Hurricanes were completely burned out and the rest damaged. It was heart breaking, both to the ground crews, and the pilots.

However when the next raid came in, just before dusk, Control had their fingers out and scrambled our serviceable a/c. The boys mixed it up with the bombers and fighters and came out on top despite the terrific odds. At the time of this writing I unfortunately have not [got] the pilots' individual claims, but 16 enemy aircraft were destroyed to-day, and no small part of them falls to our fighters. We lost no pilots or planes, but a few were damaged. A very good show.

In the original diary, claims from here on are listed on the facing page opposite main entries.

WED. APR. 1.

1st Scramble		
	P/O BECKETT P/O McKAY }	PROBABLE JU 88.
	F/SGT FLETCHER – PROBABLE JU 88.	
	SGT BOYD	– SQUIRTED – 1 JU 88
		„ – 2 ME 109s.

2nd Scramble.		
	P/O McKAY	– DAMAGED JU 87
	F/SGT FLETCHER	– 1 – JU 87 DESTROYED 1 – JU 87 PROBABLE.
	SGT BOYD	– 1 – JU 87 PROBABLE.

Thursday 2 April

Owing to our drome being u/s (bomb-holes) the Squadron operated from Takali. Only one scramble for a +35 – 88s and 87s. Despite the covering 109s our six Hurricanes engaged the bombers and shook them considerably. Again I am unable to give the individual claims, but everyone fired, and as soon as the tallies have been collected, I will put the results on the opposite page [below].

As was the case yesterday, the bombers again attacked Halfar and left it badly shaken, many more bomb-holes, planes damaged and buildings shaken. Two 1100 lbders [sic: i.e. pounders] landed on our dispersal hut, but didn't explode. However, one end of the hut fell out. No one will be able to complain of not [having] sufficient air in the dispersal hut now.

I have been informed by the fire crew, that since Dec. 9 this year, no fewer than 42 aircraft have been completely burned out on our aerodrome. This of course does not include the damaged aircraft.

APRIL. 2.

1st   { P/O BECKETT – JU 88 DAMAGED
Scramble. {   – SQUIRTED – 2 ME 109s.

      2 – JU 87s – PROBABLES.
      1 – JU 88 –   ”
      1 – ME 109 –   ”

Friday 3 April
Me 109s made four bombing raids on the drome this am. Squadron operating from Luqa but at 30 min. available [sic]. Ju 88s and 87s continued mass attacks on the Island.

Saturday 4 April
Still operating from Luqa. Came to readiness at 4 P.M. with six serviceable aircraft. Scrambled for a +50, three of us returned u/s. The rest engaged and damaged several bombers. 229 and 185 Squadrons are operating together while at Luqa. Ian Sutherland and Johnny Alderson left for ME via Wimpy.

Sunday 5 April
Germans threw three waves of 50 bombers each against the Island to-day. Squadron was scrambled with 229 and some Spits for the last wave. An interception was effected (it couldn't be helped) and the results were quite favourable. Claims on opposite page. *[None are listed either in the diary or in the squadron and station ORBs.]* Our only casualty was P/O Carsons *[sic: Sergeant Carson]* 229, shot in shoulder, but down OK. *[In fact the casualty was Pilot Officer E. Andrews of 229 Squadron who was wounded by a cannon shell.]*

Monday 6 April
Squadron stood down until serviceability is back to normal. (Normal isn't very high). Approx 300 Ju 88s and 87s and 150 Me 109s attacked the Island to-day. They concentrated on Grand Harbour.

Tuesday 7 April
Squadron still stood down. All pilots have moved to Kalafrana, where everyone will be easy to get at. It's also much quieter there.

The CO made out a roster a few days ago and everyone got 48 hrs leave. Boy, were we mad???

Our New Zealand Sgts, Robb, and Wilson have departed for home. Here's wishing them the best against the Japs.

Wednesday 8 April } ~~One.~~ ~~No scrambles.~~ Low serviceability.
Thursday 9 April

Notwithstanding the above entries, 185 Squadron was in action on 8 and 9 April. On the facing page is the following tally:

WED. APR. 8

F/L LLOYD.   – 1 – JU 88 DAMAGED
                    1 – ME 109 DAMAGED.

P/O WIGLEY – 1 – JU 88 DAMAGED.

SGT BOYD   – 2 JU 88s PROBABLE
                    1 JU 88 DAMAGED.

This corresponds with information in the squadron ORB. Flight Lieutenant Keith A. Lawrence, Flight Sergeant J.W.S. (Jack) Fletcher and Sergeant J.L. 'Tony' Boyd are also credited with damaging a Ju 88 the following day, 9 April, although it is unclear whether all three were involved in attacking the same or different aircraft. The diary records only Sergeant Boyd's success:

THURS. APR. 9.
SGT BOYD – 1 – JU 88 – DAMAGED.

Friday 10 April
Squadron came to readiness at 13.00 hrs with eight serviceable aircraft. 229 at other end of the field had four. Just after tea we were scrambled for approx 100 bombers and 50 Me 109s. Twelve took off, *[but]* by the time we were at 15,000 there were 9 left. Things suddenly happened and every Hurricane found himself surrounded by seven 109s. Then more things happened. We tried to get to the bombers but the 109s didn't think we should. A great argument ensued, resulting in too many private dog-fights to count. The first section led by F/L Lloyd and with P/Os Ormrod and Wigley got at the bombers while Yellow section led by F/Sgt Eastman with Sgts Finlay, Broad and myself more than contacted the Me 109s. In the first few minutes of the fight Sgt Broad was forcibly ejected from his aircraft by anywhere from one to fifteen 109s. However his parachute opened as

planned and he landed at Naxxar, suffering from "superficial lacerations" in other words "cuts". F/L Lloyd had a whack at the bombers, but was set upon by some 109s. He played with them for awhile, and after shaking off his allotted ten Mes he landed at Luqa with only a few holes in his plane. P/O Ormrod also landed at Luqa but in a much different manner. He was cruising around in between 109s when he suddenly spied five or six Ju 87s in line astern diving on a target. He thought they were playing so he got in behind the third one and played too. Only he played with .303 and probably got one of the 87s. Meanwhile the boys flying the 87s behind him thought he was rude, by butting in like that, so proceeded to shoot at his Hurricane till it caught fire. P/O Ormrod thought his plane would burn much better on the ground than in the air, and knowing that all good fires are at Luqa, he landed there and jumped out of his now fairly warm aircraft while it was still running along the ground. We congratulate him on getting his fire down OK on Luqa. While this was going on P/O Wigley put a lot of lead in an 87 and turned around to look for some 109s to play with. But he looked the wrong way because the 109s were all behind him. He let them shoot at him for a long time because he was too fascinated by his Rad Temp *[radiator temperature]*. He stopped looking at it when it passed 165. By this time there wasn't enough left of his Hurricane to bring back to the drome so he decided he'd entertain the people on the ground who were watching him. First he climbed out of the cockpit and grabbed the radio mast so the spectators would think he was a flag. After awhile he got tired of this and thought he'd really scare the people. So he let his aircraft come right down close to the ground (300 ft) before he let go of the radio mast. He then pulled his ripcord quickly, and deliberately tangled his legs up in the cords so the people below thought he was a bomb. But he scared himself more than he did them and untangled himself in time to save me writing an obituary, and landed safely.

While the other fellows were having their good clean fun I was also having games with eight Me 109s. But I guess I'm a poor sport because I got mad and hit one of them with my cannon, and he thoughtfully exploded and came down in flames. Everyone was tired by now, having either been shot up or shot down, so we all came back and landed. We then shot our lines to the IO and gathered in the Sergeants Mess at Kalafrana and drank many bottles of champagne and whisky to celebrate everybody shot up but not killed.

We are all very proud of today's do. We attacked 100 bombers and 50 fighters and got away without losing a man. And the man has it all buttoned up who yelled over the R/T, in the middle of the fight, "God, these Hurricanes sure can turn".

FRI. APR. 10

F/L LLOYD   – 1 – JU 88 DAMAGED.

F/SGT HORRICKS – 1 – ME 109 DESTROYED.

Saturday 11 April

Owing to yesterday's engagement the pilots and planes of 185 are u/s. No flying.

Sunday 12 April

Had four serviceable a/c but bombs dropped by Me 109s made it three. That three were put on 15 min. available [sic] but later released.

The aerodrome was heavily bombed by Ju 88s this morning in one of their largest raids on the Island. Very strong rumour has it that the Luftwaffe is leaving Sicily tomorrow. We'll soon see.

Monday 13 April

Squadron stood down. Flying consisted of air tests and ferry trips.

F/SGT Ferraby and Sgt Sim to-day accustomed themselves to the horrors of the Hurricane by doing some practice flying. The boys are new pilots in the Squad and we all wish them the best of luck.

Tuesday 14 April

At readiness with 4 a/c. Two of 229 and two of 185s. About mid-morn F/Sgt Fletcher and a 229 boy got off against a red light and patrolled the HSRL [high speed rescue launch] by Kala Bay. Two Me 109s thought the fellas looked lonely so they also patrolled the launch. Our heroes took a dim view of this and chased Hans and Fritz away, Fletch severely damaging one for good measure. A short while later light arms brought down a 109 near the drome, and our ground crews fished a cross out of the wreckage. It now hangs on our dispersal hut wall.

Just before tea time P/Os Ormrod, and Wigley, Sgt Tweedale and myself were scrambled to prevent two 109s shooting down a Beaufort near the coast. We arrived too late, however, but chased the 109s away and registering [sic] hits on them. We were ordered to patrol the Rescue Launch on its way to pick up survivors. While so doing, twelve 109s came along to interfere. However, we managed to keep them from shooting up the launch and Tweedale and myself managed to damage two of them as well. Everyone had good squirts but owing to their numbers we were unable to concentrate on any particular 109.

To top the whole day off, the Me 109s although they outnumbered us 3 to 1, frantically called up on their R/T and pleaded with Goering to send more 109s out to help, as they were being mobbed by Hurricanes.

TUES. APR. 14

F/SGT FLETCHER – 1 – ME 109 DAM.
F/SGT HORRICKS   1 – ME 109   „
SGT TWEEDALE   1 – ME 109   „

On a previous page there appears the following from The Times of Malta *which apparently relates to the above entry.*

15 ME 109 ATTACK R.A.F. RESCUE LAUNCH

Luftwaffe At Its Worst

(Malta Official Local Release)
Valetta, April 20, 1942.

In Malta one has become so accustomed to the magnificent exploits of R.A.F. fighter pilots, and of the Anti-Aircraft gunners, that one is inclined to forget some of the less spectacular efforts in the Island's struggle.

One of these recently came to light, when a R.A.F. High Speed Launch had an exciting adventure at the hands of the Luftwaffe. It survived a severe mauling and typified the indomitable spirit which enables Malta to carry on in the face of the heaviest odds against her.

OUR FIGHTERS BEAT OFF THE ENEMY

The launch was engaged in rescue work when it was attacked by a number of "ME. 109" fighters. Fortunately some R.A.F. fighters arrived on the scene in time to beat off the attackers and enable the launch to carry on with its work.

Wednesday 15 April

The only flying to-day was carried out by F/LT Lawrence, F/SGT Fletcher, and Sgt Sim who conducted a search. Squadron later placed on 30 min.

Thursday 16 April

Four a/c at 30 min. Only flying being Air Tests and ferry trips.

Gen: Our rumour of a week or so ago has proven [to be] true. A large majority of the GAF has left Sicily. Only a striking force of two hundred aircraft remaining to carry out nuisance raids on Malta.

——— *„* ———

Last Wed. the AOC C in C ME [*Air Officer Commanding Commander in Chief Middle East*], Air Marshal Tedder paid us a visit (informal) and shook hands with us all, and said we were doing a marvellous job of work and were making history. Of course we already knew that, but it was nice to hear it from him. It shows our work is recognized and appreciated.

——— *„* ———

The following day the AOC Air Vice Marshal Lloyd dropped in for a pep talk, and informed us that we would be stood down most of the next fortnight, until reinforcements arrived. He said we could expect "more Hurricanes and a lot more Spits". Bags of joy.

——— *„* ———

The next entry is the last by Canadian Pilot Officer Garth E. Horricks.

Friday 17 April

229 are doing 30 min. 185 stood down, no flying. Weather practically u/s.

On 20 April forty-six Spitfires comprising 601 (County of London) and 603 (City of Edinburgh) Squadrons were flown off the American carrier USS Wasp. The Germans waited until the aircraft landed before launching the first in a series of raids against the aerodromes.

Towards the end of the month, the 10th Submarine Flotilla left Malta for the safety of Alexandria. The submarines were not to return until the end of July. In the same period reconnaissance aircraft photographed what appeared to be three airfields being levelled in Sicily. Reports indicated that these were intended for gliders to be used in a proposed Axis invasion of Malta. Codenamed 'Herkules' by the Germans and 'C3' by the Italians, the operation was planned for that summer. The attack force was to be five times the strength of that deployed during the 1941 invasion of Crete. Yet, 'Herkules' was destined never to materialise, with Hitler instead giving priority to his offensives in North Africa and Russia. The decision ultimately sealed the fate of Rommel's Afrikakorps, thereby affecting the course of the entire war. But for Malta in April 1942, the threat of invasion was still very real, and would remain so for months to come.

There were further reinforcements in April with more to come early the following month as aircraft were flown in to replace those lost in the previous five weeks of combat. Due to the high attrition rate of its fighters, the RAF was finding it increasingly difficult to meet the enemy on an equal basis. The Bf 109s frequently outnumbered their opponents and sometimes encountered no aerial opposition whatsoever. On such occasions, the RAF adopted a rather unorthodox 'defensive' procedure, as explained by Flight Lieutenant Hugh 'Tim' Johnston of 126 Squadron:

When we can put up no aircraft at all, Fighter Control lays on a dummy R/T conversation. The other day, after a corporal in a cubicle had announced that he'd spotted four 109s and was going to attack them, the German listening device picked it up and broadcast a warning which confused the Huns so much that there was a good deal of nattering in high-pitched German and finally a burst of cannon fire!

Malta's strike aircraft also suffered losses both in the air and through being bombed while on the ground. Surviving machines were kept operational by all available means. Ground crews frequently worked through the night to service a grounded aircraft and often used spares scavenged from wrecks which littered the airfields. To protect the precious aeroplanes and service vehicles, dispersal pens were constructed from sandbags, rubble, stone and earth-filled petrol cans, and whatever else that could be utilised. By the end of April around 300 pens had been built along with twenty-seven miles of dispersal runway. This mammoth task was achieved by civilian labour, the Navy and Air Force and as many as 3,000 soldiers at a time who toiled under the most oppressive conditions, while in constant danger of air attacks.

II Fliegerkorps *was relentless in its efforts to pound Malta into submission. The recent Spitfire deliveries and Hurricane reinforcements were barely sufficient to sustain a fighter defence. Even so the Maltese displayed an unshaken belief in the RAF, the artillery, the Navy and God – and not necessarily in that order. The Governor and Commander-in-Chief, General Sir William Dobbie, himself a religious man, was not averse to expressing his own trust in Divine Providence, and in April 1942 it seemed as though nothing short of a miracle could save Malta.*

The arrival of several supply ships in early 1942, however welcome, hardly improved the worsening food shortage. The poor diet combined with the permanent stress and fear so affected the health of some that they had to be carried into air raid shelters.

The bravery and fortitude of the islanders was formally recognised on 15 April 1942 with the award of the George Cross by King George VI. It was the highest honour that an appreciative British Sovereign could bestow on a community.

General Sir William Dobbie was relieved not long after. On 7 May he was succeeded by Field Marshal Lord Gort VC.

Luftwaffe records show that between 20 March and 28 April 1942, Malta was subjected to 5,807 sorties flown by bombers, 5,667 by fighters and 345 by reconnaissance aircraft – a total of 11,819 sorties. In this five and a half week period, the weight of bombs dropped is reported to have exceeded 6,557 tonnes.

With the coming of May, the Regia Aeronautica *rejoined the* Luftwaffe *in daylight operations over Malta.*

Following the next entry by an unidentified writer, Australian Sergeant J.W. 'Slim' Yarra took over the squadron diary.

Saturday 18 April to Wednesday 29 April

As this diary has been sadly neglected during the past fortnight all that can be entered is a summary of events pertaining to the aforementioned period of neglect. We must sadly acknowledge the loss of two of our most popular members through enemy action. P/O Ormrod was the first to go followed by P/O Fletcher. All members of the squadron pay tribute to these two gallant members who gave their lives that democracy may be vindicated.

The squadron has been sadly depleted of late. P/Os Horricks and Eastman have been posted to ME owing to termination of their tour of duty on Malta, while P/O Beckett is at HQ Med awaiting posting.

Sgt Tweedale has been after the "Wily Hun" with a vengeance of late and has accounted for one JU 88 probable and one JU 87 very definitely destroyed. Said JU 87 is now reclining gracefully at the bottom of Calafrana [sic] Bay, pilot complete.

Sgt Dodd has been in action over Malta for the first time and has acquitted himself well. One JU 88 and 2 JU 87s damaged are proof of this.

Tony Boyd is still operating but has lost his faith in cannon kites. Tony reckons the Hun is getting too cheeky when the 87s turn round and want to dog-fight with a Hurricane. One jumped on Tony's tail and became very spiteful for a few seconds. We must also record the episode of the 109F who decided too much Boyd was enough. Aforementioned 109 saw Tony coming in down wind and protested strongly. His protest took the form of a diving attack which rather spoiled Tony's pansy landing. The Hurricane was badly shot up, but fortunately, or unfortunately, according to the point of view of the reader, the pilot was not even shaken (much).

Sgt Yarra is still brassed after having three different kites, in which he was doing readiness, blown up by bombs.

P/O Noble has been picking on the 109s who come over to do a spot of practice flying. It seems rather a shame when the Hun can't even get his practice flying done without interfering fighter pilots like Ron Noble spoiling it. However there is one more 109 pilot shooting a line in Hell about why he was shot down.

F/Lt Lawrence is down with the "Malta Dog". He has developed quite a distinctly new method of walking of late. Prospective sufferers may save a lot of trouble by learning the art. Laurie will take classes for tuition at a nominal fee.

There follows a list of squadron pilots compiled by Sergeant J.R. Suther-land with updates probably by Australian Sergeant Gordon R. Tweedale. (In the original diary names are grouped, according to their initials, on sepa-rate pages.)

185 SQUADRON PILOTS.

IN ALPHABETICAL *[sic]* ORDER, GIVING SCORES, ETC.

ALLARDICE   P/O   FROM 52 OTU UK 27/6/41 1 ME 110
DES 21/3/42 1 Ju 88 DAM. SHOT DOWN IN ACTION 22/3/42. (88).

ALDERSON   SGT   FROM 52 OTU UK 27/6/41 SHARED
BR20 WITH 8 OTHERS 25/7/41.

POSTED 10/4/42 MADE P/O

AMBROSE   F/O   FROM 126 SQDN MALTA, 3/10/41.
RETURNED TO 126 SQDN 7/10/41

Bamberger   Sgt   Old Original Posted UK June 6th 1941.

BAILEY   P/O   OLD ORIGINAL 2 He 111s SHARED
(DAM.) WITH F/LT HANCOCK AND F/LT WESTMACOTT 6/5/41
SHARED Mc 200 /6/41 Mc 200 DAM. 9/7/41 SHARED BR 20 WITH 8
OTHERS 25/7/41 2 E-BOATS DES. 26/7/41 F/O WEF 29/8/41 KILLED
IN ACTION 9/11/41

BRANSON   SGT   OLD ORIGINAL BAILED OUT (109)
6/5/41 SHARED BR 20 WITH 8 OTHERS 25/7/41 POSTED MNFU
1/8/41 POSTED ME 4/9/41 [sic]

BURTON   SGT   OLD ORIGINAL INJURED IN FLYING
ACCIDENT /6/41 POSTED UK 26/8/41.

BARNWELL   P/O   FROM 607 SQDN UK 30/6/41
SHARED BR 20 WITH 8 OTHERS 25/7/41 SHARED 2 E-BOATS WITH 5
OTHERS 26/7/41 POSTED MNFU 1/8/41 2 BR 20s, AT NIGHT, DES
6/8/41 DFC WEF 5/9/41. POSTED MISSING BELIEVED KILLED IN
ACTION 14/10/41 (CZ1007 DES. AT NIGHT 4/5/9/41). 14/10/41 – 1
MC 200 DEST.

BATES   SGT   FROM 52 OTU UK 27/6/41 Mc 200
PROB 4/7/41 F/SGT /3/42 POSTED HQ MED 20/3/42

BROAD   SGT   FROM 234 SQDN UK 2/3/42.

BECKETT   P/O   FROM 605 SQDN, MALTA, 18/3/42.
SHARED 1 ME 110 CONFIRMED WITH SGT ROBB, ¼ ME 110 DAM.
21/3/42

COUSENS   SGT   FROM 245 SQDN UK 30/6/41 KILLED
IN ACTION 21/11/41 (202)

COMFORT   SGT   FROM UK 13/9/41 POSTED ME WEF
25/9/41

CHAFFE   S/LDR   FROM   243   SQDN   UK   15/2/42.
POSTED MISSING 22/2/42.

DREDGE   P/O   OLD   ORIGINAL   INJURED   IN
ACTION 6/5/41 (109) POSTED OFF OPS.

DADDO-LANGLOIS P/O   FROM 66 SQDN UK 17/2/42. POSTED
249 SQDN TAKALI, 28/2/42

DODD   SGT   FROM 249 SQDN (SPITFIRES) 5/4/42

ELIOT   F/LT   OLD ORIGINAL 1st F/COMM "A"
FLT. POSTED OFF OPS 6/6/41 F/CONTROLLER.

ELLIS   SGT   FROM No 1 SQDN UK 30/6/41
SHARED BR 20 WITH 8 OTHERS 25/7/41 ¼ SHARE IN 1 Ju 88 PROB.
20/2/42 ½ SHARE WITH SGT HORRICKS IN 1 Ju 88 DES 3/1/42.

EASTMAN   SGT (RCAF) FROM 257 SQDN UK 13/9/41 F/SGT
10/4/42. P/O 20/4/42 LEFT SQUADRON 28/4/42. POSTED

FORTH   SGT   FROM 52 OTU UK 27/6/41 SHARED
SM 79 WITH P/O THOMPSON 25/7/41. SHARED 2 E-BOATS WITH 5
OTHERS 26/7/41 SHARED SM 79 WITH P/O THOMPSON 27/7/41
SHOT DOWN BY 109s – KILLED 29/12/41

FLETCHER   F/SGT (RCAF) FROM 605 SQDN MALTA 18/3/42

SHOT DOWN BY 109s KILLED 28/4/42

FINLAY   SGT   FROM 605 SQDN MALTA 18/3/42.

FERRABY   F/SGT   FROM 249 SQDN (SPITFIRES) 5/4/42

GRAY   P/O   OLD ORIGINAL BAILED OUT 6/5/41
POSTED UK 23/7/41

HAMILTON   P/O (AAF) OLD ORIGINAL (DESTROYED 5
BEFORE JOINING THE SQUADRON) PROB. 87 9/5/41 KILLED IN
ACTION (109) 14/5/41.

HALL   P/O   OLD ORIGINAL SHARED Ju 88 PROB.
WITH F/LT JEFFRIES – INJURED BY ACK-ACK 3/5/41 POSTED NON-
OPS NOW F/LT, F/CONTROLLER, MALTA.

HANCOCK   F/LT   OLD ORIGINAL 2 HE 111s DAMAGED
– SHARED WITH P/O BAILEY AND F/LT WESTMACOTT 6/5/41
F/COMM "B" FLT WEF 13/5/41. SHARED 2 E-BOATS WITH 5 OTHERS
26/7/41 1 SM 79 DES. 27/7/41 POSTED ME 17/9/41

HUNTON   SGT   FROM 59 OTU UK 30/6/41 1 MC 202
DEST. 25/10/41 ⅕TH SHARE IN 1 Ju 88 DES. 14/2/42 ¼ SHARE IN 1 Ju
88 PROB 20/2/42 F/SGT 12/3/42 POSTED HQ MED 20/3/42.

HAYES   SGT   FROM 607 SQDN UK 30/6/41 KILLED
IN ACTION (109Fs) 21/12/41

HORSEY   SGT   FROM 52 OTU UK 30/6/41 POSTED
ME WEF 25/9/41

HORRICKS   (RCAF) SGT FROM 52 OTU UK 13/9/41 ½ SHARE
WITH SGT ELLIS Ju 88 DES 3/1/42 1 Ju 88 DES. 24/1/42 1 ME 109 DES
23/2/42 1 ME 109F DES. 10/4/42. F/SGT 10/4/42. AWARDED DFM
AND MADE P/O 20/4/42 POSTED 28/4/42

HOWE   F/SGT (RCAF) FROM 605 SQDN, MALTA
18/3/42.

INNES   P/O   OLD ORIGINAL POSTED (?) 5/5/41.

JEFFRIES   F/LT   DFC OLD ORIGINAL SHARED PROB.
88 WITH P/O HALL 9/5/41. F/COMM "A" FLT WEF 6/6/41 Mc 200
DES. 4/7/41 CANT Z506 DES. 1 PROB. 1 DAM. (SYRACUSE) 9/7/41 1
MC 200 DES. 1 DAM. 11/7/41 1 MC 202 PROB. 30/9/41 POSTED ME
27/10/41.

JOLLY   SGT   OLD ORIGINAL 1 MC 200 DES. /6/41
1 MC 200 DES. 4/7/41 1 MC 202 DAM. 30/9/41 POSTED ME 20/2/42

KNIGHT   SGT   FROM   258   SQDN   UK   30/6/41
MISSING, BELIEVED KILLED IN ACTION (202) 25/10/41

LILLYWHITE   SGT   FROM   242   SQDN   UK   30/6/41.
SHARED 2 E-BOATS WITH 5 OTHERS 26/7/41 1 SM 81 DES. (LONG
RANGE PATROL) 20/10/41 F/SGT 19/12/41 P/O WEF 25/2/42.

LINTERN   P/O   FROM   504   SQDN   UK   13/9/41.
POSTED MISSING, BELIEVED POW, FROM BOMBING RAID ON
COMISO 30/9/41

LEFEVRE   S/LDR   FROM 126 SQDN MALTA 3/10/41
RETURNED TO 126 SQDN 7/10/41

LLOYD   F/O   FROM 130 SQDN UK F/COMM "B"
FLT WEF 16/12/41 1 109F DES. 29/12/41 AWARDED DFC 20/4/42

LAWRENCE   F/O   FROM 91 SQDN UK 17/2/42. F/LT
17/3/42. F/COMM "A" FLT, 17/3/42 SQD/LR

LESTER   P/O (RAAF) FROM 605 SQDN, MALTA 18/3/42.

MOULD   S/LDR   DFC AND BAR OLD ORIGINAL 1st
SQDN/COMM. CANT Z506 DES. 1 PROB. 1 DAM (SYRACUSE) 9/7/41
1 MC 200 DES 11/7/41. MISSING, BELIEVED KILLED IN ACTION (MC
202) 1/10/41

MURCH   F/O   FROM UK 1/8/41. F/COMM "B" FLT
WEF 7/10/41 POSTED ME 16/12/41

MILBURN   P/O   FROM 124 SQDN UK 17/2/42.

MORTIMER-ROSE   S/LDR   DFC AND BAR. FROM F/CONTROL,
MALTA, 17/3/42 1 ME 110 CONFIRMED 20/3/42

McGREGOR   S/LDR   FROM 126 SQDN, MALTA. 2/1/42.
POSTED ME 15/2/42

McKAY   P/O (RCAF) FROM 605 SQDN, MALTA 18/3/42.
POSTED BLIGHTY MAY 42.

NURSE   SGT   FROM   504   SQDN   UK   27/6/41
SHARED BR 20 WITH 8 OTHERS 25/7/41 1 CANT Z1007 bis DAM.
25/10/41

NOBLE   P/O   FROM   605   SQDN   MALTA   18/3/42
POSTED BLIGHTY MAY 42.

OTTEY   SGT   OLD ORIGINAL KILLED ON ACTIVE
SERVICE 2/5/41

OLIVER P/O FROM OTU UK 27/6/41 BAILED OUT (ENGINE CUT) 10/8/41 ⅓ SHARE IN 1 Ju 88 DES. 14/2/42

ORMROD P/O FROM 605 SQDN, MALTA. 18/3/42 ½ ME110 DES, ¼ ME110 DAM. 21/3/42 AWARDED DFC 20/4/42 MISSING BELIEVED KILLED 24/4/42

PIKE F/LT FROM 32 SQDN UK 27/6/41 1 MC 200 DAM. 11/7/41 F/COMM "B" FLT WEF 17/9/41 S/COMM WEF 7/10/41 1 109 DAM. 29/12/41 POSTED ME 1/1/42.

REAM SGT FROM 92 SQDN UK 30/6/41 SHARED BR20 WITH 8 OTHERS 25/7/41 19/12/41 F/SGT POSTED HQ MED 3/3/42.

REEVES P/O FROM F/CONTROL, MALTA 7/8/41 POSTED HQ MED 13/1/42.

ROBB SGT (NZAF) FROM 605 SQDN, MALTA. 18/3/42 ½ ME 110 DES. ¼ ME 110 DAM. 21/3/42 POSTED ME 14/4/42

SHEPPARD SGT (RAAF) FROM 261 SQDN MALTA, 6/5/41 SHARED MC 200 /6/41 POSTED ME 20/2/42

SUTHERLAND SGT FROM 257 SQDN UK 30/6/41 1 MC 200 DAM 4/7/41 1 ME 109 PROB. 2/1/42. 1 ME 109 DES. 1 Ju 88 DAM. 22/2/42. 1 ME109F PROB., 1 Ju 88 DES. SHARED WITH SGT STEELE AND BOFORS GUN, 17/3/42.

SWIRE SGT FROM *[sic]* UK 27/6/41 POSTED ME WEF 25/9/41

STEELE SGT FROM 615 SQDN UK 13/9/41 1 ME 109 DES. 23/2/42 1 ME 109F DES, 1 Ju 88 DAM. 9/3/42 1 ME 109F DAM, 1 Ju 88 DAM 10/3/42 1 Ju 88 DES. SHARED WITH SGT SUTHERLAND AND BOFORS GUN, 17/3/42.

SERGEANT P/O FROM 615 SQDN UK 17/2/42. POSTED 249 SQDN, TAKALI 28/2/42

STONES F/LT DFC FROM 605 SQDN, MALTA 18/3/42. FLT COMM "C" FLT POSTED HQ MED 20/3/42.

SIM   SGT (RNZAF) FROM 249 SQUADRON MALTA 5/4/42

SLY   F/LT AUS FROM UK 452 SQD 9/5/42 VIA CARRIER CRASHED ON LANDING. DIED LATER.

THOMPSON   P/O   OLD ORIGINAL SHARED SM 79 WITH SGT FORTH 25/7/41 1 MC 200 DES. 26/7/41. SHARED SM 79 WITH SGT FORTH 27/7/41 F/O WEF 29/8/41 F/LT WEF 22/11/41 – F/COMM "A" FLT 1 109F DEST. 29/12/41 1 Ju 88 DAM. – BAILED OUT – 25/1/42. DFC 1/2/42. POSTED ME 20/2/42

TWEEDALE   SGT (RAAF) FROM   [sic] SQDN, UK 2/3/42. 1 Ju 88 DAM. – INJURED (109s) 9/3/42

VARDY   SGT   FROM 261 SQDN MALTA 6/5/41 POSTED ME 20/2/42

VEITCH   P/O   FROM 238 SQDN UK 30/6/41 1 MC 202 DAM. 30/9/41 KILLED IN ACTION (OXYGEN FAILURE) 4/10/41

WALMSLEY   SGT   OLD ORIGINAL BAILED OUT – INJURED (109) 1/5/41 POSTED OFF OPS

WREN   SGT   FROM 52 OTU UK 27/6/41 POSTED ME WEF 25/9/41

WYNNE   SGT   OLD ORIGINAL KILLED IN ACTION (109) 15/5/41.

WESTMACOTT   F/O   OLD ORIGINAL F/LT WEF 12/5/41 1st F/COMM "B" FLT BAILED OUT (109s) 13/5/41 SHARED 2 HE 111s DAM WITH F/LT HANCOCK AND P/O BAILEY 6/5/41 BECAME CO OF MNFU.

WINTON   P/O   FROM 261 SQDN MALTA JUNE 1941 SHARED BR 20 WITH 8 OTHERS 25/7/41. SHARED 2 E-BOATS WITH 5 OTHERS – SHOT DOWN BY Mc 200 – ATTEMPTED CAPTURE OF E-BOAT 26/7/41 POSTED MNFU 1/8/41 F/O WEF 29/8/41

WOODSEND   P/O   FROM 56 OTU UK 30/6/41 SHARED BR 20 WITH 8 OTHERS 25/7/41 BAILED OUT (ENGINE TROUBLE) 28/9/41. BROKEN LEG – POSTED NON-EFF. 26/10/41. POSTED UK 4/3/42.

WESTCOTT   SGT   FROM 242 SQDN UK 27/6/41. CANT Z506 DAM. 9/7/41 SHARED ~~BR 20~~ 2 E-BOATS WITH 5 OTHERS 26/7/41. SHOT DOWN BY BOFORS – BAILED OUT 3/1/42 POSTED HQ MED 20/3/42.

WILSON   SGT (NZAF) FROM 605 SQDN, MALTA 18/3/42.

WIGLEY   P/O   FROM 605 SQDN MALTA 18/3/42 ½ ME 110 DES, ¼ ME 110 DAM. 21/3/42 AWARDED DFC 20/4/42 POSTED BACK BLIGHTY MAY 42

YARRA   SGT (RAAF) FROM 64 SQUADRON UK (TRANSFERRED FROM 249 SQDN MALTA) 5.4.42. 6 CONFIRMED DFM .5.42 *[sic]*

Book 2

185 SQUADRON STRENGTH

"A" FLIGHT   S/LDR MORTIMER-ROSE DFC & BAR   "B" FLIGHT

F/LT LLOYD RAF	CO	F/LT LAWRENCE RAF
P/O WIGLEY RAF		P/O NOBLE RAF
SGT TWEEDALE RAAF		P/O McKAY RCAF
SGT FINLAY RAF		SGT BROAD RAF
SGT DODD RCAF		SGT SIM RNZAF
F/SGT FERRABY RAF		SGT BOYD DFM RAAF
		SGT YARRA RAAF

The above flights list, by Sergeant 'Slim' Yarra, appears on the facing page opposite the following entries for 30 April 1942.

30–4–42

Having been allotted the important duty of recording the "Gen & doings" of 185, I must first pay tribute to the last scribe of this journal, Garth Horricks, who but recently was awarded the DFM, and also made an "officer and a gentleman" [*and*] now awaits his chance to leave this sunny isle. Garth has stalked the Hun with determination, skill daring and keenness for many moons and by his and others' example has been an inspiration to all such "new chums" who have come and gone since his arrival some eight months ago. With him will go his worthy friend P/O Eastman, and though I rarely hand out flowers to Canadians, being myself an Aussie, I must hand it to both of them, and in company with the rest of the squadron wish them good luck and good hunting.

GR Tweedale

Thursday 30 April

Today we have one Hurricane serviceable up to 4 p.m. but later on manage to augment it to three.

There were only two raids, one by 12 JU 88s, the other by 9 Italians who put up a very good show by dropping their eggs in the drink.

Great excavation works are being carried out by all and sundry to make each dispersal pen a self contained unit for refuelling, rearming and refitting, as well as being equipped with a scatter gun. The CO has been at his pen hammer and tongs and seems quite an authority on sandbags and digging implements, to the consternation of the nearest man around doing nothing.

Victories for April 1942

F/Lt Lloyd   1 109 Probable 3 109 Damaged 1 87 Damaged 5 JU 88s Damaged.

F/Lt Lawrence	1 ME 109 Damaged 1 JU 88 Damaged
P/O Noble	1 ME 109 Destroyed 3 JU 88 Damaged
P/O Wigley	1 ME 109 Probable 1 JU 87 Probable 1 ME 109 Damaged 1 JU 87 Damaged 2 JU 88 Damaged
P/O McKay	½ JU 88 Destroyed
P/O Beckett	1½ JU 88s Damaged
P/O Fletcher	1 JU 88 Destroyed 1 JU 87 Destroyed 1 ME 109 Damaged 3 JU 88s Damaged
P/O Horricks	1 ME 109 Destroyed 1 JU 88 Probable 2 ME 109 Damaged
SGT Boyd	½ JU 88 Destroyed 1 JU 87 Probable 2 JU 88 Probable 4 JU 88 Damaged 1 ME 109 Damaged
SGT Tweedale	1 ME 109 Destroyed 1 JU 87 Destroyed 2 JU 88 Probable 1 ME Damaged 1 JU 88 Damaged
SGT Finlay	1 ME 109 Damaged 1 JU 87 Damaged 1 JU 88 Damaged
SGT Dodd	1 JU 87 Probable 2 JU 87 Damaged 1 JU 88 Damaged.

DESTROYED	PROBABLE	DAMAGED
7	10	38½

Friday 1 May

The big wigs have taken us off day state to give us a spot of night flying as Jerry seems to have painted most of his aircraft black. SGT Yarra, the latest Aussie addition to the squadron fired a great burst of sparks into an '88 which induced it to fade off the plot some time later.

SGT Yarra   1 JU 88 Probable

Wednesday 6 May

Nothing of importance having occurred in the last few days I have entered into the general spirit of laziness, as far as this book is concerned anyway. [*According to the Operations Record Book of 185 Squadron, there were only air tests on 2, 3 and 4 May.*]

Our Squadron Leader Mr Mortimer-Rose is to leave us to have treatment for his ears in England so it looks as if we will lose him for good; a great pity that; as an organiser and general "live wire" he leaves nothing to be desired.

Yesterday we handed our 8 kites over to 229 Squadron who have [*sic*] for some weeks have been more or less under our wing. Today, behold, we have two left due to bombing, and one shot down by ME 109s.

This is the last entry by Sergeant Gordon Tweedale. Fellow Queenslander, Sergeant Yarra, again took over as squadron diarist and remained so until shortly before leaving Malta in July.

Thursday 7 May

Nothing much happened to-day. "B" Flight was doing the readiness with 4 kites. Only one scramble occurred and as this was just an escort job we have nothing to report. However everyone began to sit up and take notice when the boys heard that two Spitfires were coming over from Ta Kali for us to take up and become re-acquainted with. The Spits duly arrived, but rather late, and, as one became u/s on landing, F/Lt Lloyd was the only pilot able to do a few circuits. However he reported very favourably on their performance, and we are now looking forward to the not-too-distant time (we hope) when 185 shall operate as a "Spitfire" squadron.

7/5/42
SGT TWEEDALE
One 109F DESTROYED

Friday 8 May

"B" Flight was still on readiness with 4 aircraft this morning. The 4 were scrambled at about 9 P.M. They made a wizard interception on some of Joe Kesselring's 88 boys. "Tweedle" went to town with a vengeance and proceeded to shoot up everything in the sky, with the result that 1 JU 88 and 1 ME 109 "went for a Burton" and another ME 109 probably emulated the other two kites. Sgt Tony Boyd also scored a probable JU 88 while Sgt Dodd managed to intimidate an "Ice Cream boy", who was stooging about in a Macchi 202, to such an extent that he probably went into the drink. This afternoon we handed over the remainder of our Hurricanes to 229. We expect 12 Spitfires in to-morrow. Everybody is looking forward to the show and it certainly looks as if old Joe Kesselring is going to have a few headaches in the near future, and, as the Sergeants Mess has had a supply of beer in for the last two days, all the Sergeants, at least, are happy.

8/5/1942
SGT TWEEDALE
One JU 88 DESTROYED One ME 109F DESTROYED One ME 109F PROBABLY DESTROYED
SGT BOYD
ONE JU 88 PROBABLY DESTROYED
SGT DODD
ONE MACCHI 202 PROBABLY DESTROYED

On 9 May Operation 'Bowery' culminated in the delivery of sixty Spitfires flown from USS Wasp *and HMS* Eagle. *The new arrivals were quickly introduced to the desperate fighting conditions of Malta as the Germans and*

Italians timed their attacks to catch the Spitfires as they came in to land. The enemy's efforts were countered by ground crews who immediately re-armed and refuelled the aircraft, which were then taken over by experienced Malta pilots who sat strapped in their cockpits, ready to scramble. Meanwhile, enemy fighters were held at bay by the island's available Hurricanes and Spitfires.

Saturday 9 May

The balloon went up with a vengeance this morning when 11 Spitfire Vcs arrived on Halfar. The 109s kindly co operated, gratis, and initiated the "new types" who arrived in the "Spits", to the charming, if not popular, parlour game known as "109s in the circuit". However as the ground guns put up a very good cross fire, all the Spitfires, except two, landed in one piece. The aforementioned two had to be written off, leaving us with 9 aircraft. The aircraft were put in their respective pens and soon six were at readiness, owing to the magnificent work of the crews, some of whom had only seen a Spitfire once before. At two o'clock the first scramble took place and a section of four took off, led by F/Lt Lloyd. The boys got in amongst the bombers, JU 88s and 87s and there was a lot of squirting and carrying on for a while. Sgt Broad got one 88 destroyed and an 87 damaged. For once the sky seemed to be full of friendly aircraft. There were Spitfires everywhere. P/O Noble, flying a Spitfire for the first time, was unfortunately jumped by a very nasty ME 109 and managed to crash-land at Ta Kali: Ron got a couple of pieces of Jerry lead in his carcase but these injuries were only superficial. Sgt Tony Boyd, also flying a Spitfire for the first time squirted at the odd Hun but did not make any claims.

The second scramble took place at 4.30 PM. Five aircraft took part, led by F/Lt Lawrence. It is with much regret that we have to record the death of Sgt Gordon Tweedale. Tweedale, an Australian, was one of our best pilots and of late had been putting up a marvellous show. Everyone in the squadron feels "Tweedle's" loss deeply. During this show, the boys, although scrambled a little late, got right in amongst the bombers again and "took heavy toll of the enemy" as the BBC would put it. This was the last scramble of the day – and what a day. For once we had the chance to pay off a lot of old scores and give the Jerry pilots a sample of acute "ring twitch", a common ailment on Malta. As far as can be ascertained many Germans and Italians put in quite a bit of swimming practice for the next Olympic games. If, when we have settled this little argument as to who rules the world, and everything is nice and quiet again, and anyone with sixpence in his pocket can obtain a glass of beer whenever he feels the urge; if we are beaten in the aquatic events at the Olympic games by Germany or Italy, the blame may be laid on the fighter pilots of Malta, who gave the Jerries and Dagoes so much useful practice.

9.5.42
Sgt Broad: 1 JU 87 Probable, 1 JU 87 Damaged
P/O Wigley: 1 JU 87 Probable
F/Lt Lawrence: 1 JU 87 Probable

185 SQUADRON STRENGTH (SPITFIRES)
S/LEADER LLOYD DFC (RAFVR)

"A" FLIGHT	"B" FLIGHT
F/LT LAWRENCE (NZ)	F/LT PLAGIS (RHODESIAN)
P/O McNAUGHTON (CAN)	P/O HALFORD (RAF)
P/O BROAD (RAF)	P/O SHERLOCK (CAN)
SGT YARRA (AUS)	P/O KING (CAN)
F/SGT SIM (NZ)	F/SGT FERRABY (RAF)
F/SGT VINEYARD (AMERICAN)	SGT DODD (CAN.)
F/SGT MACNAMARA (CAN.)	F/SGT REID (CAN.)
F/SGT SHAW (NZ)	SGT BELL (AUS.)
	F/SGT ANDREWS (AMERICAN)

On 10 May the minelayer-cruiser HMS Welshman *completed a lone run from Gibraltar with supplies and RAF ground personnel. The enemy responded with a series of concentrated attacks countered by the efforts of the RAF and ground defences that enabled the* Welshman *to depart later that evening. Although the odds were still stacked against Malta, the situation was changing to one where the defenders could again feel that they were achieving significant results as opposed to simply disrupting the enemy's efforts.*

Sunday 10 May

Today we were on readiness with six kites, and one coming up later on. The boys, led by F/Lt – nay, Squadron Leader – Lloyd, took off at the unearthly hour of 7 A.M. This scramble, however, was rather unsatisfactory from the individual's point of view as nothing of interest happened. However 25 bombers were plotted, and, as only one crossed the coast and dropped his bombs, it was certainly a victory for the fighter squadrons on Malta.

At 1030 A.M. five aircraft took off and sailed straight into 30 JU 87s, after dealing first with some JU 88s. The JU 88s were just an appetiser, however, for when the 87s came down they were met by about 20 Spitfires. The Spits really got to work and, out of the 30 JU 87s who were misguided enough to attempt to bomb the Harbour only 2 escaped scot-free. The number destroyed amounted to 10. Old Joe Kesselring is reputed to be jumping up and down in the one spot at the rate of 75 bars to the minute. 185 Squadron figured in this show to the extent of one JU 87 Destroyed by Sgt Dodd, one JU 87 destroyed by F/Lt Lawrence, one JU 88 destroyed by P/O McKay[,]

149

one JU 88 probable and one damaged by Sgt Boyd, and another JU 88 probably destroyed by Sgt Broad. A truly welcome addition to the Squadron's score board. These recorded scores will probably be augmented when a full intelligence summary is obtainable.

Another scramble took place at 6 P.M. in which the bomber plot turned back and our own boys had to be content with worrying 109s. This gentle pastime is enjoyed by all except maybe the 109 pilots. Sgt Broad managed to get mixed up with a few of the little jobs and had a very enjoyable 10 minutes being chased. However Ernie committed one bad breach of form, by breaking the ABO which says that: "No target, whether the afore-mentioned target be drogue, ground triangle, aircraft, cow, or men on haystacks, shall return the fire of the practising machine, or machines". Sgt Broad flagrantly broke this important rule and severely damaged one of the practising ME 109s, much to the horror and disgust of the 109 pilot. Sgt Broad sneaked back to the aerodrome amidst cries of "Shame" and "Cad" and muttered remarks of "Body Line", from the 109 drivers. It has been reported from the reliable neutral sources that the German Chancellery is to make a very strong protest to the British government.

A different tally appears on the facing page, and is recorded below. Neither is corroborated by the squadron ORB, in which only Sergeant C.E. (Ernie) Broad is credited: with a Bf 109 damaged.

10.5.42.

	Sgt Boyd:	1 JU 88 Probable, 1 JU 88 damaged
✿	Sgt Dodd:	1 JU 87 Destroyed, 1 ME 109 damaged
✿	F/Lt Lawrence:	1 JU 87 destroyed
✿	Sgt Broad:	1 JU 88 destroyed 1 ME 109 damaged
✿	P/O McKay:	1 JU 88 destroyed

Monday 11 May

We still had 7 aircraft when we came on readiness at dawn this morning. We are wondering when we will receive replacements for those lost. However, the squadron has put up a fine show, with the aircraft it has.

During the morning three aircraft were scrambled to chase away some 109s who were making a nuisance of themselves. One A/C returned with engine trouble and the remaining two searched, without success, for the 109s.

Some time later the seven aircraft were scrambled to intercept a bomber plot coming in. The interception was carried out and everyone had a good time. P/O Wigley damaged a JU 88 and P/O McKay had a slight altercation with some spiteful 109s, damaging one. Owing to a rather strong crosswind the squadron had to land at Luqua *[sic]*.

[The next paragraph appears to refer to events of Tuesday 12 May.]

We were again scrambled from Luqua and had an unfortunate accident. Two of our aircraft collided taking off, which reduced our strength to five. The remaining five went up, however and met the bombers over Halfar. There were only 4 JU 88s in this raid, who managed to cross the coast. P/O Wigley damaged one of these. Sgt Yarra destroyed an ME 109. Sgt Yarra also had quite an enjoyable time playing with some Dagoes who were coming down in parachutes after some destructive person had severely tampered with their Cant 1007. The Italians took a rather poor view of Sgt Yarra's efforts to amuse them. These efforts took the form of placing the parachute canopy in the slipstream of a Spitfire. The canopy promptly collapses and the type has to fall a few hundred feet until the chute opens again. Consequently 4 very sick Dagoes landed in the water off the island.

11.5.42
P/O McKay: One ME 109 Damaged

P/O Wigley: Two JU 88s Damaged

卐 Sgt Yarra: One ME 109 Destroyed

As the battle continued, the fighting became increasingly ruthless. In February 1942 Messerschmitt Bf 109s had strafed the RAF's Air-Sea Rescue Launch 129, causing the deaths of four of the crew. Nor were Axis ASR floatplanes exempt from being attacked by Spitfires. Baled-out aircrew on both sides were never entirely safe until they had been rescued or made prisoner. As Sergeant 'Slim' Yarra's account makes clear, it was not unknown for pilots to collapse the parachute of an adversary. Flight Lieutenant Denis Barnham of 601 Squadron, who arrived on the scene shortly afterwards, had watched as three of the four Italians landed in the sea off Malta's rocky south coast. After seeing them climb on to a cliff ledge, he landed at Luqa and reported the incident. A few days later, he learned that all had been killed. Anxious Allied pilots, only too aware of the danger of being mistaken for an Italian or German if forced to bale out over Malta, prudently took to carrying identification on their Mae Wests – recognisable emblems or words such as 'Spitfire – British' written in bold letters.

Wednesday 13 May

According to the squadron ORB, there were two uneventful scrambles on 13

May. There were four or five scrambles on Thursday 14th when the following events actually occurred:

Five aircraft, led by F/Lt Lawrence, took off on the first scramble. It is unfortunate that we lost Sgt Finlay on this show. "Ginger", who was due to leave the island at any moment, was attacked by six ME 109s and crashed on the coast. *[In fact, Sergeant Colin Finlay crashed just offshore near Wied iz–Zurrieq.]*

On the second scramble we lost Sgt Tony Boyd, DFM. Tony had put up a wonderful show on the island and we can ill afford to lose pilots of his calibre. Tony was shot down by Macchi 202s. F/Sgt Ferraby managed to damage one of the Macchi 202s pretty badly.

13.5.42
F/Sgt Ferraby
> One Macchi 202 Probably Destroyed

Thursday 14 May

We are now left with three aircraft. As usual the aircraft were on readiness at dawn and spent the day chasing Reccos, searches, seagulls and each other, but no results were obtained. Old Joe Kesselring seems to be a little cautious now. He refuses to supply any more large targets – JU 88s and 87s – for the boys to shoot at and we have to be content with ME 109s and Macchi 202s.

Friday 15 May

Our three aircraft have now been reduced to two. Jerry came over last night and dropped a bomb near one: Some pieces of shrapnel entered the engine, rather spoiling the finish. However, we were on readiness again at dawn and spent the morning chasing reccos and things as usual. However, during the afternoon Sgt Sim and Sgt Yarra became mixed up with seven ME 109s and 4 Macchis. Two Macchis were destroyed and one ME 109 damaged before the boys ran out of popcorn and had to come down.

15.5.42.
⊞ ⊞ Sgt Yarra: Two Macchi Destroyed
> One ME 109 Damaged.

Saturday 16 May

To day our two aircraft carried out their usual patrols and "109 nuisance scrambles". Although some 109s were met with they would not join battle. Consequently we obtained no results to day.

Sunday 17 May

To day was practically a recurrence of yesterday, except that F/Lt Lawrence and Sgt Yarra managed to become mixed up with about 14 Macchi 202s. The dog fight which ensued was quite good fun while it lasted. Although our chaps managed to get a few good squirts in no results were obtained.

Monday 18 May

Our two aircraft were again at readiness at dawn. Sgt Yarra and Sgt Shaw were scrambled to chase some 109s away. The scramble developed into a cover for the ASR launch and from that into a regular mix up. Lots of 109s became rather obnoxious, and Sgt Yarra managed to destroy one and probably destroy another in the general mêlée. The crew of the rescue boat were rather pleased they were not shot up.

This afternoon 17 more Spitfires arrived. We received four of these as our quota. Six pilots were sent over to Luqua [sic] to do readiness from there until dusk. The boys brought our Spits back and "B" Flight will be doing readiness to morrow at dawn with six aircraft.

18.5.42.
✠ Sgt Yarra: One ME 109 Destroyed
✠   One ME 109 ~~Probably~~ Destroyed
                        confirmed

Tuesday 19 May

"B" Flight went on at dawn this morning and were instructed to operate in pairs, very high, in the hope some unsuspecting Jerry would sneak in and allow himself to be jumped. The boys met the odd ME 109 or two but could not get any satisfaction. The 109s seem to be reluctant to co-operate with us these days.

"A" Flight took over at 1 P.M. and also used the pair principle. Sgt Yarra and P/O McNaughton met a few ME 109s and were forced to come down rather fast, much to the amusement of the "A" Flight pilots on the ground watching. F/Lt Lawrence and F/Sgt Sim, our "New Zealand Combination", spotted three Cant 1007s. The Cants had their boy-friends, the Macchi tribe, with them, and the Macchis took exception to Sim diving on their bombers, and showed their displeasure in no uncertain manner, much to Sgt Sim's disgust. F/Lt Lawrence sat behind an ME 109's rudder and pumped cannon shells into him, but, as only one cannon fired, the 109 escaped, more or less in one piece.

19.5.42.
F/Lt Lawrence: One ME 109 DAMAGED

Wednesday 20 May

"A" Flight took readiness at dawn this morning with six aircraft of the genus "Spitfire". F/Lt Lawrence led four aircraft on a scramble after a recco coming in. The boys saw some ME 109s stooging about but could not pick a fight. Sgt Sim ran out of gas and had to make a "dead stick" landing at Ta Kali. It is rumoured that Sim's dinghy had to go to stores to have a few holes patched up.

Sgt Yarra and F/Sgt Vineyard went up to look for some trouble. They saw two ME 109s but could not attack. Then they spotted two "little jobs" down on the "measured mile". Muttering abuse, they both went screaming down to the attack. "Slim" was not going fast enough and when trying to shut his hood, stuck his arm out in the slipstream, very nearly tearing the aforementioned member out by the roots. Due to this clottish manoeuvre, two ME 109s were allowed to go back to Sicily, laughing like hell.

"B" Flight took over at 1 P.M. and indulged in a little practice flying, much to the disgust of the old hands. Still the fact remains, that, the "Battle of Malta" must be all our way if we can afford to do practice flying.

However, there were two scrambles during the afternoon, and, although some ME 109s were encountered, they showed no inclination to fight.

Thursday 21 May

"B" Flight were on at dawn this morning. After doing the usual practice flip, the boys were scrambled on to a plot of plus 3. For once the boys found themselves in a perfect position to jump two ME 109s. They made good use of the advantage, and a spectator might have witnessed two ME 109s going like hell, with 4 avenging Spitfires on their "respectful" tails. S/Leader Lloyd fired all his rounds at one but could not quite get within range, which was very lucky for the 109. P/O Lambert pulled off a perfect deflection shot, which sent the second ME 109 crashing into the sea in the approved fashion. F/Sgt Ferraby also managed to get a squirt in.

21.5.42
P/O Lambert:
✠   One ME 109F DESTROYED.

Friday 22 May

Nothing very much happened to day. The boys had only one scramble, on which there was no interception. They also managed to get a little practise flying in. When "B" Flight took over at 1 o'clock, however, they were scrambled on to some ME 109s. Sgt Dodd, madly gnashing his teeth, took after one ME 109 and sent the pilot on a one way trip. F/Sgt Andrews also squirted at a 109 and severely frightened the Jerry therein, if nothing more.

<u>22.5.42.</u>

✠ Sgt Dodd:

One ME 109F Destroyed.

Saturday 23 May

A very quiet day to-day. The usual scrambles after ME 109s came along, but, although the boys chased all over the sky, nothing was encountered. It seems as though Jerry has really left Sicily – or he is just waiting for a convoy to come in. However, whatever he is waiting for, it is giving us a rest, and a respite from ring-twitch. It is rumoured that we are getting some replacements from the squadrons at Luqua [sic] and Ta Kali. We need some new pilots. Quite a lot of chaps are down with that insidious malady "Malta Dog". F/Sgt Sim, is the latest victim – he even looks like a dog.

A flights list follows together with the squadron crest – reproduced below.

No. 185 SQUADRON MALTA
SPITFIRE Vc
S/LEADER LLOYD DFC (RAFVR)

"A" FLIGHT.
F/LT LAWRENCE (NZ) ("LAWRIE")
P/O BROAD (RAF) ("ERNIE")
P/O KING (CAN) ("CY")
P/O McNAUGHTON (CAN) ("ANDY")
 (KILLED IN ACTION 1/6/42)
F/SGT SIM (NZ) ("SIMMIE")
F/SGT YARRA (AUS) ("SLIM")
F/SGT VINEYARD (USA) ("TEX")
F/SGT MACNAMARA (CAN) ("MAC")
F/SGT HAGGAS (RAF)
 ("HAGGARD HAGGIS")
SGT TERRY (RAF) ("TERRY")
SGT MITCHELL (AUS) ("MITCH")

"B" FLIGHT
P/O HALFORD (RAFVR) ("HAL")
P/O LAMBERT (CAN) ("JIMMY")
P/O OGILVIE (CAN) ("BUZZ")
P/O SHERLOCK (CAN)
 ("JOHNNIE")
SGT DODD (CAN) ("DODDY")
F/SGT FERRABY (RAF) ("NICK")
F/SGT REID (CAN) ("SHORTY")
F/SGT ANDREWS (USA) (ANDY)
SGT MOYE (USA) ("CACTUS")
SGT MAHAR (AUS) (ERIC)

The Maltese 'Ara fejn hi' can be translated as 'Look for her', or 'Look for it' (feminine form). At some point the motto was altered to read 'Ara fejn hu', i.e. 'Look for him' (or 'it'), and the overall design changed to include a griffin segreant in front of a Maltese cross.

Sunday 24 May

The business gave signs of picking up a little this morning. "Hal" and "Buzz" (P/Os Halford and Ogilvie) were scrambled and vectored on to a JU 88. The JU 88 was just stooging along, quite happy and contented, until our two Spitfires arrived and commenced to disturb their peace of mind. After the rear-gunner tried a few ineffectual bursts and retired to his Anderson shelter, the boys really got to work and made quite a nice mess of the 88, giving us another one to add to our score.

24.5.42.

卐 P/O Halford } one JU 88 Destroyed.
　 P/O Ogilvie

Monday 25 May

To day was a very busy day. "A" Flight had a stand down all the morning and during the afternoon F/Sgt "Nick" Ferraby did an air-test.

Tuesday 26 May

"A" Flight took the dawn patrol this morning. F/Lt Lawrence led a section of four and went stooging off towards Sicily. Sgt Yarra was flying gaily along, making discordant noises to himself, when he noticed what he took to be slight vapour trails coming from his wings. F/Lt Lawrence very nicely informed him he had sprung a glycol leak. "Slim" was trying to work out how the glycol leak could appear in his wings when he noticed sparks coming from the gun panels and realised his ammunition was on fire. After biting a large, circular, piece out of his dinghy, Slim made for home as fast as he could. He managed to arrive OK. "Tex", who was flying No 2 was very brassed because he did not get some RT procedure practice in, calling, "Mayday for another".

Later on the boys were scrambled again, and, after stooging round for some time, spotted two exquisite specimens of genus ME 109 floating about over the water. Muttering threats and imprecations the boys went tearing down on the two suckers. However the "suckers" happened to be rather more awake than usual and spotted them. The boys could not get in any effective squirts and the 109s disappeared over the horizon. It is rumoured that the two 109s overshot Sicily and landed in Venice. However this is discredited by the Official German News service, who said that the two who did that were Italians. F/Sgt MacNamara was rather astonished when he landed and found out the Jerry kites were 109s. He was under the impression they were JU 88s.

It is rumoured that a certain pilot, while covering some minesweepers, saw a mine explode. He immediately called up his leader and with a marked Canadian accent spouted forth: "Say, Red One, did you see that bomb explode by that ship down there?" We are not mentioning names, but if F/Sgt MacNamara gives any more information away to the enemy, Joe Kesselring will probably award him an Iron Cross 999th Class.

During the afternoon the boys had two scrambles and were unfortunate to be jumped twice. F/Sgt Ferraby did some quick thinking when he discovered some ME 109s coming down, and found the rest of the formation unable to receive him on the RT. He immediately turned into his No 2, who did a quick break to avoid collision, causing the sky to become littered with Spitfires doing amazing evolutions [sic: revolutions?]. However the Hun was foxed completely and beetled off home, muttering threats.

In addition to the seventeen Spitfires already ferried to the Island by HMS Eagle, aircraft had also arrived for the island's strike force. With sufficient Spitfires to hand, 229 Squadron was allowed to depart.

Wednesday 27 May
Today was very quiet. "B" Flight was on at dawn readiness, but all they could find when they were scrambled were large formations of SFA [*sweet Fanny Adams/sweet fuck-all*], flying at various altitudes. When attacked these formations disappeared into thin air, so no results were obtained.

No 229 Squadron went back to the Middle East to-day taking with them the last of the Hurricanes. We were not sorry to see the Hurricanes go. Now that the boys are back flying Spitfires again they don't want anything more to do with Hurricanes.

"A" Flight had one scramble during the afternoon, and although the enemy fighters still outnumbered us slightly, they would not come down and fight, much to the chagrin of the boys in the air. Sgt Yarra chased a couple of ME 109s out to sea. He squirted but did not do any damage.

Thursday 28 May
A very quiet day to-day. All the boys could do was a little practise flying.

S/Leader Lloyd, our CO went home last night. We were all sorry to lose him, but he had completed his time on the island and done his job very well. F/Lt Lawrence is now CO of 185 Squadron. However the old boys who knew F/Lt Lawrence during the blitz would not recognise him now. That moustache, which was once the pride and joy of 185 Squadron, met with a fatal accident recently and is now being mourned by all and sundry.

Friday 29 May

Squadron Leader Lawrence led the only scramble we had to-day, but the Jerries again refused to co operate with us. This is a darned poor show: Everyone is becoming browned off and if Jerry continues to refuse to mix it we will have to appeal to the referee for victory or a technical knock out.

We were lucky in being able to obtain F/Lt West as one of our new flight commanders. F/Lt West has been pursuing the Hun with deadly intent and dark thoughts in his mind for quite a long time now. He has been with 249 at Ta Kali since the Blitz started, and it is indeed a privilege to obtain a man of his calibre for the squadron.

Facing page:

29.5.42.
F/SGT YARRA AWARDED DISTINGUISHED FLYING MEDAL

No 185 SQUADRON (REVISED)

SQUADRON LEADER K.A. LAWRENCE COMMANDING OFFICER

"A" FLIGHT	"B" FLIGHT
F/LT WEST (RAF)	P/O HALFORD (RAF)
P/O BROAD (RAF)	P/O LAMBERT (CAN)
P/O KING (CAN)	P/O OGILVIE (CAN)
P/O McNAUGHTON (CAN)	P/O SHERLOCK (CAN)
(KILLED IN ACTION 1/6/42) √	F/SGT FERRABY (RAF)
F/SGT YARRA DFM (AUS)	F/SGT ANDREWS (USA)
F/SGT SIM (NZ)	F/SGT REID (CAN) √
F/SGT VINEYARD (USA)	F/SGT MOYE (USA) √
F/SGT MACNAMARA (CAN.)	SGT DODD (CAN)
F/SGT HAGGAS (RAF) √	SGT MAHAR (AUS)
SGT TERRY (RAF) √	
SGT MITCHELL (AUS)	

Ticks, above, indicate fatalities.

Saturday 30 May

"The Three Twerps" came over again to day, escorted by their tribe of Macchi 202s and RE 1001s [sic], but the boys were waiting for them. They went right in and soon the sky was filled with Italians doing violent aerobatics, trying to dodge the Spitfires. However most of the old boys had trouble with their cannons. Some very satisfying dog fights took place and, although we only claimed damaged REs we certainly shook the Italian war merchants and they'll think twice about peddling their wares on this island for some time.

To day we have 70 Spitfires serviceable on the island. Quite a difference from the days when six Hurricanes and 4 Spitfires were considered amazing serviceability.

30.5.41 *[sic]*
F/Sgt Ferraby
 1 RE Damaged.

By the end of May developments in the Western Desert and on the Eastern Front again led to the departure of most Sicily-based Luftwaffe *units. As in 1941, operations against Malta were left primarily to the Italians and, as before, the reduction of German aircraft in Sicily provided a temporary respite that enabled Malta to strengthen and reorganise its defences.*

Sunday 31 May
To day was very quiet. We had two negative scrambles, and spent the rest of the day listening to swing records on the Radio.

INDIVIDUAL SCORES FOR MAY 1942

S/LDR LAWRENCE: 2 JU 88s DESTROYED – 1 ME 109F DAMAGED

P/O WIGLEY DFC: 1 JU 87 PROBABLY DESTROYED – 2 JU 88s DAMAGED (POSTED)

P/O McKAY: 1 JU 88 DESTROYED – 1 ME 109F DAMAGED (POSTED)

P/O BROAD: 1 JU 88 DESTROYED – 1 JU 87 PROBABLY DESTROYED – 1 JU 87 DAMAGED – 2 ME 109Fs DAMAGED

F/SGT YARRA DFM: 3 ME 109Fs DESTROYED – 2 RE 1001s *[sic]* DESTROYED – 1 JU 88 PROBABLY DESTROYED – 1 JU 88 DAMAGED – 1 ME 109F DAMAGED

SGT TWEEDALE: 1 JU 88 DESTROYED – 2 ME 109Fs DESTROYED – 1 ME 109F PROBABLY DESTROYED. (DECEASED)

SGT BOYD DFM: 2 JU 88s PROBABLY DESTROYED – 1 JU 88 DAMAGED. (DECEASED)

SGT DODD:	1 JU 87 DESTROYED – ~~1 MC 202~~ 1 ME 109F DESTROYED – 1 MC 202 PROBABLY DESTROYED – 1 ME 109 DAMAGED
F/SGT FERRABY:	1 MC 202 PROBABLY DESTROYED – 1 RE 1001 DAMAGED
P/O LAMBERT:	1 ME 109 DESTROYED
P/O HALFORD:	1 JU 88 DESTROYED
<u>TOTAL:</u>	DESTROYED: 16 PROBABLY DESTROYED: 8 DAMAGED: 11

We lost 3 Pilots.

Monday 1 June

"A" Flight were scrambled to day on to a bogey plot which developed into 4 ME 109s doing their usual stooge over the island. There was some wizard cloud cover and the boys made good use of this to jump about 8 ME 109s just east of Calafrana. P/O Broad damaged one ME 109, while F/SGT YARRA chased two others and shot one down. Unfortunately P/O McNaughton was shot down during this engagement. Andy, who had joined the squadron only recently, was very popular with everyone. We cannot afford to lose men like Andy – they are too hard to replace.

    1.6.1942.
    P/O Broad: 1 ME 109 Damaged
✠ F/SGT YARRA: 1 ME 109 Destroyed

Tuesday 2 June

"B" Flight were on at dawn this morning and took the dawn patrol. However it was just the usual stooge patrol – nothing sighted. But later on in the morning things began to happen. The "Ice Cream Vendors" came over peddling their wares, at their usual height. The parade was composed by 3 Cants and about 20 RE 2001s, 2 boys blowing bugles marching out in front, and a couple of dogs bringing up the rear. Four Spitfires went up to watch the proceedings, and, in their usual style, waited until the Italians were not looking before commencing to make a series of dirty darts at the enemy aircraft. F/Sgt "Shorty" Reid damaged one Cant and one RE 2001 in the ensuing mix-up. The boys are getting rather annoyed at the Italians for poaching on our preserves. We don't mind them coming over if they ask permission first, but when they just sneak over and use up a lot of our air to fly their aeroplanes in it is becoming a bit too thick. We had to teach the Jerry Bombers a sharp lesson when they were doing it and we cannot see our way clear to let the Italians get away with it. We don't poach on their preserves – much, so why don't they keep on their own side of the fence. They've got lots of room to fly over there – Sicily is much bigger than Malta.

2.6.42.
F/SGT REID: 1 CANT 1007 DAMAGED
                        1 RE 2001 DAMAGED

On 3 June thirty-one Spitfires took off from HMS Eagle. *All but four reached Malta.*

Wednesday 3 June
To day was "Air Test Day" and was celebrated with great gusto by the boys. They were busy getting a new delivery of Spitfires ready for combat. We obtained 4 of these new jobs as our quota bringing our strength up to sixteen aircraft. We will be able to put 12 aircraft on the line from dawn to dusk every day now and still have some spare. We are a little short of pilots, but received some new ones to day, which will help a lot.

Thursday 4 June
Today was another quiet day. The boys did some stooge scrambles but could not contact anything. The only thing that looked worthwhile was an Italian plot, but as soon as they realised our fighters were airborne they turned back and went home.

Friday 5 June
A very good day to day. We were at one hour's availability all day and not a single kite left the runway. The day was spent in the respective messes.

Saturday 6 June
"A" Flight took the dawn patrol today and for once something happened. F/Sgt MacNamara and F/SGT Haggas were sent after a JU 88 who was beating up the sea some distance from the island. The boys went out and picked on the JU 88. They had to share it with another type, however, who stuck his nose in. Still Mack and "Haggard Haggis" obtained ⅓ each. Everyone was highly elated at the promise of some activity in the future on an otherwise stooge dawn patrol.

"A" Flight had quite a little activity. We were kept busy all the morning scrambling after ME 109s, "Blood waggons", seagulls and plots of SFA. However an enjoyable time was had by all and the party finally broke up when "B" Flight arrived to take over.

"B" Flight had their share of fun and games during the afternoon. F/Lt Plagis DFC and his boys went up and captured the "blood waggon". Johnny picked on a bunch of RE 2001s and induced one pilot to bale out. The second guy was not so lucky – he was last seen going into the drink doing about 500 MPH. It is considered unlikely that he survived. "Shorty" Reid also did a little beating up and destroyed an RE 2001 and damaged another. P/O Lambert, Sgt Dodd and Sgt Russel found the "blood waggon" stooging along and did some OTU style practise attacks on it. However they used live ammunition and made quite a nice mess of the floatplane. We did not lose one a/c, but according to the Italian Radio the boys in the RE 2001s destroyed six Spitfires.

6.6.1942.
F/LT PLAGIS DFC
⊕ ⊕   2 RE 2001s DESTROYED
F/SGT REID
⊕   1 RE 2001 DESTROYED
    1 RE 2001 DAMAGED
P/O LAMBERT ⎤
⊕   SGT RUSSEL   ⎬ 1 FLOAT PLANE DESTROYED
    SGT DODD   ⎦
✠   F/SGT HAGGAS   ⎫
    F/SGT MACNAMARA ⎬ ⅔ JU 88 DEST.

Sunday 7 June

"B" Flight were on dawn readiness to-day. F/Lt Plagis and a section of four went off to intercept a plot of 12 plus. They found four ME 109s stooging about and proceeded to bounce them properly. F/Lt Plagis destroyed an ME 109F and F/Sgt "Shorty" Reid probably destroyed another. This combat made the second engagement in two days in which F/Lt Plagis figured, during which period he destroyed three enemy aircraft, bringing his total up to 11 destroyed.

During the afternoon another section of four were scrambled and chased some ME 109s. However contact was not established. F/Sgt Yarra was returning to base with a "dud" motor when he was jumped by 4 RE 2001s. During the ensuing mix up two of the RE 2001s flew across "Slim's" sights and stopped some lead. At the same time as this mix-up was taking place F/SGT Sim was chasing two ME 109s who had their noses down going for home. However the 109s had their "tits" pressed as usual and disappeared over the horizon to the tune of muttered curses from F/Sgt Sim.

7.6.1942
F/LT PLAGIS DFC
✠   1 ME 109 DESTROYED

F/SGT REID
   1 ME 109 PROBABLY DESTROYED

F/SGT YARRA
   2 RE 2001s DAMAGED

Monday 8 June

The whole Squadron were stood down to day.

The next day another thirty-two Spitfires arrived after being ferried towards Malta on HMS Eagle.

Tuesday 9 June

To day we received 4 more Spitfires to add to our collection. This brings our strength up to 20 aircraft.

The day was spent doing patrols and scrambles over the island but nothing was encountered. P/O Halford was stooging along with his section and made a dirty pass at four a/c. However these aircraft turned out to be four seagulls who were doing a practice formation. The seagulls were very annoyed and threatened to dive-bomb our dispersal if the incident is repeated.

Wednesday 10 June

"B" Flight were on the dawn patrol today. It turned out to be the usual stooge job. The Hun seems rather chary of getting out of bed before 8 A.M. these days. The rest of the day was spent doing the usual scrambles and nothing was encountered.

Thursday 11 June

The squadron was at 1 hour's availability all day and spent the day swimming.

Friday 12 June

"A" Flight were on at dawn this morning. Two JU 88s dashed in and dropped some bombs on Safi Strip about 7 A.M. They took us by surprise, but one section were scrambled and chased the 88s. However, ME 109s interfered and the boys had to deal with them. Sgt Terry damaged one of the little jobs, but by the time the 109s beetled off home, the JU 88s were out of sight.

For the rest of the day the Jerries were very inactive. We did some escort work but did not have any more joy.

Saturday 13 June

S/Ldr Lawrence did two more air tests to-day.

In mid-June convoys 'Vigorous' and 'Harpoon' made a simultaneous attempt to reach Malta, the former from the Middle East and the latter via Gibraltar. After suffering heavy losses, 'Vigorous' was aborted. With Malta-based aircraft providing air cover, the survivors of Operation 'Harpoon' continued to battle through. Two merchantmen reached the island, as did the Welshman *on another unescorted run.*

Sunday 14 June

Today was a quiet day. We only had two scrambles. One plot was an Italian effort which turned back. The other was a Baltimore on delivery from ME.

There have been a lot of various aircraft coming to the island during the last few days. Baltimores, Marylands, "Wimpys" and Beaufighters have been arriving at Luqua [*sic*] to do escort work on the convoy which is expected in at any time now. The Luqua boys are all fitting long range tanks on to their Spitfires to do long range protective cover over the convoy. In fact, everyone is looking forward to the promise of some large scale trouble with the Jerries and Italians.

Monday 15 June

To day the boys did a protective patrol over the "Welshman". This is the first sign of the convoy we have seen so far. However it is rumoured that the ships will be within range of our Spits to morrow or the next day.

S/Ldr Lawrence did an escort for some Beaufighters who were returning from a prang on some Italians who were sailing their boats in "Mare Nostrum".

Two more scrambles took place in the morning but were only protective patrols over the island.

During the afternoon however things started to happen. F/Lt West led a section of four out to the convoy, which had magically appeared on the horizon. During the patrol some JU 88s appeared and prepared to lay a few eggs. However the boys got right amongst the Jerries, much to the consternation of the 88 pilots, most of whom ditched their bombs in the sea.

F/Lt West destroyed an ME 109 who was trying to spoil our boys' fun, and then dashed into the JU 88s and probably destroyed one of the big jobs.

F/Sgt Sim was beetling along after an 88 who was making rapidly for home. He was having some difficulty in catching the 88 when he noticed another one flying in formation with him. The pilot in the 88, noticing the evil look on F/Sgt Sim's face immediately buzzed off, hotly pursued by "Simmie", who proceeded to shoot great pieces off the enemy bomber. However, the aforementioned pieces kept bouncing off Sim's Spitfire and tore some holes in various places, but did not prevent the destruction of the JU 88, or the safe return of F/Sgt Sim.

P/O Stenborg also got mixed up in the fun and damaged two JU 88s.

P/O Broad took four out to relieve F/Lt West's boys and run into the end of the scrap. P/O Broad destroyed an ME 109 after a hectic few minutes. P/O Baril was shot down by another ME 109, but he bailed out and was picked up by one of the escorting destroyers.

The excitement was continued for the rest of the day and finished off with a very nice forced landing on the aerodrome by Sgt Drew whose motor failed in the circuit.

15 6 42
- F/LT WEST: 1 ME 109F DESTROYED
                 1 JU 88 PROBABLY DESTROYED
- F/SGT SIM: 1 JU 88 DESTROYED
  P/O STENBORG: 2 JU 88s DAMAGED
- P/O BROAD: 1 ME 109 DESTROYED

Tuesday 16 June

"A" Flight took over at dawn this morning and a section of four, led by S/Ldr Lawrence, were scrambled. The plot turned out to be a raid on Grand Harbour by three JU 88s escorted by ME 109s. However the boys did not get amongst the bombers.

Later on F/Sgt Yarra was scrambled with his section. The boys went up looking for ME 109s. They found what they were looking for – 12 of genus ME 109 coming down out of the sun. Four Spitfires broke in all directions, but as F/Sgt MacNamara turned into the 109s a very spiteful one shot his controls away and "Mac" was forced to take to the silk, landing in the sea with a juicy splash, much to his disgust. F/Sgt Vineyard pulled out of a spiral dive and his seat promptly came loose and pinned him against the dash-board. "Tex" also had to bail out and had some trouble getting loose from his machine. One of the "Gremlins" in the cockpit grabbed him by the foot and refused to let go for some time. However Tex managed to trade his flying boot for his life and got away. He came floating down about 3 miles away from "Mac", mouthing uncouth Texan oaths. F/Sgt Yarra damaged a 109 and promptly spun off in the attempt, collecting a bullet through the exhaust during the fray. All the boys then went up and did some Air-Sea Rescue patrols until the boys were safely in. "Tex" was none the worse for the enforced swim, whereas "Mac" got off with minor bruises.

16.6.42.
F/SGT YARRA DFM
    1 ME 109F DAMAGED.

On the same page as the above claim a revised flights list is also provided:

No 185 SQUADRON MALTA

S/LDR K.A. LAWRENCE. COMMANDING OFFICER (POSTED UK)

"A" FLIGHT	"B" FLIGHT
F/LT WEST (RAF) (POSTED UK)	F/LT PLAGIS DFC (RHODESIA) (POSTED UK)
P/O KING (CAN)	
P/O BROAD (RAF) (POSTED UK)	P/O HALFORD (RAF) (POSTED 1435)
F/SGT YARRA DFM (AUS) (POSTED UK)	P/O LAMBERT (CAN) (WOUNDED IN ACTION)
F/SGT SIM (NZ) (POSTED UK)	P/O OGILVIE (CAN)
F/SGT VINEYARD (USA) (POSTED 1435 SQDN)	P/O KENT (RAF) (KILLED IN ACCIDENT)
F/SGT MACNAMARA (CAN) (POSTED 1435 SQDN)	P/O SHERLOCK (CAN)
SGT MITCHELL (AUS)	F/SGT FERRABY (RAF) (WOUNDED IN ACTION)
SGT TERRY (RAF) (KILLED IN ACTION)	SGT DODD (CAN) (POSTED UK)
F/SGT HAGGAS (RAF) (KILLED IN ACTION)	F/SGT REID (CAN) (KILLED IN ACTION)
P/O BARIL (CAN)	F/SGT ANDREWS (USA)
SGT REID (AUS)	SGT MAHAR (AUS)
F/O STOOP (RAF) (WOUNDED IN ACTION)	SGT DREW (RAF)
P/O STENBORG (NZ)	SGT PARKER (RAF) (POSTED UK)
P/O JAMES (RHODESIA) (POSTED UK)	P/O CHARNEY
SGT CONWAY (NZ) (WOUNDED IN ACTION)	SGT RUSSEL (CAN) (KILLED IN ACTION)

Wednesday 17 June

Very quiet to day. The "Yellow Noses" seem content to sit back and shoot a line to each other about their victory yesterday. Only one plot came on the board all day and that was too hard to catch, so we did not get a chance for revenge.

There is no entry for Thursday 18 June, but the squadron ORB mentions one uneventful scramble involving four pilots at 12:45 hours for +1 aircraft.

Friday 19 June

Squadron stood down all day. F/Lt West did an air-test.

Saturday 20 June

The boys are still determined to give the ME 109s some sorrow for the way they beat us up on the 16th, but the Jerries seem determined not to give us the chance. They absolutely refuse to play with us these days. Today was a succession of scrambles without interception.

Sunday 21 June

To day started off in the usual fashion. "B" Flight were on from dawn and had only one scramble. "A" Flight took over at 1 pm and did not scramble until 7 pm, when two sections took off to intercept a 12+ plot which turned into a lone JU 88, protected by fighters, doing a recco. F/Sgt Yarra and his section managed to trick 4 ME 109s into coming down. The boys engaged and F/Sgt Yarra sat on one ME 109 and shot his tail off with a juicy crunch. F/Sgt Terry had a cannon shell explode over his cockpit and had to crash land on the aerodrome. F/Sgt Yarra then spotted the poor old Recco JU 88 and, madly gnashing his teeth, went down to attack. He managed to damage the JU 88, but was in turn attacked by ME 109s. A merry mix-up ensued in which one ME 109 was shot down. F/Sgt Yarra returned with large pieces bitten out of his dinghy, but otherwise was quite OK. Thereby was the ignominious defeat of the 16th avenged. AMEN.

Not content with this victory, F/Sgt Bob Sim picked on an ME 109F who was endeavouring to beat up a Spitfire. Sitting behind the Jerry, he poured a 12 second burst into the very surprised "Yellow Nose", causing it much trouble. The 109 could not do much about this unprecedented attack and now the pilot is probably learning to play "Tuxedo Junction" on a harp, under the tutelage of a venerable old fellow with a long white beard and a halo.

Unfortunately, F/Sgt Conway was shot down in this engagement and is now in hospital with an injured spine.

> 21 6 42
> F/SGT YARRA DFM
> 卐 卐　　2 ME 109Fs Destroyed
> 　　　　1 JU 88 DAMAGED.
>
> F/Sgt SIM
> 卐　　1 ME 109 DESTROYED

Monday 22 June

The boys managed to get into some more trouble to day. They were scrambled for a fighter sweep and met some ME 109s who were doing their usual practise formation over the Island. "Shorty" Reid and Nick Ferraby took exception to this flagrant breach of etiquette and proceeded to enter a mild protest. F/Sgt Reid's protest took the form of a long burst of cannon fire which stopped the engine of one ME 109 and induced the pilot to bale out. "Nick" was satisfied with severely frightening his ME 109, who was last seen heading for Sicily at a terrific rate of MPH.

22 6 1942
✠   F/Sgt Reid. 1 ME 109F Destroyed

Tuesday 23 June
The boys had some fun with the Italians to day. It was unfortunate that through bad controlling they missed the bombing force until it was on its way home. However P/O King and F/Sgt Vineyard chased the "Ice cream boys" half way back to Sicily and "Tex" got very nasty with an ME 109 who tried to interfere. These Italians are in for a rude shock one of these fine days. They have been getting away with too much lately. There was quite a little activity to day. The squadron was scrambled twice and different sections kept going and coming all day. The boys got a few operational hours in, but apart from the episode of the Italians, nothing was encountered.

23.6.1942.
F/Sgt Vineyard:- 1 ME 109F Damaged

Wednesday 24 June
The squadron only had two scrambles to day. The first was in the morning, and, although the section saw the ME 109s in the distance they could not make contact. The second scramble was the usual stooge job after ME 109s who refuse to cross the coast.

Thursday 25 June
The squadron was stood down all day.

Friday 26 June
To day was very quiet up till six o'clock when the Italian "Regia Aeronauticae" [sic] came over giving another practical example in the series, "The Bombing of Malta – High Level". The squadron was scrambled and vainly chased the retiring bombers half way back to Sicily. F/Lt West managed to catch up with an RE 2001 and severely battered him. The RE 2001 finally gave up the ghost, and one more Italian fighter pilot went off the active list. Mussolini claimed six Spitfires shot down in this engagement and air official "gen" sheet stated "none of our aircraft are missing", so someone is lying and in the words of the prophet "it sure ain't us, boy".

The boys in "A" Flight had one more scramble during the afternoon but just stooged about the sky getting some operational time up.

Facing page:

<u>26 6 1942</u>
F/Lt West: 1 RE 2001 Destroyed

<u>185 SQUADRON SCORE FOR JUNE 1942</u>

<u>F/LT PLAGIS, DFC & BAR</u>:-	2 RE 2001s DESTROYED 1 ME 109F DESTROYED. ⊕ ⊕ ⚝
<u>F/LT WEST DFC & BAR</u>:-	1 ME 109F DESTROYED, 1 RE 2001 DESTROYED 1 JU 88 DAMAGED ⚝ ⊕
<u>P/O BROAD</u>:-	1 ME 109F DESTROYED 1 ME 109F DAMAGED ⚝
<u>F/SGT YARRA DFM</u>:-	3 ME 109Fs DESTROYED 2 RE 2001s DAMAGED 1 JU 88 DAM. 1 ME 109F DAMAGED ⚝ ⚝ ⚝
<u>F/SGT REID</u>:-	1 RE 2001 DESTROYED, 1 ME 109F DESTROYED, 1 ME 109 PROBABLY DESTROYED, 1 CANT DAMAGED 2 RE 2001s DAMAGED ⚝ ⚝
<u>F/SGT SIM</u>:-	1 ME 109 DESTROYED, 1 JU 88 DESTROYED. ⚝ ⚝
<u>F/SGT HAGGAS</u>:-	⅓ JU 88 ~~DAMAGED~~ DESTROYED
<u>F/SGT MACNAMARA</u>	⅓ JU 88 DESTROYED
<u>P/O LAMBERT</u>	⅓ "BLOOD WAGGON" DESTROYED
<u>SGT RUSSEL</u>	⅓ "BLOOD WAGGON" DESTROYED
<u>SGT DODD</u>	⅓ "BLOOD WAGGON" DESTROYED

Saturday 27 June

Most of the day's work consisted of protective patrols over minesweepers operating out from Grand Harbour. However, "Johnny" Sherlock, in his inimitable style, managed to get mixed up with four ME 109Fs. Johnny squirted, the ME 109s squirted, the "ack ack" squirted, and nothing whatsoever was hit. Must have been good shooting on everyone's part.

Sunday 28 June

Lots of negative scrambles to-day. F/O Stoop and his section careered madly out to sea in search of some enemy bombers which were rumoured to be stooging about with evil designs on this beautiful??? island.

However, much to the disgust of the section the "Enemy bombers" developed into a tribe of Beauforts who were coming back after doing a lot of "no good" to an Italian convoy.

There are no entries in the diary or squadron ORB for Monday 29 and Tuesday 30 June. At 05:00 hours on the 29th, delayed action and anti-personnel bombs were dropped at Hal Far among the dispersal areas and on the aerodrome, which was rendered unserviceable until the evening. One soldier was injured, a Swordfish was destroyed and four Spitfires sustained damage. The squadron was stood down at 19:00 hours and remained so throughout the 30th.

In Libya on 21 June Tobruk had changed hands yet again, this time falling to the Deutsche Afrikakorps. Shortly afterwards, 601 Squadron departed Malta to join the hard-pressed RAF in North Africa. Meanwhile, II Fliegerkorps was bolstered by Ju 88s and Bf 109s transferred from other sectors, and the Regia Aeronautica commenced a build-up of its forces in Sicily.

July began with a renewed Axis offensive that continued unabated for two weeks. On the 14th Air Vice-Marshal Keith Park took over from Air Vice-Marshal Lloyd as Air Officer Commanding. Soon afterwards, the new AOC issued an order for raids to be intercepted en-route to Malta in an attempt to force the bombers to jettison their loads before they could cross the coast. The tactic duly became standard procedure.

Wednesday 1 July

To day started off very well. An Italian merchant vessel was reported some 40 miles away from the island and two Spitfires were despatched to investigate. All the boys were on their toes with visions of pranging a full size merchant ship, but when the recco section returned and reported nothing there, their hopes began to fall. When a second recco section also failed to contact the "Flying Dutchman", the boys gave it up as a bad job.

However, during the afternoon, "B" Flight found lots of fun waiting for them. The Italians came in again and the whole Flight was waiting for them. F/Sgt Reid destroyed an ME 109 and damaged another. This brings "Shorty's" score up to 4 destroyed, which is a very good performance on the part of "The Kid". "Johnny" Sherlock beat up an ME 109 and came back curling his moustache, with a look of triumph on his handsome? face. P/O Halford also damaged an ME 109, very severely, which rather discouraged the Jerry pilot therein, while P/O Charney damaged an ME 109 and a MACCHI 202. Sgt Mahar also managed to get amongst the enemy and also damaged a MACCHI 202. The combined efforts of these boys must have produced a few grey hairs in our old pal, Joe Kesselring's, hair.

1/7/42
F/Sgt Reid.
✠ 1 ME 109F Destroyed
   1 ME 109F Damaged
P/O Halford
   1 MACCHI 202 Damaged
P/O Sherlock
   1 ME 109 Damaged
Sgt MAHAR
   1 MACCHI 202 Damaged
P/O Charney
   1 ME 109 Damaged
   1 Macchi 202 Damaged

Thursday 2 July

It looks very much as if the old days are are [sic] returning with a vengeance. JU 88s have made a reappearance over the island. They bring a terrific escort of ME 109s and Italian fighters over with them these days and the boys are really having some fun. "B" Flight were on the early readiness to day and the boys went up and got right amongst the Jerries. "Shorty" Reid destroyed one ME 109. "Buzz" pulled off a very nice forced landing at Ta Kali after being badly shot up by some particularly nasty ME 109s. He got in wheels down, rather a difficult thing to accomplish on this island. F/Sgt Moye also landed at Luqua [sic] but was able to fly his aircraft back to Hal Far OK.

"A" Flight took over at 1 o'clock and their show started almost before they had taken over. Eight aircraft were scrambled with F/Sgt Yarra leading and they intercepted the bombers over the island. F/Sgt Sim sat behind a JU 88 and squirted all his ammo into the black B— but the JU 88 failed to come down – against all laws of nature – and Bob had to be content with a damaged. P/O Stenborg also got into a good position behind an ME 109 but his cannons jammed, much to the relief of the 109 pilot.

A second show developed later in the day. F/Sgt Haggas beat hell out of a Macchi 202 and sent it down in the sea a little too fast for comfort. F/O Stoop also performed a very neat operation on an MC 202 who was flying around the sky, and caused the sudden demise of one more Dago. Sgt Len Reid damaged an ME 109 who was trying to shoot a Spitfire down. On the whole we had a very good day today and everyone went home satisfied with the day's work, except of course the Jerries and Dagoes.

2.7.42.
✠ F/Sgt REID: 1 ME 109F DESTROYED
⊕ F/Sgt Haggas: 1 MC 202 DESTROYED

⊕ F/O STOOP: 1 MC 202 DESTROYED
   F/Sgt SIM: 1 JU 88 DAMAGED
   F/Sgt [sic] REID: 1 ME 109F DAMAGED

Friday 3 July

Today started off with the same activity as yesterday. Johnny Halford, who is now a Flight Lieutenant, led a section on an interception. The interception, however, was not successful, but Sgt Parker found a nest of ME 109s near Gozo and beetled in and shot one down in the approved fashion. Tony Drew also managed to get mixed up in a spot of bother, and, although he squirted at some 109s, he did not claim. The rest of the day was spent in scrambles but no interceptions were made.

3.7.42.
Sgt PARKER: 1 ME 109F DESTROYED

Saturday 4 July

A very quiet day to day – only one scramble.

Sunday 5 July

The boys started off to day with the luck right against them. On the first scramble 5 out of 8 pilots had to return to base with trouble – mostly R/T. However F/LT Halford managed to damage a JU 88 in spite of the luck. When "A" Flight took over at 1 o'clock, however, the luck seemed to change. On the first scramble a section of 8 led by F/Sgt Yarra ran into a very nice party of JU 88s and ME 109Fs. The boys engaged over the island and treated the Malts to the spectacle of enemy aircraft being severely beaten up. F/Sgt Yarra became mixed up with the "Gaggle" and destroyed a JU 88, probably destroyed an ME 109 and damaged another. P/O Stenborg sailed into a flock of ME 109s and shot two down, much to the disgust of the ME 109 pilots, who beetled off home at high speed to complain about the episode. Once again everyone returned to the billet happy.

5.7.1942
P/O STENBORG: 2 ME 109Fs DESTROYED
F/Sgt YARRA DFM: 1 JU 88 DESTROYED
                 1 ME 109F PROBABLY DEST
                 1 ME 109F DAMAGED
F/LT HALFORD: 1 JU 88 DAMAGED.

Monday 6 July

The activity on the part of the Jerries has been continued now for the past week and today he really started to go to town. Although this phase cannot be compared with the period of the "Blitz", there certainly is plenty of action going for all and sundry. This morning "B" Flight were scrambled and really became mixed up with the "Hostiles". F/Sgt MOYE was the only one who failed to return, being shot down by some ME 109s. "Cactus" had not been in the squadron long, but it was a blow to lose him so soon. The rest of the Flight put up quite a score amongst themselves. Squadron Leader New [*who assumed command on 29 June*] probably destroyed a JU 88 and damaged another, Johnny Sherlock damaged an ME 109F, "Buzz" Ogilvie got into quite a mix up, but did not claim anything, P/O Charney destroyed an ME 109F. F/LT Halford was leading one section and every member of that section scored. "Hal" damaged 1 JU 88 and 2 ME 109s, Tony Drew destroyed a JU 88, "Shorty" Reid probably destroyed an ME 109F and damaged a JU 88, while F/Sgt Andrews squirted at numerous things but did not observe any results. The boys were scrambled again later in the day and Sgt Dodd destroyed one ME 109 while Sgt Drew damaged another. Sgt Dodd also destroyed one ME 109 in the first scramble. There was one more scramble during the day but the plot turned back just when the boys were up in a very good position to bounce them if they had attempted to come in over the island. That finished all activity for the day.

6.7.1942.

✠	P/O Charney:	1 ME 109F Destroyed
✠ ✠	Sgt Dodd:	2 ME 109 Fs Destroyed
✠	Sgt Drew:	1 JU 88 Destroyed
		1 ME 109F Damaged
	S/LDR NEW:	1 JU 88 Probably Destroyed
		1 JU 88 Damaged.
	P/O SHERLOCK:	1 ME 109F Damaged.
	F/LT Halford:	1 JU 88 Damaged
		2 ME 109Fs Damaged
	F/Sgt Reid:	1 JU 88 Probably Destroyed
		1 ME 109 Damaged.

6.7.1942.
F/LT WEST AWARDED DISTINGUISHED FLYING CROSS AND BAR.

Tuesday 7 July
"B" Flight were on the early readiness again this morning. The Jerries seemed to quieten down a little however, and the flight only got one scramble all the morning. During this show Sgt Dodd damaged one ME 109F while Sgt Eric Mahar destroyed another one in the approved fashion. "Nick" baled out. "A" Flight took over at one o'clock. On the first scramble the Italians brought in a flock of SM 84s and indulged in a spot of their usual high level bombing. Our boys were right with them doing their little

bit to hinder proceedings as much as possible. During this engagement both Sgt Haggas and Sgt Terry were shot down. These two boys had been with the squadron for some time and both had flown very well and done their job. They both died fighting against far superior odds and will be remembered as long as No 185 Squadron remains in operation during the war. The rest of the flight did a very good job. The bombers were forced to ditch their bombs and not one fell in the target area. F/Sgt Yarra destroyed two RE 2001s before being shot up and forced to return to base. F/Sgt MacNamara damaged two SM 84s. P/O Broad was in a beautiful position behind the SM 84s but his cannons would not fire. Only one more scramble took place today but the plot did not materialise.

7.6. [sic] 1942.
F/Sgt YARRA DFM: 2 RE 2001s Destroyed
F/Sgt MacNamara: 2 SM 84s Damaged.

Wednesday 8 July
The air operations to day were confined to scrambles after plots which did not come in. The boys became browned off after a while, with going up to 30,000 and sitting there freezing. However as no bombs were dropped on the Island it was a victory to us.

Thursday 9 July
To day was a repetition of yesterday except that the boys did one search for a pilot who was spotted in the sea. He was not found, but as it was a Jerry or Italian pilot nobody cared very much. The water would do him good, and it is said that drowning is a pleasant death, which is much too good for a German.

Friday 10 July
Rumour has it that the new batch of Spitfires we are expecting are to arrive to-morrow. It is about time as we are getting rather short of aircraft. F/Lt Jimmy Lambert went to Gibraltar some weeks ago to lead the new boys here. He is probably enjoying himself in Gibraltar getting very drunk. Only one scramble took place – no results – and F/Sgt Yarra and P/O Baril conducted a search for a dinghy reported in the sea. An investiture was conducted in Valletta during the afternoon at which F/Sgt Yarra was presented with a DFM ribbon by Lord Gort VC.

Facing page:

No 185 SQUADRON (PRESENT STRENGTH)
S/LDR NEW CO

"A" FLIGHT	"B" FLIGHT	
F/LT LAMBERT	F/LT CHARNEY	
P/O KING	P/O OGILVIE	NON EFFECTIVE
F/O BRUCE	P/O SHERLOCK	PILOTS
P/O BARIL	P/O GUTHRIE	P/O STENBORG DFC
SGT DREW	F/SGT ANDREWS	F/SGT YARRA DFM
SGT MITCHELL	SGT MAHAR	F/SGT PARKER
SGT REID	SGT MACLEOD	SGT DODD.
SGT LIVINGSTONE	SGT GUNSTONE	P/O Ferraby
SGT WEAVER	SGT HARTNEY	F/O Stoop
	SGT FORRESTER	

Saturday 11 July

Most of the day was spent in doing protective patrols over two Sunderlands in Calafrana Bay. However the boys took time off to get mixed up with one bombing raid and F/Sgt Yarra destroyed an ME 109. The other boys could not get amongst the Jerries so we had to be content with one victory for the day.

11.7.1942.
F/Sgt Yarra DFM
  1 ME 109F DESTROYED

Sunday 12 July

"B" Flight were on readiness at dawn this morning and were scrambled after a plot of 17+, which later developed into a 30+. The two sections got mixed up with the fighter escort and F/Lt Charney destroyed one Macchi 202. Squadron Leader New damaged another Macchi 202. Sgt Russel squirted at some more Italian fighters but did not observe any results. The boys did two more scrambles during the day but could not contact anything except a few seagulls.

12.7.1942.
F/LT Charney: 1 MC 202 Destroyed
S/Ldr New: 1 MC 202 Damaged.

Monday 13 July

Six of the boys were stood down from flying to day preparatory to going back to England, which produced great rejoicing amongst said pilots. They were P/O Broad, F/Sgt Sim, F/Sgt Parker, F/Sgt Yarra DFM, Sgt Dodd and F/Sgt Ferraby.

However the rest of the Squadron carried on. "B" Flight went up on one scramble after the usual early morning bombing raid. The boys had a little trouble with the fighter escort and only Sgt Drew managed to get in to the JU 88s, damaging one severely. Sgt Mahar squirted at various Jerries but did not claim. "A" Flight took over at 1 o'clock but only did a search and one scramble. The search, which was for a pilot from Ta Kali, was successful, but the scramble was not, owing to the fact that the Jerry fighter sweep did not cross the coast.

Tuesday 14 July
"A" Flight took the early readiness to day. They also took a pretty solid crack at the Jerry raid which came in about nine o'clock. The boys intercepted perfectly and completely disorganised the "gaggle" of JU 88s. P/O "Cy" King damaged one JU 88, Sgt Mitchell damaged a JU 88 and Sgt Reid also damaged one of the big jobs. Sgt MacNamara <u>Probably</u> destroyed a JU 88. F/O Stoop was shot down by a flock of ME 109s and had to bale out. Unfortunately he was burned about the face, but should be back on flying in a few weeks.

F/Lt Halford and P/O Baril carried out a very efficient search for F/O Stoop, finding him some 15 miles east of Calafrana.

This is the last entry by Flight Sergeant Yarra. Alongside the next entry is written: <u>As recorded by P/O Sherlock</u> *– F.J. Sherlock came from Canada.*

"B" Flight took over at 1:00 p.m. and spent a very enjoyable afternoon sitting in dispersal thinking of Jerry who spent all the afternoon sunbathing in Sicily with bags of feminine company.

14/7/42
P/O King   – 1 JU88 damaged
Sgt Mitchell   – 1 JU88   „
Sgt Reid   1 JU88   „
F/Sgt MacNamara – 1 JU88 probable.

F/O Stoop shot down and picked up by HSL.

Recent RAF losses were alleviated on the 15th when the Eagle *arrived off Malta with thirty-one Spitfires.*

Wednesday 15 July
Today some new Spits arrived, being ably led by our new "Flight Loot" – J.F. Lambert. They are certainly a very welcome addition to our "clapped-out" VCs which have done noble work. There were no scrambles today by 185.

Thursday 16 July

"A" Flight took over at dawn and had an early scramble to shake the cobwebs loose, but failed to contact the wily Hun – supposedly 12+. Another scramble proved to be a stooge job. "B" Flight took over at noon but it proved to be a quiet afternoon and no a/c left the ground at Hal Far.

Friday 17 July

B Flight took over and were scrambled very late after 3 ME109s over 20,000′, which were picked up by "Eagle-Eye" Mahar while still 10,000′ above us but they beetled off home for breakfast of ham and eggs and waffles.

A Flight took over at noon and started out in great style, F/Lt Halford knocking down an optimistic Hun and Shorty Reid, who is now an "A" Flight type with the pretty ribbon known as the DFM under his wings, with Sgt Weaver, one of the new boys, each accounted for a 109F type. The boys also escorted the HSL who went out of their way to pick up the Jerries.

F/LT Halford – 1 ME109 destroyed ✠
F/Sgt Reid DFM 1 ME109   „   ✠
Sgt Weaver   1 ME109   „   ✠

Saturday 18 July

A Flight continued to dice with death but only spent an hour chasing unobtrusive Huns, who appear to like the climate over our Isle, but unfortunately the Huns kept out of their way, to return some other time.

B Flight kept the chairs occupied in dispersal all afternoon – and very nice, too.

Sunday 19 July

B Flight continued to sit around and three brave types, including the CO, "volunteered" to do air tests. Unfortunately one of the new boys, Sgt Hartney, landed down wind and crashed into "E" Pen, knocking himself out, and fracturing his skull. The Doctor, however was quite reassuring in that Sgt Hartney would soon be up and around again.

A Flight took over at noon but nothing turned up for 185.

Monday 20 July

A Flight was still on at dawn but was scrambled on a plot which did not materialize, the boys gnashing their teeth at being so rudely disturbed for nothing.

B Flight kindly turned up at noon to take over from A Flight and were scrambled almost immediately for a large plot. Blue Section, led by F/Lt Lambert, attacked 7 JU88s escorted by about 20 109s and 202s.

Unfortunately Sgt Russel, a Canadian ~~of the better~~ as all Cans a good type was shot down and killed. F/Lt Lambert, also a Canadian, was shot down but bailed out, although wounded, and was picked up by a minesweeper. The only redeeming feature was that "Ginger" Parker got a 109F. P/O Sherlock got very frightened. The boys put up a continuous search for "Russ" but unfortunately nothing was sighted. The CO and P/O Sherlock were subsequently scrambled to cover the minesweeper but nothing of any importance occurred.

20/7/42
Sgt Parker – 1 ME109F Destroyed. ✠

On the 21st twenty-eight more Spitfires were delivered courtesy once again of HMS Eagle. Subsequently, 1435 Flight, previously rendered ineffective as a Hurricane unit, was re-formed as a Spitfire squadron. 229 Squadron was also reconstituted with pilots and Spitfires of 603 Squadron after it ceased to operate as a Malta-based unit.

Tuesday 21 July
Black Section, under the leadership of the "Black Knight of Malta" (F/Lt Charney) were scrambled after 6+ 109s who apparently were trying to intercept a new bunch of Spits. However the "Red Knight of Malta" (Buzz Ogilvie) capably led the sprogs in without loss and in record time. There were two more scrambles of two sections of two, who covered the minesweepers.
A Flight took over at noon but were not scrambled.

Wednesday 22 July
A Flight continued on duty and were scrambled after a plot of +15. We announce, and I speak for every pilot of 185, with deepest regret, that one of the ablest, keenest and most popular pilots on the Island, F/Sgt "Shorty" Reid DFM, a Canadian, is missing from this scramble. Sgt Weaver maintained his good work, this time shooting down two nasty ME109Fs.
B Flight took over at noon and continued to search in the hope of finding Shorty but with no success. The Black Knight (F/Lt Charney) covered the minesweepers and succeeded in getting bounced, Sgt Mahar being the unlucky individual. However, Eric brought his kite back OK and landed it without further damage.

22-7-42
Sgt Weaver – 2 ME109s destroyed. ✠ ✠

Thursday 23 July
B Flight were scrambled before they were awake after 3+ 109s but no

interception took place. The Black Knight covered the minesweepers without an incident.

A Flight took over at noon and went to town on a plot of 15+ – Sgt Mitchell, an Aussie, shooting down an Itie in a MC202, and Sgt Weaver scoring another double – 2 ME109s again – a really excellent record.

In the morning, P/O Dave Kent, while practising in a Hurricane for bombing Sicily, had the engine pack up on him on a take-off and crashed into the wrecked hangar and was unfortunately killed. Dave was a very keen type and we cannot afford to lose men like him.

Sgt Mitchell – 1 MC202 Destroyed ✠
Sgt Weaver – 1 ME109F   „   ✠
　　　　　　　1 ME109F   „   ✠

Friday 24 July

A Flight continued the good work and got well and truly into a gaggle of JU88s, everyone squirting madly. P/O "Cy" King, "Mitch", "Tony" Drew and Sgt Weaver each claiming ½ a JU88 – the two former damaged, and the latter two, destroyed. Len Reid, an Aussie, wanted to be different and destroyed an 88 by himself. Jimmy Guthrie also damaged an 88. Lord Gort VC and the AOC personally congratulated each of the boys on their very fine effort.

P/O King   – ½ JU88 ⎱ damaged
Sgt Mitchell – ½ JU88 ⎰   „
Sgt Reid   – 1 JU88 destroyed ✠
Sgt Drew   – ½ JU88 ⎱   „   ✠
Sgt Weaver   – ½ JU88 ⎰   „
P/O Guthrie – 1 JU88 – damaged.

Saturday 25 July

A stand-down today so Monico's did a little extra business in the way of JCs [presumably John Collins (cocktail)].

Sunday 26 July

The Black Knight led B Flight into the azure blue after some dirty JU88s and their little brothers – ME109s. The Red Knight, however, was first to attack, he and Joe Sherlock squirting at JU88s while F/SGT Andy Andrews went into the fighters alone, splitting them enough for the other two to get in and out again. However, the shooting was bloody awful on both sides and nobody got hurt.

A Flight took over at noon and the intrepid Cy King took the flight into the air against 24+ of our hostile neighbors. However, nobody intercepted nothing, as Shakespeare would say, and all a/c returned safely.

Monday 27 July

P/O Cy King again led the A Flight types into battle and this time P/O Jimmy Guthrie got himself a nice little ME109F, replete with dirty black crosses and all. A little later they took the air again but after chasing the usual squadrons of SFA around they inflated.

B Flight had 2 scrambles of two a/c, but all they got was very browned-off.

Tuesday 28 July

B Flight were scrambled after a plot of 18+ but made no contact with the Hun. However, in a late scramble F/Sgt Andrews mixed it up with a gang of 109s, two of whom bit large rings out of their dinghy.

28-7-42
F/SGT Andrews – 2 109s damaged.

A Flight took over at noon and continued to increase the Jerries' ring-twitch. P/O Baril and P/O Jimmy Guthrie shared a JU88 with another squadron. Hal Far was bombed and the boys landed at Luqa, leaving the kites there all night.

28/7/42 –
P/O Baril }
P/O Guthrie } ½ JU88 destroyed ✠

Wednesday 29 July

A Flight returned to Hal Far and shortly after landing were scrambled after a plot of 24+ consisting of 8 JU88s and fighter escort. Unfortunately no contact was made.

B Flight then took over and were scrambled twice after ME109Fs but after dashing around the ozone, the Black Knight failed to make contact with Joe Kesselring's band of buggers and nothing happened. Tomorrow being a stand-down, everybody staggered over to the Sgts mess for a few noggins.

Thursday 30 July

185 Squadron U/S on account of they all have headaches. A stand-down. F/O Bruce carried out some rather necessary air-tests.

Friday 31 July

Black Section took the air first at 6:00 am but found bags of SFA in echelon, weaving like hell. P/O Stenborg of A Flight thoroughly cheesed off the B Flight types by going up on a test flight and shooting down 1 of 3 ME109s he found.

1. The nucleus of 185 Squadron was created with pilots of 261 Squadron. This included the original squadron diarist, Pilot Officer H. W. 'Chubby' Eliot, shown here shortly before he joined the new unit.

2. 15 August 1941. Initially the composition of 185 Squadron was distinctly British. Back, L–R: Pilot Officer Philip M. Allardice, Sergeants Arnold W. Jolly, T.E.J. Ream, C.S. Hunton, Johnny Alderson, A.J. 'Jimmy' Forth, Ernest G. Knight, Brian Hayes and Horsey. Middle, L–R: Pilot Officer R.M. Oliver, Sergeant Trevor H. Bates, Pilot Officer G.G. 'Gay' Bailey, Sergeants R.A. 'Dicky' Cousens, Peter Lillywhite and J.R. Sutherland, Pilot Officer A.J. 'Tony' Reeves, Sergeants W.F. Nurse and Vardy. Front, L–R: Flight Lieutenants S.A.D. Pike and Charles G. St. D. Jeffries, Squadron Leader P.W.O. 'Boy' Mould, Flight Lieutenant N.P.W. 'Pat' Hancock and Pilot Officer Peter D. Thompson (squadron diarist, August to 25 December 1941).

3. Hawker Hurricane Z2421 after Sergeant H. 'Stanley' Burton's flying accident on 11 June 1941.

4. Italian MAS 452 which was 'captured' by Pilot Officer Denis Winton in unusual circumstances on 26 July 1941.

5.   Some pilots of 'B' Flight in autumn 1941. Back, L–R: Flying Officer G.G. 'Gay' Bailey, Sergeant P. Lillywhite, Sergeant F.G. Sheppard (Australia). Front, L–R: Sergeant J. Alderson, Sergeant Arnold W. Jolly, Flight Lieutenant S.A.D. Pike, Sergeant W.F. Nurse, Sergeant J. Westcott.

6.   Burnt-out Junkers Ju 88 of 2./K.Gr. 806 after it was shot down on 3 January 1942. Among those involved in bringing down this aircraft was Canadian Sergeant Garth E. Horricks, whose Hurricane received ten bullet holes from the resolute German rear-gunner.

7.   9 March 1942. A Ju 88 of II./K.G. 77 burns moments after crashing at Hal Far. Note the descending parachute of one of the crew.

8.   Bomb damage at Hal Far.

9, 10. The officers' mess at Hal Far before and after it was bombed.

11. Line-up of 185 Squadron Hurricanes.

12. Remains of a Hurricane in a bombed-out hangar.

13. Hurricane Z4941 landing at Hal Far. This particular aircraft was operational with both the RAF and the Royal Navy before it was struck off charge at the end of April 1945.

15. Among those who lost their lives in 185 Squadron were fighter pilots from the United Kingdom, Australia, New Zealand, Canada and the United States. On 28 April 1942 Canadian Flight Sergeant J.W.S. 'Jack' Fletcher baled out of his Hurricane only for his parachute to stream over the tail before tearing free and causing him to fall to his death.

14. Spring 1942. Squadron Leader Edward B. Mortimer-Rose manning twin Browning machine guns at an airfield defence post.

16. SNCOs J.W. 'Slim' Yarra (Australia) and, on his left, C.E. 'Ernie' Broad (UK). Yarra was the squadron diarist for three and half months, until 14 July 1942.

17. Pilot Officers Philip Wigley (left) and Ron Noble both served in 605 Squadron before it was amalgamated with 185.

18.   After Hauptmann Karl-Heinz Krahl was shot down and killed by ground fire on
14 April 1942 a wing section was recovered from the wreckage of his Messerschmitt
Bf 109. This photograph, taken shortly afterwards, reflects the cosmopolitan make-up of
185 Squadron at the time. L–R: Sergeant R.J. 'Bob' Sim (New Zealand), Sergeant J.W. 'Slim'
Yarra (Australia), Pilot Officer J.I. 'Skip' McKay (Canada) and Pilot Officer Ron Noble (UK).

19.   May 1942. Enjoying a day off at
the Dragunara Palace, St Julians. L–R:
Pilot Officer D.E. Llewellyn (soon to
join 601 Squadron in the Middle East)
and Canadians Pilot Officers A.A. 'Andy'
McNaughton and J.F. 'Jimmy' Lambert.
McNaughton was killed within a month of
arriving at Malta.

20.   Australian Sergeant J. L. 'Tony' Boyd
who was shot down on 14 May 1942 and
was still in his Spitfire when it crashed and
exploded at Luqa aerodrome.

21.   Flight Sergeant Haydn 'Vic' Haggas (left) from the UK was lost on 7 July 1942; New Zealander Flight Sergeant 'Pop' Conway crash landed and was seriously injured on 21 June.

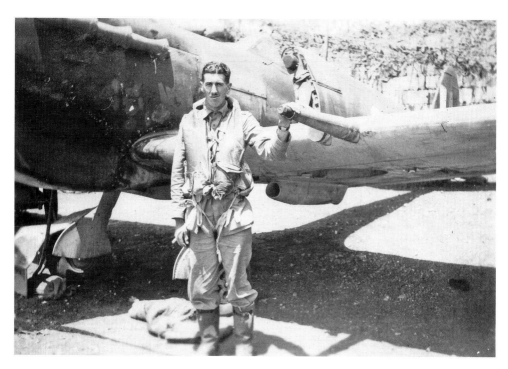

22.   New Zealander Squadron Leader K.A. 'Lawrie' Lawrence.

23, 24. Two experienced fighter pilots who arrived as flight commanders from 249 Squadron: Flight Lieutenant Ronald West from Scotland seen with his ground crew in mid 1942, and Greek-Rhodesian Flight Lieutenant John A. Plagis.

25. Ground crew of Supermarine Spitfire 'S' in mid 1942.

26. Crew of *'B' for Beer.*

27. Wing Commander H.L. Dawson (New Zealand) and others shelter during a raid.

28. 'A' Flight, mid 1942. Sitting on aircraft nose: Flight Sergeant J.W. 'Slim' Yarra (Australia); on wing: Flight Sergeant Peter C. Terry (UK); standing L–R: Pilot Officer J.W.P. 'Paul' Baril (Canada), Flying Officer J.R. Stoop, Sergeant L.S. 'Len' Reid (Australia), Pilot Officer C.E. 'Ernie' Broad (UK), Flight Sergeant M.W. 'Tex' Vineyard (USA), Pilot Officer C.A. 'Cy' King (Canada), Flight Sergeant Haydn 'Vic' Haggas (UK), Flying Officer Jones (adjutant), Squadron Leader K.A. 'Lawrie' Lawrence (New Zealand), Flight Lieutenant Ron West (UK), Flight Sergeant R.J. 'Bob' Sim (New Zealand), Flight Sergeant J.E. 'Mac' MacNamara (Canada), probably Pilot Officer James (Rhodesia), Sergeant K.R. 'Ken' Mitchell (Australia), Pilot Officer Gray Stenborg (New Zealand).

29.   Spitfire GL-N (BR305) in which Canadian Sergeant D.J. 'Danny' Hartney was injured when he crashed into the wall of a blast pen on 19 July 1942. Hartney returned to the squadron in October, but died due to ill health three months later.

30.   185 Squadron baseball team, winter 1943. Standing: Pilot Officer S.S. 'Bill' Williams (New Zealand), Sergeant W.A. 'Al' Laing (Canada), Flight Sergeant John N. 'Dusty' Miller (Canada), Pilot Officer Al Eckert (USA) and, behind, Flying Officer E.G. 'Gordon' Lapp (Canada), Sergeant James Tarbuck (UK), Sergeant George F. Mercer (Canada), Squadron Leader J.D. Ashton (UK), Flight Lieutenant Harold C. Knight (South Africa), Flying Officer Len Cheek (UK), Sergeant G.D. 'Jerry' Billing (Canada). Kneeling: Flight Sergeant Cornelius J. Carmody (Canada), Sergeant J.M. Maffre (Canada), Sergeant George C. Warcup (Canada), Flight Sergeant R.A.G. 'Georges' Nadon (Canada), Flight Sergeant D.J. McLaren (Canada), Sergeant J. Thorogood (UK).

31. Pilots of 'A' Flight, probably late March 1943. L–R: Sergeant William A. Cruickshank (UK), Flight Sergeant Robert M. 'Zip' Zobell (Canada), Pilot Officer J.M. 'Matt' Reid (Canada), Pilot Officer James Tarbuck (UK), Flight Sergeant Al Sinclair (Canada), Flight Lieutenant Harold C. Knight (South Africa), Flight Sergeant R.A.G. 'Georges' Nadon (Canada), Pilot Officer C.J. Webster (Canada), Flying Officer E.G. 'Gordon' Lapp (Canada), Sergeant J. Thorogood (UK).

32. Wrapped in a blanket, Canadian Flight Sergeant George Mercer about to step ashore at St Paul's Bay after being rescued by HSL 107 on 6 May 1943.

33.   Clipped-wing Spitfire Mk LF IX (ML404) landing at Pontedera, Italy, in 1945.

34.   Campo Formido, Italy, 4 June 1945. Front: unidentified except for Flight Sergeants George Y. 'Jock' Nisbet and K.R. 'Piggy' Pickersgill (both sitting with arms folded). Standing, L–R: Warrant Officer J.T. 'Squire' Lynch, Flight Lieutenant G.A. Hurn (adjutant), Squadron Leader M.V. Christopherson, unidentified, Pilot Officer L. 'Blondie' Liversidge, Flying Officer L.W.A. 'Bill' Stretch, next two unidentified with Flying Officer D.W. 'Mac' McFarlane and Flying Officer C.E. 'Brownie' Brown standing behind. Back: unidentified except for Pilot Officer Douglas S. Weedon who is third from left.

A Flight took over at noon and were very unfortunate. Ops had their finger well and truly inserted and vectored the boys under a gaggle of ME109s who took advantage of their position and did the "bounce perfect" act. Doc Livingstone was shot down, bailing out and being picked up very quickly out of the drink. Fortunately he was uninjured. F/O Bruce, however, had a rather more unfortunate experience, spending 17 hours in a dinghy, coming ashore in the early hours of the morning. He was uninjured but very stiff and swollen. The boys searched all p.m. for him but although he saw them they could not locate him.

So endeth the Month of July/42.

31-7-42
P/O Stenborg DFC 1 ME109F destroyed ✠

A revised flights list appears on the facing page of the original diary and is reproduced below.

No 185 SQUADRON. JULY 31/42.

S/LDR NEW – C/O RAF (HAWK-EYE)

"B" FLIGHT		"A" FLIGHT.	
F/LT Ken Charney RAF (THE BLACK KNIGHT)		P/O Cy King (CY)	RCAF
		P/O Guthrie (JIMMIE)	RAF
P/O Ogilvie (Buzz) RCAF (THE RED KNIGHT)		P/O Baril (PAUL)	RCAF
		P/O Stenborg (DFC)	
P/O Sherlock	RCAF (JO)	(STEN)	RNZAF
F/Sgt Andrews	RCAF (ANDY)	Sgt McLeod	RNZAF
Sgt Mahar	RAAF (ERIC)	Sgt Reid (LEN)	RAAF
Sgt Smith	(Rhodesia) (SMITTY)	Sgt Mitchell (MITCH)	RAAF
Sgt MacLeod	RCAF (MAC)	Sgt Drew (TONY)	RAF
Sgt Gunstone	RAF (JIMMIE)	Sgt Weaver (WEAVE)	RCAF
Sgt Walker	RAF (BILL)	Sgt Harmer (BOB)	RCAF
Sgt Forrester	(Rhodesia) (TREES)	Sgt Livingstone (DOC)	RCAF

NON-EFFECTIVE.
F/O Bruce	–	RAF
Sgt Hartney		RCAF
F/O Stoop		RAF
P/O Ferraby		RAF
F/LT LAMBERT		RCAF

On 1 August another writer assumed the duty of squadron diarist. Although unidentified, the spelling indicates that he was either American or Canadian.

Saturday 1 August

And with the start of the month we get a new, albeit a temporary scribe, who I fear will lack greatly in literary style. Early in the morning, at 06:10 Sgt Drew led a section of "A" Flight on a search for F/O Bruce before we heard he had arisen from the briny deep demanding a drink. Later, at 09:30, after a hasty if not tasty breakfast in dispersal, P/O Guthrie led six of "A" Flight's valiants up toward a plot of 15+ but nothing came of it. The rest of the morning was spent doing air-tests. In the afternoon P/O Ogilvie led a scramble of one section each [of] which made no contact with our friends (?) from Sicily. The rest of the day "B" Flight spent doing air-tests.

Sunday 2 August

"B" Flight was on at dawn but spent the morning quietly playing cards. "A" Flight came on at 1:00 and promptly at 14:00 hrs were scrambled. They were vectored up under the raid and were well and truly bounced. Here I have to regretfully report that P/O Guthrie has been shot down and killed and Sgt McLeod is missing. P/O Guthrie was well liked by the squadron and altho new to us was very experienced, having done over 80 sweeps over France. We can ill afford this type of loss. P/O King then led a search for Sgt McLeod but saw nothing. Next at 16:50 Sgt Drew led a section after a plot of 3 small jobs but couldn't find them. Then Sgt Mitchell and Sgt Reid went out and had another look for Sgt McLeod but still were unable to find him. "Mac" was from NZ and altho also new to our squadron will be missed by the types for he was always smiling. In the shambles when the flight was jumped, Sgt Weaver by adroit squirting was able to poke a few holes in one of the nasty Nazis and claims a 109 probable.

2/8/42
Sgt Weaver – 1 Me 109F – Probable.

Monday 3 August

And a quiet day dawned altho the Nazi did his best by way of fighter sweeps to disturb us – "Cy" King leading two scrambles for "A" Flight which intercepted nothing, and the CO – S/Ldr New led one equally successful one for "B" Flight. These three were after fighter sweeps and there were no engagements. Sgt Gunstone must have been told that even air tests on Malta are operational – for he did an air test that lasted 40 minutes.

Tuesday 4 August

Squadron was stood down, bars all over the island were busy – Those in Sliema in particular. F/LT Charney had a slight altercation with numerous and sundry including the police and returned to B'Bugia at 05:00 in a very bedraggled condition while "Killer" Stenborg upon perceiving that the Black Knight had failed to follow his leap aboard the departing ferry boat in Sliema shouted "Women and children first" and leaped overboard in full blue. With peak cap firmly clamped on his head he paddled ashore to the delight of the watching Maltese.

Wednesday 5 August
The Red Knight of Malta, Buz Ogilvie led his gallant section out after a Blood wagon but failed to intercept it and that was all of 185's efforts for the day. The rest of the time was spent resting up after our day of rest.

Thursday 6 August
Today "A" Flight chased a plot of 109s about the sky – funny thing – the Hun was outnumbered for once – 6 Huns and 8 of 185 Squadron –. What a shame they didn't meet!

Friday 7 August
The only flying was a scramble by three aircraft of "A" Flight – they still don't know what it was they were looking for – maybe the swallows again.

Saturday 8 August
Sgt Walker – a new type – from Yorkshire – who seems to have had some experience went up on an air test. Sgt Mahar and F/Sgt Andrews went out on a search but saw nothing – not even the usual turtle dinghy. At 19:35 P/O Ogilvie and P/O Sherlock went on an "E" Boat Recco which took them within 5 miles of the coast of Sicily for 11 minutes. The whole squadron stood out in the falling dusk listening for their noise of approach. Needless to say – with such an incomparable pair, they got away with it –. Altho undercarts [i.e. undercarriages] were severely strained by the dusk landings.

Sunday 9 August
The squadron was again stood down but with the convoy "do" coming up the types for once kept fairly well away from John Barleycorn. This did not however stop the other two Malta pastimes of swimming and attempted seduction of women.

Monday 10 August
Action again today, "B" Flight led by the intrepid Black Knight was well and truly bounced in a turn by some 109s they had already seen. Sgt Mahar, who was shot up, insists that there were at least 20 or 30 of them.

Sgt Walker tried out his guns on an obliging Hun who posed momentarily as a target. However he was a bit out of practice and the Hun went home. "Johnny" Sherlock had fun and games with a pair of 109s up north of Grand Harbor but his shootin eye was out too so he didn't get anything. Sgt Mahar went down to take a Hun off Johnny's tail and his port cannon fired 2 shots and the s'board didn't fire at all. He used up his MG on him and then decided to go home. A dirty great Me crept up his tail and let him have it. Eric got to Luqa only to have a bullet hole in his tyre and completely wrote off the kite on landing. However he wasn't hurt, but I bet he looks behind the next time he comes home alone.

At this point the diary is continued by another anonymous writer.

"A" Flight took over as usual and after one abortive scramble, the only action was when Capt Swales and P/O Stenborg on recco for "E" boats made mince-meat of a poor Wop pill-box on the Sicilian coast.

On 11 August thirty-seven Spitfires took off for Malta from HMS Furious *as part of Operation 'Pedestal' – the most famous of all Malta convoys. Although there was now a significant number of Spitfires on the island, the overall situation was still critical. Operation 'Pedestal' had left Scotland on 3 August on the first stage of its journey to the Mediterranean. 'Pedestal' consisted of fourteen merchantmen under Royal Navy escort. By the time the convoy reached beleaguered Malta, nine cargo vessels and four warships had been sunk. Among the five surviving merchant ships, was the Texaco oil tanker,* Ohio. *After being disabled during torpedo and bombing attacks, in which one bomber actually crashed on to her deck, the battered ship finally reached Grand Harbour lashed between two destroyers and with another secured to the stern as an emergency rudder. The date was 15 August, the Feast of the Assumption, known locally as the Feast of Saint Mary. Ever since, the Maltese have referred to Operation 'Pedestal' as* Il-Convoy ta' Santa Marija.

Tuesday 11 August
"A" Flight once again took the air after a 15+ but apart from seeing 4 Macchis who immediately turned tail, nothing materialised.

"B" Flight in the afternoon had two scrambles which turned out to be "stooges".

Wednesday 12 August
Today the squadron got its 100th victory – a poor, innocent He 111 which "Buz" Ogilvie together with Capt Swales and "Johnnie" Sherlock really "gave the works". The convoy long suspected is now almost within range and everyone is really keyed up for action. The rest of the day was

spent doing the usual "stooge" patrols.

Thursday 13 August

I am glad to say that the convoy except for one straggler is now safely in Valetta Harbour. From 10 am the boys have been doing dozens of patrols but just like the last convoy, the Huns decided that the Malta convoy patrol service was too much for them. The convoy has cost us dearly in ships including HMS Eagle but the five merchantmen which did get here are indeed a godsend. The only incident to mar a good day's work was Sgt Clewley's crash on take-off. Luckily, however, his injuries were not as bad as was feared and we all hope to see him soon.

Friday 14 August

The day started off again with patrols over the stragglers entering harbour. The Huns haven't even approached the island but we are all hoping for some excitement while the ships are being unloaded – stooges aren't really in our line.

Saturday 15 August

The Huns have actually woken up and a 20+ approached the island. The valiant "A" took to the air and Sgt Tarbuck on his first flight of this type got a Me 109 but unfortunately had to bale out owing to engine failure and had to spend a few minutes in his dinghy until being rescued by the HSL. Still a very good show.

"B" Flight spent the rest of the day patrolling the Harbour in pairs – cheap operational hours.

Sunday 16 August

Today passed quite peacefully and except for one scramble in the evening which flopped miserably, the boys spent the day sleeping in the dispersal.

Thirty-two Spitfires were launched from HMS Furious *on 17 August. Twenty-nine reached Malta. During the second half of the month, Allied attacks against Sicily increased with fighter sweeps by Spitfires, and raids by Hurri-bombers flown by Royal Naval Air Service pilots – until they were curtailed in September due to fuel shortages. During this period there was a noticeable decline in enemy air activity. Nevertheless, the Axis Command was still very much concerned about the ongoing disruption of Rommel's Mediterranean supply routes.*

Monday 17 August

Once again "A" Flight had the luck this morning when P/O Stenborg and Sgt Weaver managed to get the height on the Huns and bounced them. Weaver got two and Sten after blowing one up, was shot to pieces himself and had to bale out and take to his dinghy quite unhurt. But it was still a very good show.

"B" Flight under the CO weren't so lucky and nothing resulted from their scramble.

The above is the last entry by the present writer. His successor was Pilot Officer P.A.J. O'Brien.

The following pilots arrived from UK by carrier on the 11th and 17th of August.

Lieut Kuhlmann SAAF	11th August.
P/O Paul	killed 19/11/42
P/O O'Brien RAFVR	
Sgt Garvey NZ	
Sgt Tarbuck RAF	Died APRIL 1943. P/O.
Sgt Guy	killed 7/12/42
Sgt Vinall	killed 12/10/42 Sgt Clewley RAAF
F/O Lindsay	killed 23/10/42
F/O Woodger	Shot down POW 27/8/42	17th August
P/O Cheek	
P/O Maynard	killed 22/11/42.
Sgt Bolland	
Sgt Gore	
Sgt Swain	killed 13/9/42
Sgt Houlton	

There were no entries for the period 18 to 23 August. The squadron ORB records uneventful scrambles and/or patrols between 18 and 22 August, while the entry for the 23rd reads:

Notification has today been received from Air Ministry, that Sgt; Pilot Hayes, late member of the Squadron, and reported missing on the 21st December, 1941, is now officially presumed dead.

Monday 24 August
A Flight under G/C Churchill DSO DFC carried out an 'offensive sweep' on Sicily, the first by Spitfires from Malta. However the enemy was not sighted and no engagements took place.

Tuesday 25 August
On a scramble today Sgt Weaver had a squirt at a 109F and claimed a probable. Good show Weave!

25-8-42. Sgt Weaver DFM one ME109F PROBABLE ✠

Wednesday 26 August

S/Ldr New has left us for the Middle East and Major Swales has taken over command of the squadron. Keith Kuhlmann has taken over 'A' Flight with the rank of captain. We wish them both every success in their new posts.

B Flight, under the intrepid 'Black Knight' escorted the Navy Boys in Hurribombers, on an attack on Biscari. Hits were seen on the aerodrome and all our aircraft returned safely.

Thursday 27 August

This was a great day! A Flight took part in a Wing Sweep on three Sicilian dromes. Comiso was our target. The attack was made at sea-level and we were fortunate in catching several 88s on the circuit which were promptly dealt with. Unfortunately F/O Woodger was shot down but made a safe landing and is now a prisoner of war.

G/C Churchill was shot down by flak and killed. The success of this mission can be judged by the score on the opposite page [*see below*].

27-8-42. Major Swales.	one Ju 88 DESTROYED ✠	
Sgt Weaver DFM	⎰ one Ju 88 DESTROYED	
	one JU 88 PROBABLE	✠ ✠ ✠
	⎱ one 109 DESTROYED	
Capt Kuhlmann	one Ju 88 DESTROYED ✠	
W/C Thompson DFC	one Ju 88 PROBABLE ✠	
Sgt Reid	one Ju 88 DESTROYED ✠	
F/LT Charney	one Ju 88 PROBABLE ✠	
	one Ju 88 DAMAGED ✠	
F/Sgt Mitchell	one Ju 88 PROBABLE ✠	

F/O Woodger shot down (POW)

The above is the last entry for August 1942. The squadron ORB records uneventful scrambles on 28 and 29 August and on the 30th a sweep over Sicily by ten aircraft led by Major C.J.O. Swales. There was another scramble, again with no claims, on the 31st. Also recorded on this date is the following:

The death of S/L PD Chaffe, Late Sqdn Commdr. reported missing of the 22nd Feb. 1942, is officially presumed by A.M. The body of P/O OO. Ormrod DFC late member of the Squadron was today discovered at Cospicua. P/O Ormrod was reported missing on 22nd April, 1942. He was buried at the R.N. Capuccini Cemetery.

September 1942.

This month a considerable number of our 'old faithfuls' left for UK.
viz. Buzz Ogilvie
    Johnny Sherlock
    Cy King
    Paul Baril
    Dutch Stenborg DFC
    Tony Drew (now P/O)
    Andrews (now P/O)
    Jimmy Lambert and P/O Ferraby (out of hospital)
Others went to the ME
    F/O Bruce
    Bob Harmer
    Doc Livingstone.

This was more or less a month of peace and quiet. Both flights carried out a considerable number of 'offensive sweeps' over Sicily but only on one occasion did the enemy attempt to interfere. On this occasion about half a dozen Macchi 202s were run into and Keith Kuhlmann promptly shot one down. Weave went down after the others and the last we saw of him was sitting on the tail of a Macchi (or ME 109) which was going down almost vertically. The other 'Itis' had put their noses down and beat a hasty retreat. As the flight made for home, Weave called up on the R/T and told us that he was on fire and was going to land on the beach – he also mentioned something about stealing a rowing boat and coming back as soon as possible. He claimed an ~~109~~ enemy a/c destroyed. The Italian Radio next day said that their "chasers" had forced a British aircraft to land and that the pilot, an American had been taken prisoner. They also announced the loss of two Italian aircraft.

On the 5th Ken Charney intercepted some Italians over Malta and shot a Macchi 202 down.

High flying fighter sweeps were carried out almost every day this month by the axis. They usually came in at about 28–30,000 feet flying at about 600 mph (?) and out again with their noses well down. Needless to say engagements were few and far between but the boys got quite an amount of 'practice' flying in. The intrepid pilots of B Flight did a 'recco' of Lampedusa and met with quite a dose of 'hot flak' so they didn't hang around too long.

We regret that Sgt Swain was killed in an accident on the 13th. He was doing a practice dog fight and spun in.

5-9-42 F/LT Charney.   one Macchi 202 destroyed ⊕

9-9-42. Capt Kuhlmann   one Macchi 202 destroyed ⊕
        Sgt Weaver DFM one Macchi 202 destroyed ⊕
        Weaver shot down (P/o war.)

Facing page:

No 185 Squadron   October 1942

Major Swales (SAAF)

'A' Flight	'B' Flight
Capt Kuhlmann	F/LT Charney
P/O Reid	F/O Lindsay † KILLED
P/O Cheek	P/O Park. † KILLED
P/O O'Brien	P/O Maynard † KILLED
F/Sgt Mitchell	F/Sgt Mahar
F/Sgt Gore	Sgt Smith
Sgt Gunstone	Sgt Bolland
Sgt Tarbuck	Sgt Garvey
Sgt Vinall † KILLED.	Sgt McLeod [sic] † KILLED.
Sgt Walker	F/Sgt Hartney
	Sgt Guy † KILLED.
	Sgt Houlton

By October the Luftwaffe *had gathered a formidable force in Sicily. The final Italo–German offensive against Malta began early on the 11th. Raids were almost invariably carried out by small formations of bombers heavily escorted by fighters. After seven days, during which both sides suffered substantial losses, the enemy changed tactics, resorting instead to attacks by fighters and fighter-bombers. But at last it was becoming increasingly clear that Hitler had lost the opportunity of ever defeating Malta.*

October 1942.

This month started as September finished with the enemy doing high flying fighter sweeps almost three or 4 times a day. On the 10th the squadron was released and the Hun naturally enough chose this day to start his blitz tactics once more. In the afternoon he attacked with 88s and bombs were dropped on Gozo. Next morning B Flight engaged some 109s without any results. In the afternoon A Flight opened the scoring with 3, 109s destroyed. W/C Thompson, P/O Len Reid and Les Gore got one each. Good show boys!

11-10-42. W/C Thompson DFC one ME 109 destroyed ⚡
          P/O L. Reid   one ME 109 destroyed ⚡

Sgt Gore   one ME 109 destroyed ✠

Monday 12 October
A Flight were scrambled for a 40+ and Keith destroyed a 109F. Vinall damaged an 88. One section did an air sea rescue patrol and sighted 3 dinghies (2 Jerries and 1 Spit).

A third scramble for 27+ came shortly afterwards and W/Co damaged a 109F, and Len Reid damaged an 88. Unfortunately Sgt Vinall was shot down and his body was washed ashore at Dingli later on in the day.

B Flight were scrambled twice in the afternoon but without any results.

12-10-42 Capt Kuhlmann   one ME 109 destroyed ✠
         Sgt Vinall   one Ju 88 damaged   ✠
         W/C Thompson DFC   one ME 109 damaged   ✠
         P/O Reid   one Ju 88 damaged   ✠

  Sgt Vinall shot down (killed).

Tuesday 13 October
A 40+ plot was intercepted by B Flight this morning and Ken Charney got a probable 109, Major Swales damaged a 109, P/O Maynard damaged an 88 and a 109, and Eric Mahar damaged an 88. A scramble for 36+ followed and Major Swales got a probable 88. Sgt MacLeod missing.

13-10-42 F/LT Charney one ME 109 probable   ✠
         P/O Maynard   one ME 109 damaged   ✠
                       one Ju 88 damaged   ✠
         Major Swales one ME 109 damaged   ✠
                       one Ju 88 probable   ✠
         F/Sgt Mahar   one Ju 88 damaged   ✠

  Sgt MacLeod missing (killed)

Wednesday 14 October
'A' Flight scrambled to intercept a 40+. Some other Spits jumped them over the island and the sections split up. (Finger trouble?) W/C Thompson damaged a 109 and squirted at a Macchi but did not claim for the latter. Len Reid claimed a 109 damaged as did P/O O'Brien (humble self).

Later we were again scrambled to meet a 50+ but once again we were split up, by 109s (this time). However the results this time were very good (see opp. page) *[below]*.

In the afternoon Sgt Guy got a 109 probable and F/Sgt Tubby Mahar destroyed an 88.

14-10-42

W/C Thompson	one Ju 88 destroyed	⚡
P/O L. Reid	one ME 109 destroyed	⚡
	one Ju 88 damaged	⚡
Capt Kuhlmann	one ME 109 destroyed	⚡
P/O Len Cheek	one Ju 88 damaged	⚡
	one Ju 88 probable	⚡
Sgt Tarbuck	one ME 109 damaged	⚡
	one Ju 88 damaged	⚡
P/O O'Brien	one ME 109 damaged	⚡

Thursday 15 October

'B' Flight were scrambled for a 36+ this morning <u>but the bombers did not come in.</u> It seems as if the Hun is weakening now.

One section was scrambled for a 3+ and surprised some Macchis. Tubby Mahar destroyed a 202 and Major Swales and Sgt Garvey damaged one each. 'Black Knight' Charney destroyed a 202 which was out with some others as escort to a blood wagon. Ken seems to hypnotise these Itis.

In the afternoon, Len Cheek destroyed an 88 and Tarbuck damaged a 109F.

15-10-42. F/Sgt Mahar	one Macchi 202 destroyed				⊕
Major Swales	"	"	"	damaged	⊕
Sgt Garvey	"	"	"	damaged	⊕
F/LT Charney	"	"	"	destroyed	⊕
P/O Cheek	one Ju 88 destroyed				⚡
Sgt Tarbuck	one ME 109 damaged				⚡

Friday 16 October

'A' Flight scrambled for a 70+ and intercepted them north of the Grand Harbour. The squadron dived on the 88s which were about 5,000 feet below and forced them to jettison their bombs in the sea. They turned round and fled for home. Sgt Gore shot a 109 off the Wing Co's tail and damaged it. Len Reid got a probable 88, Keith Kuhlmann damaged an 88 and O'Brien also. We were travelling at such a hell of a speed that we nearly all blacked out and got split up. Sgt Tarbuck damaged a 109 also but did not claim.

Scrambled again a few minutes later but plot did not materialize. As we were refuelling the crafty Hun sent over some 88s and caught us in our pens. A very comical sight was the Wing Co and Keith with their heads tucked under a dirty bit of netting hiding from the crackerjacks like a couple of ostriches.

The Wing Co's section was scrambled shortly afterwards but the plot faded and it was suspected of being a blood wagon party.

And yet another scramble and once more the bombers turned back before reaching the island.

16-10-42. P/O Len Reid   one Ju 88 probable
        P/O O'Brien   one Ju 88 damaged
        Capt Kuhlmann one Ju 88 damaged
        Sgt Gore.   one ME 109 damaged

Saturday 17 October

B Flight were scrambled this morning for a 30+ and Ken Charney gave a hearty squirt at a Macchi 202 and damaged it. They were again scrambled and this time Ken got an 88 destroyed and Bob Park damaged 2 JU 88s and one 109F. Sgt Smith also damaged a 109F. Sgt Garvey however was shot up and crashed just off the drome. The aircraft caught fire but thanks to the prompt action of the Wingco and F/O Lindsay, Garvey was brought clear in time. Fortunately he was not seriously injured and should be with us again in a few weeks. We must congratulate the W/Co and F/O Lindsay on a very good show!

Later in the afternoon A Flight were scrambled for a 36+, which turned out to be some 109 bombers escorted by fighters. No engagement took place as they were flying "balls out" and they dropped their bombs or rather jettisoned them and went out at sea level. The Wingco had to suffer the indignity of landing with his wheels up as his undercarriage would not come down.

The following tally and subsequent entries are written in another hand:

17.10.42. F/Lt Ken Charney. 1 Mc 202 damaged ⊕
                        1 Ju 88 damaged   卐
        P/O Bob Park.   1 Ju 88 damaged   卐
                        1 Me 109 damaged 卐
        Sgt Smith.   1 Ju 88 damaged   卐

Sunday 18 October

Today we started fairly early 50+ turned up soon after 7 o'clock. A Flight was scrambled and jumped by 6 – 109s but got away with it OK. Len Reid got a probable. Again at 10 o'clock 35+ came in but although A Flight were up in good time no E/a were seen. At a quarter to four 75+ E/a came in and B Flight were sent up far too late. Some E/a were seen and chased but they had height advantage and were able to beat it home.

18.10.42. P/O Len Reid. 1. Me 109 probable 卐

Monday 19 October

Jerry started off on us this morning. 109 Bombers let us have the benefit of their presence at half past six. Two Hurrys were damaged otherwise all well. At a quarter to eight "B" Flight at 20,000′ saw 6 – 109s 8000′ above them south of the Island but could not get near them. The same thing happened at 10 o'clock when 15 E/a were seen but couldn't be got at. "A" Flight got to work soon after midday when they managed to get among 20 bomber fighters and fighters 5 miles north of the Island. Keith Kuhlmann and Sgt Gunstone each managed to damage a 109. Again at 5 o'clock E/a were seen but no getting them to fight.

19.10.42. Capt Keith Kuhlmann 1 Me 109 damaged ✠
         Sgt Gunstone   1 Me 109 damaged ✠

Attached is a flights list compiled by Pilot Officer O'Brien.

<u>185 Squadron Pilots.</u>   19/X/42.
                                                    23A

'A' Flight	'B' Flight
Capt Kuhlmann	F/LT Charney UK
P/O O'Brien	F/O Lindsay ×
P/O Cheek.	P/O Park ×
P/O Lapp	P/O Maynard ×
P/O Reid.	
F/Sgt Mitchell UK	F/Sgt Mahar UK
Sgt Gunstone UK	Sgt Smith P/O ME
Sgt Walker B [remainder unreadable]	Sgt Guy ×
Sgt Tarbuck	Sgt Bolland √
F/Sgt Gore	Sgt Hartney √
	Sgt Saunders ×
	U/S Sgt Garvey √
U/S Sgt Forrester.	Sgt Houlton. ME

Tuesday 20 October

20th October was a very quiet day. There were only three raids during the day but nothing happened. Sgt Saunders and P/O Lapp arrived.

Wednesday 21 October

No flying at all. Sgts Mahar, and Mitchell left and Sgt Houlton arrived.

Thursday 22 October

"B" Flight were up for half an hour on a 15+ but saw nothing, but at half past eleven 109s dive bombed the aerodrome. 60+ turned up in the afternoon for "A" Flight but again no luck.

Friday 23 October

Two quick fighter bomber raids this morning. "B" Flight got in amongst 109s over Dingli, Ken Charney damaged one and Sgt Saunders destroyed another *[but]* unfortunately F/O Lindsay was shot down and killed. "A" Flight had a stooge patrol in the afternoon but nothing turned up.

23.10.42. F/L Ken Charney. 1 Me 109 damaged ✠
          Sgt Saunders   1 Me 109 destroyed ✠

      F/O Lindsay. shot down (Killed).

Saturday 24 October

"A" Flight had a quiet morning, one section being up for a 20+ but they would not mix it. "B" Flight were up at one o'clock for a 15+. 10 were seen heading Northwards over Dingli but too far away to catch. Soon after this they were jumped by 109s and Sgt Saunders was shot down. F/S Zobell and Sgts Laing[,] Dunning and Harwood arrived.

24.10.42. Sgt Saunders. shot down (Killed).

Sunday 25 October

Both Flights each had one sortie today but nothing happened.

Monday 26 October

"A" Flight had a chase with 8 – 109s but could not get them to fight while in the afternoon 40+ fighter and fighter bombers dropped bombs on Birzebbugia. "B" Flight were airborne but no luck. Sgt Smith got his Commission through. F/O Knight, P/Os Reid, Williams and Eckert arrived.

Tuesday 27 October

Only one patrol during the day. Nothing doing.

Wednesday 28 October

"A" Flight again had an early chase when they went 20 miles North of the Island with no result, while just after midday "B" Flight saw 2 109s in the distance.

On 29 October HMS Furious *launched another batch of Spitfires from a departure point west of Malta. All twenty-nine aircraft reached their destination. Meanwhile, in Egypt, a successful Allied offensive at El-*

Alamein was followed, on 8 November, by Anglo–American landings in French North Africa, prompting the diversion of Axis resources in Sicily to these battle fronts. For a while, attacks on Malta continued, but never with the same tenacity as before.

Thursday 29 October

Another stooge day. Two patrols were done in the morning by "B" Flight but no E/a crossed the coast. F/Ss Vance and Miller, Sgts Billing and Thorogood arrived.

Friday 30 October

A little attack today "B" Flight did a recce of Pachino and Scalambria. No E/a seen.

This last week has been dull.

Saturday 31 October

1 Section "B" Flight did another recco this morning in the same area as last night. Very uneventful. "A" Flight did a stooge patrol in the afternoon. P/O L.S. Reid left.

October has seen the Hun beaten in his second attempt to put Malta off the map. From the 11th to the 18th 88s escorted by fighters made heavy attacks, by the later date we had shot down 40 bombers and 40 fighters. From the 18th to the 28th fighter bombers on tip and run raids made things unpleasant, but even these failed and the last two days of the month were raid free.

The main problem now was the shortage of provisions, although the situation was alleviated somewhat by supply runs undertaken by individual ships and submarines. It was not until 20 November 1942 that the siege was finally lifted with the arrival of all four merchantmen during Operation 'Stoneage'.

Following the October Blitz, Axis efforts to neutralise Malta were dramatically scaled down and Malta-based aircraft were able to take the battle to the enemy. Offensive sorties clearly lacked the heady excitement of defensive operations, however, and this is reflected in the sometimes all too brief entries that follow. Often, diarists neglected altogether to record events.

November 1942.

The first three days saw a recurrence of the tip and run raids. On November 2nd a section up on a training flight were jumped by 109s [but] luckily [there were] no casualties. November 3rd bombs were dropped on the a/d and destroyed a Spit. "A" Flight were up and Sgt Gunstone got a Mc 202. On the 3rd Major Swales left [with] the new CO S/L White taking over on the 4th. F/L Atkinson arrived on the 1st from UK. On Nov. 14th and 15th a deck level recco over Lampedusa and Linosa. No E/a seen. From the 18th to the end of the month all the patrols were as protection to shipping. P/O Park was killed on the 19th November, and P/O Maynard on the 22nd.

On the 25th November we started bombing with Spits, going to Gela. On one of these trips Sgt Houlton saw 9 – Ju 52s and managed to get a squirt at two of them, result 2 – Ju 52s damaged. No one else saw them. Comiso a/d was also bombed.

Pilots arriving and departing in addition to those mentioned were, F/L Charney left on 17th P/O Smith on 21st while *[the rest of this sentence, listing three new arrivals, has been deleted].*

engine failure over convoy – baled out
19.11.42 P/O Park ~~shot down~~   (Killed)

flew into the sea on anti E-boat patrol
22.11.42. P/O Maynard ~~shot down~~   (Killed)

29.11.42. Sgt Houlton 2 Ju 52s damaged.

December 1942.

Tuesday 1 December
4 Spit Bombers + 4 escort set off to bomb Comiso. W/C Thompson's engine cut when just South of Sicily. He jettisoned bombs. Everyone else did the same. All returned. From noon onwards shipping patrols.

There are no entries for 2 and 3 December. According to the squadron ORB only uneventful patrols were flown on these dates.

Friday 4 December
Scramble to intercept 3/109s over Grand Harbour. They dived away as we were climbing.

Saturday 5 December
Protective patrols to shipping in Grand Harbour.

On the facing page alongside this entry is written:

W/C Stephens returned with Spit IX from Gib

Sunday 6 December
"B" Flight did a patrol of Lampedusa and Linosa. Accurate Flak. "A" Flight in the afternoon went to bomb Comiso. 10/10ths cloud so bombs

jettisoned over Sicily.

Monday 7 December
Scramble to intercept Ju 88 20 miles South. E/a attacked but not knocked down. Sgt Guy shot down in sea.

Facing page:

7th Dec   Sgt Guy Shot down (Killed)

There are no entries for the period 8 to 10 December. The squadron ORB records three searches each by four aircraft for Sergeant Daniel G. Guy on the 8th and one patrol over shipping in Grand Harbour. On the 9th Hal Far aerodrome was unserviceable due to rain. On 10 December the squadron was involved in one uneventful scramble and two patrols over Grand Harbour.

Friday 11 December
Again bombed Comiso.

Saturday 12 December
Comiso again.

Nothing was entered for 13 December, while the squadron ORB records only one shipping patrol over Grand Harbour.

Monday 14 December
4 scrambles *[but]* nothing seen.

There are no entries for 15 December in either the diary or squadron ORB.

Wednesday 16 December
W/C J.M. Thompson becomes Section Commander vice W/C Dawson. W/C M.M. Stephens DSO DFC becomes W/C Flying.

Thursday 17 December
Bombed Lampedusa and shot it up. Good show all a/c on aerodrome shot up.

Friday 18 December
ASR search. Pilot found and rescued. Shipping protection.

Friday 18 December to Tuesday 22 December
Protective patrols for shipping. A lot of rain *[made]* a/d serviceable and u/s alternately *[with]* quite a lot of the latter.

The next two entries are by Flying Officer O'Brien.

Wednesday 23 December
Four intrepid types of 'B' Flight under the C/O made a bombing attack on Lampedusa. 8 x 250 lb bombs were duly dropped but wispy cloud made observation of results difficult although two hits were seen on the aerodrome. There was some flak and Sgt Laing got a piece in his radiator which fortunately, was not serious.

Later there was a scramble for a +4 but nothing was seen. F/Sgt McLaren had glycol trouble and his engine conked out 20 miles N of the island at 25,000. He however managed to make a wheels up landing safely on the drome.

Thursday 24 December and Friday 25 December
Unfortunately (or was it?) the rain put the drome U/S and we had to spend Xmas on the ground – perhaps it was just as well.

Flying Officer O'Brien also compiled the following flights list. Another diarist was responsible for entries after 25 December.

No. 185 SQUADRON   DECEMBER 26th 1942.

S/LDR WHITE C/O.

'A' FLIGHT	'B' FLIGHT.
CAPT K.C. KUHLMANN	F/LT R. ATKINSON
F/O L. CHEEK	F/O KNIGHT
F/O P.A.J. O'BRIEN	F/O WITHY killed May 43
P/O G. LAPP	P/O ECKERT
P/O M. REID	P/O WILLIAMS
F/SGT GORE	P/O NESBITT
F/SGT ZOBELL	F/SGT LAING
F/SGT VANCE	F/SGT MILLER killed March 43
F/SGT CARMODY killed Feb 43	F/SGT McLAREN
SGT TARBUCK died April 43	SGT GARVEY
SGT DUNNING	SGT BILLING
SGT THOROGOOD	SGT MAFFRE

NON-EFFECTIVE (AWAITING POSTING TO UK).
F/SGT WALKER
F/SGT FORRESTER
F/SGT HARTNEY died on ship to UK
SGT BOLLAND

Saturday 26 December

The morning past [sic] quietly with an uneventful patrol. F/O Cheek, during a standing patrol in the afternoon, chased and damaged a ME 109 staying with it almost to Sicily before getting near enough for a "squirt".

Sunday 27 December

One uneventful patrol.

Monday 28 December

F/Lt Atkinson took a section to have a look round the Lampedusa area, nothing was seen.

'A' Flight were scrambled in the afternoon for what turned out to be a friendly aircraft.

Alongside this entry is written:

W/Cmdr Thompson DFC and Bar left Hal Far to take up duties of Wingco Flying LUQA, and W/Cmdr Hanks DSO DFC took over Station Commander Hal Far.

Tuesday 29 December

Two scrambles this day but the Hun didn't play.

Wednesday 30 December

The CO and 'B' Flight commander both took a section to look for trouble around Lampedusa in the early hours. Unfortunately nothing was seen, and the day was completed with a fruitless scramble by 'A' Flight.

Thursday 31 December

1942's last day was "full of flying". This was started by 'A' Flight when Captain Kuhlmann led a section on convoy patrol at 06.50. Two more patrols followed in the morning, and 'B' Flight took over with a sweep round Lampedusa. This was followed by 6 a/c attacking the aerodrome at Lamp: [Lampedusa] with bombs led by W/Cdr Stephens. The only results observed were two strikes – in the sea! – cloud made accurate observation difficult. So the last day of the old year passed without seeing any enemy a/c.

1943

185 SQUADRON
1st JANUARY
1943
S/Ldr WHITE

"A" FLIGHT	"B" FLIGHT
CAPT KUHLMANN	F/LT ATKINSON
F/O CHEEK	F/O KNIGHT
P/O O'BRIEN	F/O WITHY
P/O LAPP	P/O ECKERT
P/O REID	P/O WILLIAMS
F/SGT CARMODY	P/O NESBITT
F/SGT GORE	F/SGT McLAREN
SGT TARBUCK	F/SGT MILLER
SGT THOROGOOD	SGT LAING
SGT DUNNING	SGT BILLING
F/SGT VANCE	SGT GARVEY
F/SGT ZOBELL	SGT MAFFRE

Friday 1 January
Two a/c only up on practice flying.

Saturday 2 January
'A' Flight had two sections on patrol Lampedusa Linosa area without result. In the afternoon 'B' Flight did two Island Patrols without any activity, and the CO led a "Spoof" exercise. (Gun laying practice.)

Sunday 3 January
'B' Flight first section under the lead of F/Lt Atkinson were scrambled after a H 111 [sic: He 111] which had been damaged by a section [of] 126 Sq and then lost. Low cloud and bad visibility did not help and after searching round Gozo the Hun was assumed to have 'gone in' and the section was recalled. Another scramble soon followed but was a blank. 'A' Flight did not take the air.

Monday 4 January
Practice flying and a dusk patrol by 'B' Flight.

Tuesday 5 January
'B' Flight had another fruitless scramble.

Wednesday 6 January
A section was ordered off to search for the Tunis Train (transport a/c)

without success. However between Lampedusa and Linosa S/Ldr White led the attack on two F-boats which were well shot up by the 4 a/c. Two Macchi 202s joined in and one was probably destroyed (F/O Withy). Another section led by F/Lt Atkinson were at the same time bombing Lampedusa Aerodrome but results were difficult to see. Harold Knight and Al Eckert tried to join in with the Macchis but did not intercept.

Thursday 7 January

The CO took a section of 'B' Flight round Linosa–Lampedusa while 'Atty' took his section the opposite way. Nothing was seen, but the latter section were given a warm 'flak' reception, much to Bill Williams' discomfort being the nearest to the island. In the afternoon a 6+ caused 'A' Flight to rush into the air but no contact was made. Two sections later went over to Lamp: Wingco Stephens leading the bombers with satisfactory results. The 4 escort with the Flight Commander [sic]

Friday 8 January

'A' Flight again bombed Lampedusa Aerodrome with 4 escort (8 a/c in all) again with satisfactory results. In the afternoon 9 a/c started off led by the CO for a Balbo with W/Cmdr Hanks above to criticize and make helpful suggestions. Sgt Laing had to fall out with undercart trouble so the Wingco joined in. A creditable exhibition of pair landings made up for rather ropey formation flying.

Saturday 9 January

No flying – 'drome u/s except in emergency.

Sunday 10 January

Four bombers and six fighters from 'A' Flight visited Gela aerodrome. The bombing was somewhat inaccurate and flak was encountered. Some 109s followed them back and Matt Reid received 4 cannon shells and some m/g for a memento near Comino, as a result of not hearing Sgt Thorogood's "Break" due to 'Jerry Jamming' on the R/T. Sgt T got in a squirt and claimed a damaged.

In the afternoon an escorted bomber attack on Lamp: was made but clouds prevented observation of results. The cover saw 3 e/a a/c [sic] but no action was joined.

Facing page:

10th F/Sgt Nadon, F/Sgt Sinclair and Sgt MacRae arrived from UK. The Lib: [Liberator] crashed on landing! No one hurt.

Monday 11 January
'A' Flight patrolled a convoy with no diversions.

Tuesday 12 January
An escorted bomber sweep on Lampedusa Aerodrome by 'A' Flight with no results observed. 'B' Flight went on a nought feet sweep round the same area led by our USA enthusiast, Al Eckert, P/O. The three new arrivals had a look at Malta from the air with F/Lt Atkinson.

Wednesday 13 January
No flying, 'drome u/s wet.

Thursday 14 January
'A' Flight took another crack at Lamp: aerodrome with escort. The CO followed about 15 minutes after to do a lone attack and had the satisfaction of seeing his bombs do good work. The others also created some havoc. No e/a/c [enemy aircraft], but some flak. In the afternoon 9 a/c, 'B' Flight, repeated the morning's work. Harold led the four top cover, being joined by Wingco Hanks. The CO led a section of three bombers and pressed home the attack with excellent results (eventually – first try bombs did not go!) in a new mode of attack, bombing in vic.

Friday 15 January
Bill Williams led his first section with the CO as No 3 to look at Lamp: with another section going round t'other way. Bad weather somewhat spoiled the trips.

Keith Kuhlmann and Paddy O'Brien stood down, to await transport to England.

Harold Knight received his second ring and much celebrating was done by the bar that night.

Best of luck Harold with 'A' Flight.

Saturday 16 January
In spite of last night Harold led six bombers over Lamp: 'drome. F/O Lapp took the lead of the escort 4 a/c.

Sunday 17 January
Two offensive patrols to Lamp: nothing sighted. One section scrambled to 20,000´ for a 9+ but they did not intercept. B Flight.

Facing page:

17th Sgt Warcup arrived from UK.

Monday 18 January

'A' Flight another fruitless scramble, this time at 0635 hrs thus putting an end to all further sleep. 'A' Flight visited Lamp: with 6 bombers with some effect.

In the afternoon a new diversion was started for us by W/Cmdr Hanks who, with S/Ldr White and F/Lt Atkinson paid a '0' feet visit to Sicily with Spit-bombers and pranged a passenger train good and proper, afterwards shooting up the engine.

Facing page:

18th Sgt Mercer arrived from UK.

Tuesday 19 January

Another Lampedusa patrol with no joy.

This morning we much regret to record that S/Lt Pratt (NZ) RNAS while doing a practice trip on one of our a/c went into the sea. It is assumed that he was low flying, and [was] dazzled by the sun. He had done excellent work and his loss to the station will be much felt. A search revealed no wreckage or sign of oil. [*Sub-Lieutenant (A) Ernest F. Pratt was a pilot in the Royal New Zealand Naval Volunteer Reserve.*]

Wednesday 20 January

W/Cmdr Stephens led 'A' Flight over Sicily to bomb a bridge near Rosolini. A train was shot up by S/Ldr White on his own and the others shared a train further South. The CO found his near Noto.

At night (moon period) six a/c went over at half hour intervals to achieve what damage they could in Sicily. The night's bag was 2 engines, a building road junction and probable damage to a bridge and two lorries. F/Lt Knight bagging the two trains with cannon and mg [*and*] the other damage being [*done with*] bombs and guns.

Thursday 21 January

'B' Flight took another look at Lamp:, one section. Thanks to a new R/T mod: [?] to cut out Hun interference inter-a/c communication is practically nil. C/O went sick with 'flu.

Facing page:

S/Ldr Ashton took over 185 Sqdn pending S/Ldr White's recovery.

Friday 22 January

'A' Flight visited Licata with 5 bombers and 5 escort experiencing considerable flak but no fighter opposition. Also another scramble with no result. 'B' Flight visited Lamp: in the afternoon with 3 a/c (F/O Withy falling out with R/T trouble). At night another ½ hourly invasion of Sicily [*with*] Wingco Stephens pranging a warehouse, F/O Cheek a factory and engine shed and Bill Williams visiting Syracuse (by mistake!) and extinguishing a searchlight. Wingco Hanks dropped two bombs in an engine shed but they failed to explode.

Saturday 23 January
'B' Flight put up six a/c in 3 sections of 2 to rhubarb Sicily, one a/c in each section carrying bombs. The bombs were not seen to do any serious devastation but two stations and some MT were successfully shot up.
'A' Flight were scrambled in the afternoon but did not make contact.

Facing page:

23rd The 8th Army entered Tripoli and the town fell. Good show – Now for leave in TRIPOLI instead of St Paul's Bay.

Sunday 24 January
'A' Flight sent two sections to Sicily, Harold Knight leading the bombers and Len Cheek the escort. After some attentions from Me 109 the bombers returned somewhat shot up and Harold increased his score by 1 probable Me 109. In the escort section F/O Lapp and F/Sgt Carmody shared a probable Ju 88. 'B' Flight acted as rear cover to Krendi wing later.

Facing page:

Capt Kuhlmann and F/O O'Brien left for UK.

Monday 25 January
S/Ldr Ashton led a section through some considerable cloud to see how many a/c were on Lampedusa 'drome. Three were seen from 5,000 ft, and the gun posts speeded the parting 'guests'.
B Flight took another look later but saw little.

Tuesday 26 January
Apart from the Spit IX returning to Hal Far little flying was done today and none of it operational.

Wednesday 27 January
At 6.35 Al Eckert took a section to cover 4 returning Beauforts but saw nothing. Later Lampedusa was approached but cloud prevented the release, profitably, of bombs so they were brought back. The Squadron was released for 24 hours at 1300 but owing to the ban on public places Valetta was not visited, and a quiet time had by all.

Thursday 28 January
'A' Flight bombed Lamp: 'drome thro' a gap in the cloud and results were not noted clearly.

Friday 29 January
Eight a/c of 'A' Flight swept the sky round Pachino. F/O Cheek damaged a 109 Me.

'B' were scrambled but were unable to intercept. They then did a sweep over Sicily but, altho' the Hun was patrolling parallel to them, did not make contact.

Saturday 30 January
'B' Flight did a high cover sweep between Sicily and Malta but saw nothing. In the late morning Liberators from N Africa bombed Sicily and two sections went up as high cover but made no contacts altho' plenty of e.a/c came up.

In the afternoon 'A' Flight did a sweep to Pachino and F/O Cheek and Sgt Warcup fired at 109s but made no claim.

Facing page:

Sgt Garvey returned to UK.

Sunday 31 January
Len Cheek again – dived on 2 Me 109s on a sweep over Sicily at 450 mph then blacked out as the Hun rolled away at the critical moment. Earlier there was a convoy patrol, and our first attempt at long range escort which was not successful as the 'Babies' were lost at rendezvous.

Monday 1 February
'B' Flight put up a section of 4 a/c to go out West of Linosa to search for and escort back some damaged MTBs. En route however these were reduced to one only which was picked up N of the island and circled for some 3 hours, a very interesting trip!! 229 were with us for ¾ of the time. Later 8 a/c took off to sweep Sicily, S/Ldr Ashton returned with engine trouble so Bill Williams took over. Nothing was seen on either sortie. Squadron released 1300. F/O WITHY takes over 'B' FLIGHT as F/LT ATKINSON returns UK.

Facing page:

F/Lt Atkinson ("Atty") owing to trouble with an old injury had to give up flying pending an operation on his hand. Much to our regret this necessitated a return to UK so the flight (B) and Squadron lose a capable flight commander. He left Malta on the night 2nd–3rd February.

Tuesday 2 February

'A' Flight visited Lampedusa and Linosa at deck level but saw nothing, F/Sgt Zobell leading.

Wednesday 3 February

Eight Spits from 'A' Flight swept the Sicilian skies without contacting the enemy.

Thursday 4 February

This morning 'B' Flight took a look at Sicily from near Syracuse to Comiso. Large numbers of e/a came up and at least 6 were sighted [but] none however came near enough to engage or be engaged. On the way home Tom Nesbitt at 18,000 ft, informed us his engine wasn't working any more. He very creditably and coolly glided back to within 15 miles of Grand Harbour, baled out at 5000 ft and to everyone's relief was duly picked up by the ASRS little the worse for his hour's immersion. Unfortunately his dinghy failed to inflate and he had a cold and wet 60` [sic: minutes]. 'A' Flight brought three replacement a/c from Krendi.

Friday 5 February

Practise flying and camera gun only today. Stand down 1300 hrs.

Facing page:

5th FEBRUARY

S/Ldr Crafts came over from Krendi (229 Sqdn) to take over 185 Sqdn and we wish him the best of luck and congratulations.

Saturday 6 February

Bad weather, air tests only.

Sunday 7 February

Another uneventful sweep on Lampedusa by 'B' Flight. Thick cloud at 6000 ft obscured the island. Release 1510 hrs.

Monday 8 February

Today 'A' Flight had a similar experience to that of 'B's on the 4th. Unfortunately it did not end so happily, and it is with regret that we record the loss of F/Sgt Carmody. He reported engine trouble and glided some distance towards base but no one saw him bale out. There is a faint possibility he <u>may</u> have made it and been picked up by the Hun but, we fear, very faint. [*Canadian Flight Sergeant Cornelius J. Carmody was killed.*] There were several e/a about at the time and Sgt Warcup fired but made no claim. Two ME 109s collided however and both are believed to have gone in. In the afternoon S/Ldr Crafts took a section to Sicily but owing to R/T difficulties and lack of information the e/a present were not intercepted. It appears that the pilots over the water must have definite instructions not to engage as they have had plenty of opportunity. This would seem to show a/c shortage?

Tuesday 9 February
The CO led a scramble after a 9+ plot but as is now usual no interception was possible as they soon turned back.

Wednesday 10 February
This morning a convoy of 4 merchant vessels with 8 destroyers and 1 cruiser escort approached the island. 185 supplied 4 patrols equally distributed between the flights with no interest.

Thursday 11 February
Bad weather, 'drome U/S. Release 11.45 hrs.

Friday 12 February
Same again, no flying, recovering from party in Sliema.

Saturday 13 February
'A' Flight sent up a high cover escort for a returning PRU job with Sgt Tarbuck leading. No joy. In the afternoon the CO led a 'B' Flight section on another profitless Krendi sweep withdrawal cover.

Sunday 14 February
A short and abortive scramble by 'B' Flight.
No flying for 'A' Flight.

Monday 15 February
Practice flying only for 'A' Flight then 'B' put up an Island Patrol, Al Eckert returning with R/T trouble and Sgt Billing taking over.
Later 4 "bombers" and 4 fighters joined with 8 bombers of Krendi to attack warehouses at SCICLI, Sicily, '0' ft to near the coast climb to 10,000 and bombing at 1500 to 2000. A very successful show, at least 80% of the bombs going home, finished off by the CO's fighter section ground strafing the target, or what was left of it. Krendi lost one.

Tuesday 16 February
Another fruitless withdrawal cover by 'B' Flight only. No flying for A Flight. F/Sgt Miller took off, with others, in Hurricanes for Tripoli leave. Tom Nesbitt and Len Cheek returned from their trip not very impressed. The town is still not settled down and they found little in the line of wine,

women or song. *[Written in margin:* Release 1300 pm*]*

Wednesday 17 February
Practice flying for "A" Flight.

Thursday 18 February
Practice flying for both flights.

Friday 19 February
No flying.

Saturday 20 February
'A' Flight had a section of two scrambled. Airborne for 10 minutes only. No other flying.

Sunday 21 February
'B' Flight had to put up a long range section to search for a missing Mosquito near Pantelleria. Nothing was found and no e/a seen. They returned, very "foot" sore after 3 hrs *[and]* 35´ flying, to a late lunch at 4.15 hrs and a 48 hr stand down. 'B' Flight stood down.

We congratulate Sgt Tarbuck on his commission which came thro' today.

Monday 22 February
Another convoy *[consisting of]* 4 m/v and 2 tankers arrived this morning and three sections were needed. 'B' Flight were still off so 'A' spent the afternoon doing Island Patrols with the addition of 2 'B' types to make up 12 pilots. As each flight now has but 9 pilots replacements and additions are required rather urgently. Especially as both the Hun and Itie have recently promised Malta more attention shortly. We trust this is no idle threat but will materialize 'ere *[?]* long.

Tuesday 23 February
More convoy cover (Island Patrols). A tanker is unloading in Pretty Bay having travelled 18,000 miles from Texas bringing some 1,500,000 galls of 100 Octane.

Wednesday 24 February
Another day of uneventful Island Patrols.

Thursday 25 February
'A' Flight sent 4 a/c on a weather recco over Sicily quite early with no result from the enemy. Later another section did a high cover patrol for a returning sweep. In the afternoon 'B' Flight did a similar cover which Sgt

Billing was to have led but owing to R/T trouble had to take over No 3. There were apparently plenty of Huns about but none were sighted.

Friday 26 February
Camera gun work only.

Saturday 27 February
'A' Flight with Krendi went out to bomb Syracuse. Results as far as could be seen were very pleasing [with] bombs bursting on hangars (seaplane) jetties, one ship and warehouses also a fire was started in the town.

The next day another writer took over the diary.

Sunday 28 February
'A' Flight started early by sending out a section to look for a "Wimpy" in distress which they found OK – the big job arrived back soon after. Camera gunning followed till "B" Flt took over. "B" Flt went bombing with 249 the target being the power station at Cassibile, however cloud obscured the target area and no results were seen. On the way back at deck level the boys were pleased to see a submarine off Avola, so they proceeded to make its ventilation much better and did a very good job too – the CO collecting some portion of it in his radiator.

Monday 1 March
B Flt started the day by stirring up the opposition with a fighter sweep over Noto and Ragusa. 3 109s were seen and Sgt Maffre damaged one of them – on the way back F/Sgt Miller's kite got temperamental and its engine stopped but he glided for quite a time and jumped 30 mls out from the island and was picked up by HSL – a very good show. Apart from the above Air/Sea Rescue escort the rest of the day's flying was taken up with practice and local patrols. In the last few days 5 new pilots have arrived from the UK – P/Os Sinclair and McKee and Sgts Warr, Roberts and Yates – we all wish them the best of luck and a pleasant stay.

Facing page:

P/O Sinclair ⎫
P/O McKee ⎪ Arrived 185 from UK
Sgt Roberts ⎬ 26.2.43.
„ Warr ⎪
„ Yates ⎭

Tuesday 2 March

"A" Flt on recco over Lampedusa this morning sighted 4 big jobs on the drome – so they hurried back and 4 bombers with 4 escort went out to prang same – unfortunately the bombs overshot and hit the 'drome perimeter. Except for one practice trip by B Flt in the afternoon that was all the day's flying.

Wednesday 3 March

"B" Flight were off fairly early 8 strong to search for a dinghy about 15 miles S of Scalambri – they found the job and F/Sgt Laing was low down circling when an 88 joined in – Al Laing let off at this job but no results were seen and the 88 left them. Again at 1215 the two sections were scrambled after 9+ at great height – the boys were jumped at 17,000´ and Sgt Mercer was shot up and did a crash landing back at Halfar – Sgt Billing was less fortunate and had to jump 20 mls N of St Paul's Bay and was picked up by HSL – luckily the only damage was a few bruises on Sgt Billing. After that very hectic morning the Sqdn was stood down until 1300 on the 4/3/43. F/O Cheek left the Sqdn today for the UK and we all wish him the best of luck there.

Thursday 4 March

F/Sgts Zobell and Laing took two Hurricanes to Tripoli this afternoon (our "rest" camp) – later on both Red and Yellow sections of "A" Flt were scrambled but no contact was made.

Friday 5 March

No flying today due to duff weather.

Saturday 6 March

"B" Flt did two convoy patrols today, and apart from that there was no flying – another slack day.

Sunday 7 March

"A" Flt had one section scrambled this morning but the plot did not come in at all – practice flying was the only other activity of the day.

Monday 8 March

"B" Flt did one camera gunning exercise this morning, and the Sqdn was stood down at 1300 hrs today.

"A" Flt however decided to do a Mars practice the same afternoon and 12 Spits had a happy time in numerous jumps etc.

Tuesday 9 March

Only one practice trip this afternoon.

Wednesday 10 March

No trips this morning and in the afternoon "B" Flt did a Balbo practice.

Thursday 11 March

Practice trips were done by both "A" and "B" Flts today and nothing unusual happened.

Facing page:

F/O Schuren. } Arrived from UK
P/O Webster }   11/3/43.

Friday 12 March

"A" Flt with 126 Sqdn did a sweep to N of Comiso today but were not engaged – (126 were engaged by 1 109 but no results were forthcoming) – "B" Flt took over and did a spoof, shipping cooperation and practice trips – no other flying today.

We welcome two more pilots from the UK, F/O Schuren and P/O Webster, – the best of luck and a good stay.

Saturday 13 March

The Sqdn was stood down at 1300 hrs and "B" Flt just did one practice trip today – in the afternoon the Officers played the Sgts at soft-ball and won by 1 run – there should be a future in that series!!!!

Sunday 14 March

"A" Flt took the stand at 1300 and apart from practice there was no other flying today.

Facing page:

SGT CRUICKSHANK } arrived from UK
SGT CROSS   }   14-3-43.

Monday 15 March

No flying at all today.

Tuesday 16 March

"A" Flt had one section scrambled today after +2 but nothing doing – that was all for today.

Wednesday 17 March

Three convoy stooges were put up by "A" Flt this morning for an incoming job. – in the afternoon "B" Flt did a mass effort with 10 machines and many were the bounces thereof!!

In the evening (full of spirit after seeing "Malta GC") *[motion picture]* four pilots of "A" Flt did some night flying.

Thursday 18 March

No flying this morning and the Sqdn released at 1300 – RAIN!!!

Friday 19 March

It rained all stand down and the 'drome was still damp today, so we were only serviceable and so no practice was done and of course no Huns came over.

Saturday 20 March

This morning "A" Flt put up a long range section patrol over a tanker, and followed it up with 2 short range patrols – that was all for the morning.

"B" Flt in the afternoon took over and sent a Rhubarb over to Sicily – ~~on the way back~~ *after bombing a railway bridge flak caused* F/Lt Withy's engine *to* pack~~ed~~ in and he was forced to jump about 8 mls off their coast. F/Sgt Miller who orbited the dinghy was unfortunately shot down by 2 109s – a great pity to lose Dusty and a very gallant show on his part staying with F/Lt Withy – F/Lt Withy was eventually picked up by the Walrus (after quite a hectic time) and brought home OK despite the 109s' intentions on the Walrus – a very good show. *Two of the Walrus' escorting Spits were lost.*

This evening four of "A" Flt did some uneventful night flying. *[An unknown hand deleted and rewrote part of the above entry, shown in italics.]*

Sunday 21 March

Apart from a weather recco (which put out any ops today) and a spot of practice flying there was no flying of any note today. Again this evening 4 of "B" Flt did uneventful night flying.

The following day Pilot Officer Sinclair took over as squadron diarist.

Monday 22 March

"A" Flight was on dawn readiness but nothing came up. Practice flying was all that was done. Night flying was done by "A" Flight but not more than was absolutely necessary.

Tuesday 23 March

Nothing but practice. We ought to be about "perfect" now.
Stand down 13:00 hrs.

Wednesday 24 March

"A" Flight was scrambled after 3+ but as usual nothing happened. That was all for the day. Squadron released 1800 hrs.

Thursday 25 March

Again "A" Flight was scrambled, this time 4+. Business looking up???

An air-sea rescue patrol was carried out by F/O Reid and 3 others (SGT ROBERTS, F/S ZOBELL AND THOROGOOD.) F/O STOVEL, OF 126 SQDN, (MK IXs) was picked up and everything under control.

Local patrol was carried out by "B" Flight in the afternoon. That is all.

Friday 26 March

"B" Flight put up a search patrol (long range), nothing turned up and one of the boys had trouble on landing.

A scramble then came up for "B" Flight but again nothing happened.

Outside of air tests and practise flying by "A" Flight nothing more was done.

Saturday 27 March

"A" Flight

F/O Lapp was sent over Sicily on a weather recco. While he was up a section was scrambled against 6+. Later on, it was learned that the 6+ were after our F/O Lapp. But he reported that he saw nothing, so all ended happily. (for Jerry.)

"B" Flight

F/LT Withy did another recco but nothing turned up and another uneventful day came to a close.

Sunday 28 March

Nothing but practise flying by "B" Flight.

Squadron stood down 1300.

Monday 29 March

"A" Flight, very kindly, went on the line for 3½ hrs, on their morning off, while other sqdns did practise Balbo.

After a little practise flying "A" Flight scrambled a section of 4. One never got off the ground and a second had engine trouble and had to return. This a/c (under F/LT Knight) did a very nice forced landing. Fortunately for the remaining two nothing came along.

Tuesday 30 March

"B" Flight carried out an uneventful fighter sweep over Sicily. Two a/c had engine trouble but returned safely.

Wednesday 31 March

Two scrambles by "B" Flight and air tests and practise by "A" Flight finished flying for the month of March.

Thursday 1 April

Scramble by "B" Flight, as usual nothing came.

Facing page:

P/O TARBUCK. died to-day after a short period of illness. After being on the island for nine months he was well known by many and his absence is felt by all. He was a very valuable man to his squadron and he is missed especially by the rest of the boys in "A" Flight.

Friday 2 April

Again "B" Flight had a scramble but nothing again.
Stood down 13:00.

Saturday 3 April and Sunday 4 April

Nothing but practise.

Monday 5 April

"B" Flight did a search patrol.

"A" Flight put up 8 a/c with 8 a/c from 229. Altogether there were 12 bombers and 4 escort. For this little show they went to Porto Empedocle. They approached at 16–18000 ft and dived and released bombs at 8000 ft. All of 185 Sqdn's bombs landed in target area. Light and some heavy AA was encountered but no enemy a/c.

Tuesday 6 April

Nothing again but practise for both flights.

Wednesday 7 April

We, "A" Flight, had a quiet day until just at dusk, when we were scrambled after 1+. Only two took off and they intercepted an a/c which turned out to be friendly – bad luck.

Thursday 8 April

No action at all.

Friday 9 April

Same.

Saturday 10 April

F/LT WITHY and F/O SCHUREN went out on a search patrol. The search was fruitful indeed for they shot down an [sic] Ju 88. It was a very quick and neat job and was an example for others to follow.

Later in the day "B" Flight put 12 a/c up as escort to 8 Beaufighters and went on a bombing show to Pantelleria. All returned safely.

Facing page:

10-4-43 F/LT Withy } 1 Ju 88 DESTROYED ✠
      F/O Schuren }

Sunday 11 April

"A" Flight stood by with 4 long range jobs at dawn, but the special "do" was cancelled. Four of our a/c were later sent out on a search for a Wellington but had no luck. Four more long range jobs went on an offensive sweep to Pant. [*Pantellaria*] and Sicily. One a/c was sighted but it was too close to base and didn't take long getting back. Outside of a few fishing boats that is all that was seen. All returned safely.

Monday 12 April

"B" Flight again put out 4 long range a/c on an offensive sweep but no dice. Practise flying and an island patrol completed the flying for the day.

Tuesday 13 April

"A" Flight put out 4 long range jobs on an offensive sweep but again no fun. Practise flying and local flying by W/C Hanks in a Kittyhawk.

Wednesday 14 April

Four long range jobs were put out by "B" Flight on an offensive sweep to within 5 miles of Malita [*sic:* Melito] di Porto Salvo (Toe of Italy). Two A/C were sighted but out of range. Nothing more occurred. All returned.

In the afternoon "A" Flight had a quiet afternoon until nearly dusk when they scrambled a section. However this ended only in an island patrol.

Thursday 15 April

After a session of cine-gun practise "A" Flight put out 8 a/c with 126, 249 and 1435 Squadrons for a fighter sweep over Sicily. Before the sweep ended however there were only 4 a/c of 185 still in the air. The others had returned for various a/c failures. All of our boys returned safely and nothing was seen except a/a.

"B" Flight did some night flying.

Friday 16 April
"B" Flight sent out 4 A/C to protect destroyers off Sicily. During a hectic time 2 of our boys had a crack at a *[Focke-Wulf]* 190 observing strikes but a/c dove away. One of our boys had an accident while landing but no one was hurt.

Later in the morning, after a scramble, B Flight again went out on a sweep over Sicily. Two returned early but didn't miss anything. No enemy a/c were seen.

Facing page:

16-4-43 F/LT WITHY ⎱ FW 190 – DAMAGED
      P/O McKee ⎰

Saturday 17 April
"A" Flight put out 8 a/c, four bombers and 4 fighters to bomb Syracuse (along with 3 of 229 and 1 of 229). *[According to the ORBs of 229 and 249 Squadrons, the former unit provided three Spitfire-bombers plus four Spitfires as escort and the latter one Spitfire-bomber.]* No enemy a/c were encountered and a good job was done by the bombers. Heavy and light a/a was all the opposition received.

Sunday 18 April
Local flying, air testing and many co-op was the complete flying for the day.

Monday 19 April
"B" Flight came on pre-dawn but only did a spot of air firing practise for the war effort.

"A" Flight did air testing.

Pardon me – "B" Flight also did night flying.

Tuesday 20 April
"A" Flight started out the day by air-firing practise.

"B" Flight continued on with a bomber sweep on Porto Empedocle. Sixteen a/c took part. 8 from 185 and 8 from 229. Twelve bombers and four escort. No enemy a/c but a/a.

Wednesday 21 April
"B" Flight carried out an offensive patrol but failed to become offensive. Practise flying and air tests finished flying for the day.

Thursday 22 April
"A" Flight came down for dawn readiness and two sections were

scrambled after 3+ but Jerry got cold feet and didn't want to get them wet too.

"A" Flight finished off the morning with air firing. Squadron was stood down at 13:00 hrs.

Friday 23 April
Practise flying by B Flight.

Saturday 24 April
"B" Flight started a busy morning at pre-dawn and started with a long range sweep. They swept between Cape Bon and Pant. then South West Sicily. This was done at zero feet with the same results. Then came a scramble with same results.

Later in the morning 8 of our bomber Spits took off with a/c from 229 and 249. Altogether twenty four a/c took part. However finding the target, which was Pantelleria, obscured by cloud they jettisoned their bombs into the sea and swept the sea at zero feet from Pant. to 5 mi[les] south of Keliba and back. All that was achieved was piling up hours.

"A" Flight did only practise flying.

Sunday 25 April
"A" Flight did dawn readiness and started out with 2 a/c on air sea rescue. Then a couple of the boys did air to air firing. This was followed by an uneventful scramble.

"B" Flight finished the day with a convoy patrol and a scramble.

Monday 26 April
In the afternoon "A" Flight did a bomber sweep on Augusta along with 229 Squdn. There was no interference and some good bombing was done. Light and heavy a/a was inaccurate and no bother. No enemy a/c were seen going or coming home. All returned safe including one bomb.

Tuesday 27 April
Four of "A" Flight were out on an offensive sweep, long range (for the use of). But nothing was seen. Practise flying ended the morning and squadron was stood down at 13:15 hrs.

Wednesday 28 April
Nothing to do.

Thursday 29 April
Scramble by "A" Flight was recalled.

Friday 30 April

Four of "A" Flight (again) went out on a long range stooge but (again) failed to contact anything except a couple of enemy surface craft which they left alone. The surface craft fired on them but our boys didn't attack because of proximity of Pantelleria. All returned safe.

A scramble was again recalled.

"B" boys did some practise flying to finish the day.

In May 1943 the Afrikakorps *surrendered in Tunisia. For 185 Squadron the routine continued.*

Saturday 1 May

"A" Flight started the month off by being 1st and 2nd off all afternoon. Not a very pleasant do. We had one scramble after 1+ which turned out to be friendly.

Sunday 2 May

"A" Flight sent out 2 a/c on a weather recco to Pant. but weather was pretty thick. Two air tests finished the morning and squadron was stood down at 13.00 hrs.

Monday 3 May

"B" Flight took over at 1300 hrs doing air tests then a bomber sweep on Lampedusa was organized. Altogether 23 Spits took part (8 of 185, 7 of 229, 4 of 249 bombers and 4 of 249 fighter escort). Bombs were dropped on aerodrome but results were not seen on account of bad visibility. Heavy a/a was to be had. All returned safely.

Tuesday 4 May

"B" Flight did dawn readiness and were scrambled to search for missing PRU.

Island Patrol was done by both flights for the remainder of the day.

Wednesday 5 May

Pre dawn was done by "A" Flight and also more island patrol.

"B" Flight also did more island patrol.

Thursday 6 May

"B" Flight did an offensive patrol led by Sqd Ldr Crafts. They managed to damage 1 F-boat but one of the boys F/Sgt Mercer had to bale out but was picked up by HSL.

"B" Flight put in more hrs on island patrol and 1 uneventful scramble.

Facing page:

LT BOSCH – ARRIVED FROM UK.

Friday 7 May

"A" Flight had 8 a/c scrambled but no action took place.
Sqd released 1300 hrs – stood down.

Saturday 8 May

"B" Flight took part in a bomber sweep on Porto Empedocle. Altogether there were 36 Spits on the show [including] 10 of 185. The power station was the target and many bursts were seen around and on target. Several buildings east and west also hit. Intense heavy and light a/a was to be had. All returned safely. Two scrambles were had to finish off the ~~morning~~ (pardon me) afternoon.

Sunday 9 May

"B" Flight started the morning with 2 a/c on a search patrol. A couple of scrambles and cine gun practise was all the flying for the day.

Monday 10 May

"A" Flight did pre dawn stuff and got an early scramble. Nothing doing. Camera practise and a scramble to help HSL finished "A" Flight's morning.

"B" Flight did camera gun and practise flying in the afternoon.

Tuesday 11 May

"B" Flight supplied 8 a/c for escort to Libs over Sicily. Three had tank trouble and one engine trouble. All returned OK.

"A" Flight did FA.

Wednesday 12 May

"A" Flight sent 4 a/c out on an offensive patrol and managed to really shoot up a train on the toe of Italy. They had practically the whole Luftwaffe up after them but none were sighted. However a/a around the train got Sgt Yates and on the way out he was last seen crashed in the sea. Although one of the newer fellows Yates was liked by all and is sure missed by the boys.

Facing page:

Sgt Yates – killed in action – shot down by a/a. Crashed in sea off east coast of ~~Italy~~ Sicily near toe of Italy.

SGT HARRIS
SGT HENDERSON } Arrived from England via Africa – "A" Flight

SGT BUCHANAN ⎤
SGT WILSON   ⎦ "B" Flight „   „   „   „

Practise flying finished "A" Flight's morning but one of the boys crashed on landing due to u/c [*undercarriage*] collapsing. No one hurt.

Thursday 13 May
A couple of air tests for the whole day.

Friday 14 May
After a couple of air tests "A" Flight put 8 a/c up on a bomber sweep on Comiso aerodrome along with 9 from 126 Squdn. The target was found but owing to cloud results were not observed. Enemy a/c were airborne but no contact was made. However P/O Zobell returned early with engine trouble. On jettisoning his bombs before landing one bomb hung up. It looked perfectly safe but after touching down the bomb fell off and exploded a few seconds later. Fortunately no one was seriously hurt. The u/c of the a/c collapsed and shrapnel caused damage – Cat II – but pilot was alright. All the rest returned safe.
Later in the day 8 a/c were scrambled but no contact was made.

Saturday 15 May
"A" Flight had two new fellows practise flying.
"B" Flight escorted Beaus with 7 a/c on a bomber sweep, long range. Nothing was sighted.
Later in the day F/O Reid flew the AOC's a/c over to Safi for the opening of said aerodrome.

Sunday 16 May
Practice flying and one scramble was all the flying for to-day.

Monday 17 May
Same again.

Tuesday 18 May
One air test – oh–hum!

Wednesday 19 May
Practise flying by both flights again.

Facing page:

F/O LAPP
F/O WILLIAMS
P/O LAING   } were stood down and are returning to Blighty
F/S DUNNING   to-morrow. (20th)
F/S BILLING

Thursday 20 May

"A" Flight started with two sections flying practice and were vectored onto enemy a/c. However no contacts were made. Another scramble after 2+ resulted in the same. "B" Flight did a bomber sweep on Comiso with 8 a/c, 1 returning – engine trouble. 8 a/c from 229 and 4 of 1435 accompanied them. After bombing the aerodrome the formation was attacked by 4 Me 109s – enemy broke away. Then 6 Me 109s attacked at 8–10,000′ [and] one of the a/c had a shot but no results were seen. Two Spits of the other Sqdns were hit but returned safely.

Friday 21 May

Well at 6:30 this morning Jerry gave us a real surprise by coming over with 36+ 190s and 109s and dive bombed Hal Far from about 15000′ down to about 5. They were engaged by Spits from other squdns but not before they had dropped 6 on Hal Far destroying 3 Albacores [and] 1 Spit and damaging another Spit. One 190 was destroyed and several a/c damaged. Two Naval chaps were injured one seriously. One 1000 lb bomb landed unexploded on the wall of a pen. It was soon taken care of. More raids came in during the day but no more bombs. Our boys had to be content with convoy patrol and island patrol. Later on the first of our Mk IXs came in from Africa. At last we may get above the Hun.

Saturday 22 May

While doing Island patrol 4 of "A" Flight were vectored after enemy a/c. They saw them (12) above and going in opposite direction. After turning into them a few times the enemy a/c headed home. No action. A couple of scrambles resulting in sweet FA finished the day.

Sunday 23 May

"B" Flight had a couple of scrambles but no contacts were made. Sqdn stood down at 1300 hrs.

Monday 24 May

To-day the IXs did all the flying although the Vs were also on the line. On one scramble three of our IXs sighted the enemy actually being above them. However they lost them on a turn and that was that.

Four of the IXs went on a sweep over Sicily and again they were above the Hun but no contact was made.

Another, unidentified, diarist took over on 25 May.

Tuesday 25 May

A Flight had a scramble for the IXs with no results and also did some practise flying. In the afternoon B Flight had two scrambles, one section of 5s and one of IXs, with no combat. This was a sad day for the squadron, however, as F/L Withy crashed into the sea in a Spit IX while on a scramble. The squadron has lost a first class member, and all concerned were deeply grieved at the loss of such a capable flight commander, who was liked and respected by everyone.

On a previous page:

F/LT FOSTER WITHY – CRASHED INTO SEA FROM 26 THOU' WHILE ON A SCRAMBLE IN A SPIT IX – PRESUMABLY THROUGH OXYGEN FAILURE.

Wednesday 26 May

The CO and F/O Schuren were scrambled uneventfully in the IXs early. Later the same two aided in escorting Liberators to bomb Sicily, a job which was well done. Later in the morning a rare "double green" was fired and two sections of Vs were airborne when two plots came in but no contact was made. In the P.M., A Flight had two scrambles, one being done by a section of IXs, but with no result. Three new IXs arrived from Maison Blanche through the courtesy of Messrs Reid, Nesbitt and Bosch.

Thursday 27 May

"A" Flight accounted for three air tests this AM and a spell of unbroken dawn readiness. In the afternoon B Flight did some air tests, and the two IXs were scrambled, piloted by F/O Schuren and Lt Bosch. A vector to Linosa ensued without result, the section returning early as F/O Schuren had an oxygen leak.

Friday 28 May

Eight aircraft (IXs and Vs) of B Flight scrambled almost simultaneously on a plot of 9+ with no results. Later the "fives" nipped off again on a plot of 15+ which faded early. F/O McKee and Sgt McRae carried out a Naval Coop exercise, F/S MacLaren soared aloft in a IX for his first trip, and lastly the CO led a section of IXs in a short and uneventful scramble. The squadron stood down for a day off at 1300 hours.

Saturday 29 May

The "nines" scrambled early after coming on duty but were immediately recalled. F/Lt Knight, leading, had the misfortune to hit a lorry on the runway when landing and crashed, ripping off a wing and writing the aircraft off in general. Very luckily he escaped unhurt. The lorry driver (who was at fault) was likewise uninjured. The IXs scrambled again later on but met with no combat. At eight o'clock in the evening the Vs did an unexciting island patrol, led by F/O Reid, and this ended the day's activities.

Sunday 30 May

F/O Reid's section of Vs scrambled on a short-lived fade out this morning, and later A Flight indulged in practise flying and one air test. The CO led four IXs on a show over Sicily, and though there were plots up, nothing happened. In the afternoon a IX arrived, via Sgt Roberts, from Luqa and McRae did an air test. A section of Vs and IXs were scrambled in that order about an hour apart but on each occasion the intrepid Teutons lost heart and fled for base again, which was disappointing. The IXs flew into some flak while flying over Halfar, which was a poor show, but even though the "take cover" was fired no Jerries were seen or attacked. To wind up another day, three new IXs, flown by Ireland, Webster and Sinclair, arrived from Maison Blanche at Algiers, appearing suddenly over the drome in typical 185 style of shoot-up.

Monday 31 May

This morning B Flight accounted for one scramble which was unfruitful, and a sweep by three IXs on Comiso which was also comparatively quiet. A couple of convoy and island patrols rounded off B Flight's tour. In the afternoon A Flight accounted for a couple of air tests, to be followed by three scrambles, the last two of which were almost simultaneous, IXs and Vs. However, nothing developed, and so ended the day.

Tuesday 1 June

Twelve on this A.M., the IXs being on the line all morning, with nary a scramble for their pains. Two island patrols were done and B Flight took over at noon: The afternoon saw an island patrol, an air test and two scrambles, the last being the IXs for 25+. The "take cover" was fired and the Jerries were visible overhead from dispersal, but unfortunately our boys made no contact much to their disappointment, and another day passed.

Wednesday 2 June

This morning B Flight, assisted by 3 A Flight boys carried out two escorts for incoming destroyers east of the island. The IXs also scrambled twice, but with no result. Sgts Cross and Wilson rounded off the morning's work by doing their first flips in a Spit IX. In the afternoon although the squadron was officially stood down, F/S Mercer took part in a camouflage exercise (with various Wincos [sic: Wingcos] and Group

Captains acting as his Nos 2 and 3!!!!).

Thursday 3 June

A Flight took over at noon and the Vs scrambled with no combat. Several kites were tested and a few flown to Luqa. An island patrol and two more scrambles, IX and V, with no results ended the day.

Friday 4 June

Today was the most eventful in many a weary month. Firstly most of the pilots had the chance to meet our new CO of 185, S/Ldr MacDougall DFC. Our former CO, S/L Crafts leaves the squadron with best wishes for continued good luck and good hunting from all who had the pleasure of serving on the squadron with him. With the same sentiments we welcome our new CO and trust he will have a long and happy term with his new command. Congratulations are also in order to F/LT McKee who puts up his second strip and takes over B Flight, much to the pleasure of all. Today A Flight made history for us by destroying a FW 190 (F/L Knight) and probably destroying an Me 109 (Sgt Cruickshank) while on a scramble in the IXs – well done! A couple more scrambles, in IXs and Vs were fruitless, and likewise, unfortunately, a search patrol for a baled-out pilot. In the afternoon B Flight did a brace of air tests, a couple of local flying trips (individual) in the IX, and two uneventful scrambles, Vs and IXs.

On a previous page:

<u>4-6-43</u> F/L KNIGHT – FW 190 – DESTROYED   ✸
SGT CRUICKSHANK – ME 109 – PROBABLY DESTROYED. ✸
<u>S/L MacDougall DFC takes over 185 from S/L Crafts.</u>

Saturday 5 June

This morning's readiness of B Flight consisted of one sole scramble in the Vs, but the Jerries did not venture to cross the coast. In the afternoon the squadron very sadly packed up to move to Krendi, all aircraft being flown there by 4:30 and all kit. Old 185 had been on Halfar for two years, and was the oldest squadron on the island, having built up a proud score on that station. What with being well established on airfield and having a very congenial atmosphere among the pilots in the excellent quarters and messes, the boys were "browned off" with the move. However, "ours not to reason why –"

After 185 Squadron relocated to Qrendi the diary was resumed by Pilot Officer Sinclair.

Sunday 6 June

"A" Flight came on at 13:00 hrs and the nines were scrambled after a plot of 15+. On our first day at Krendi Flight Sergt Nadon got a probable and F/O Reid had a squirt. All in all it was a very good start.

Facing page:

F/SGT NADON:- ME 109 PROBABLY DESTROYED. ⚼

Monday 7 June

"A" Flight did dawn readiness and started off with a convoy patrol. Nothing happened.

Then the IXs were scrambled after a plot of 12+. One enemy a/c was seen but was too far away and going like h—— for home.

"B" Flight came on at 13:00 hrs.

They had two uneventful scrambles and a couple of destroyer escort flips.

Facing page:

P/O BAXTER.
P/O WYNDHAM.
F/S ERSKINE.   } ARRIVED FROM UK.
SGT MEAGHER.
SGT STEWART.

Tuesday 8 June

"B" Flight started this morning with a visibility test. After that they had two scrambles but no action.

In the afternoon the new chaps did practise flying for the first time. "A" Flight had a scramble but no luck. While on practise flying a section was vectored onto enemy a/c but did not see it.

Wednesday 9 June

Seven of our nines were flown by "A" Flight on an escort job for Liberators. Altogether there were forty Spits airborne on this due [sic] 185 did not get any action, although they saw enemy a/c. All returned safely. Good job of bombing by Libs.

"B" Flight finished the day with a practise flip.

Thursday 10 June

"B" Flight started the day off with a scramble in the IXs but nothing was done.

Then 4 of the Vs and 6 of the IXs were airborne on a bombing do as escorts to Spits of [sic]

Practise flying by "B" Flight finished their morning.

"A" Flight started out by practise flying the new fellows.

Then the IXs were scrambled after 3+. One 109 was destroyed by F/O Kennedy and his number 2 P/O Sinclair. F/S Sinclair's guns jammed but not before he had a squirt. No. 4 failed to join the formation. The enemy a/c was chased right back to Sicily and was reported to have crashed into the sea. The pilot bailed out.

Later the IXs were again scrambled and vectored right off the coast of Sicily. After flying around for awhile they spotted the "Blood Wagon" picking up a pilot. Hard as it was, they left it alone. Then a Macchi 202 was spotted. F/S Sinclair got in a squirt and observed strikes on wing. Then Macchi headed north and F/O Kennedy came up under it and observed strikes in the engine. A/c was last seen on fire. All our a/c returned. Two air tests finished the day's flying.

Facing page:

F/LT KNIGHT – Stood down – but not returning immediately

F/O REID
P/O ZOBELL } Stood down – returning to UK tomorrow
F/S MAFFRE

F/O KENNEDY } 109G – DESTROYED. ࿕
P/O SINCLAIR

F/O KENNEDY } MACCHI 202 – DESTROYED. ⊞
F/S SINCLAIR

Friday 11 June

"A" Flight did predawn readiness but no flying was done until 11:00 hrs, that was practice. Then came an uneventful scramble.

"B" Flight then took over and did a fighter sweep over Sicily. But nothing happened. Island patrol and practice wound up a long day.

Saturday 12 June

"B" Flight came on at dawn and filled in a morning with practice flying. Squadron was stood down at 13:00 hrs.

Sunday 13 June

Nine Mk IXs flown by "B" Flight under Sqdn/Ldr MacDougall went as escort to Libs bombing Gerbini and Catania. No action was had by our boys. But 229 and 249 got a probable and damaged. However they lost three Spits. One was W/Cmdr Ellis. *[All three pilots including Wing Commander John Ellis, Krendi Wing Leader, were taken prisoner.]* Two other Spits crashed on landing. Altogether it was a rather costly do.

Four of our Spit IXs flown by "A" Flight were airborne on a scramble of 12+ but no luck.

Monday 14 June

"A" Flight did dawn readiness but only got airborne on practice flights. "B" Flight did the same.

Facing page:

14/6/43. Sgt MILLWARD } ARRIVED.
         Sgt RUSSUM

Tuesday 15 June

"B" Flight again did practice flying.

"A" Flight had two a/c on a convoy patrol – nothing doing. The IXs were scrambled but no contacts were made.

Wednesday 16 June

"A" Flight started in the morning and about half-way thru' the IXs were scrambled but no fun was had. Practice flying finished "A" Flight's tour of duty for the day.

"B" Flight, lucky as usual, got flying time in by practice flying and two informal scrambles.

Thursday 17 June

After doing dawn readiness "B" Flight took six nines over to Safi to co-operate with 1435 Sqdn as high cover to Libs bombing Biscari and Comiso aerodromes. Enemy a/c were seen but no contacts were made – all returned safely.

Sqdn stood down at 13:00 hrs.

Friday 18 June

"A" Flight did practice flying on their stand down morning. Then five of our IXs went to Safi to do a diversionary sweep over Sicily with 126 Sqdn and 1435. No action but accurate a/a near Comiso and Biscari.

"A" Flight then came on and more practice flying was done. An uneventful island patrol was carried out later in the day.

Saturday 19 June

Dawn readiness was done by "A" Flight. A scramble in the IXs later on was uneventful.

"B" Flight came on at 13:00 hrs and did practice flying. Later on they had a scramble then carried out an island patrol. No action took place.

Facing page:

F/LT WILLMOTT – arrived to take over Flight "A".

Sunday 20 June

"B" Flight struggled thru' a practice flip in the morning then all the boys went to Luca to see the King. *[This was an impromptu visit by King George VI.]*

Monday 21 June

"A" Flight did a spot of practice and air tests and then "B" Flight took over.

"B" Flight took nine Mk IXs under W/Cmdr Drake on a fighter sweep over Sicily. No contact was made.

Tuesday 22 June

"B" spent a busy morning practice flying.

"A" Flt then carried on and later put up two sections of Mk IXs to catch the Hun. Although the section under the CO saw the Hun they failed to make contact. Bad luck.

Wednesday 23 June

"B" Flt put up 4 Mk IXs on a sweep over Sicily but no fun was had.

Facing page:

F/LT KNIGHT – left for UK.

Thursday 24 June

"B" Flt did practice flying – that is all.

Friday 25 June

"A" Flt did the practice flying this morning.

Saturday 26 June

"A" Flt then did dawn readiness and got a scramble in the IXs after 1+. No luck. One of the boys landed at Luqua *[sic]*.

"B" Flt came on in the afternoon. They did practice formation, camera gun and aerobatics. Later on four IXs under F/Lt McKee were scrambled on a plot of 6+. They succeeded in sighting 3 x 109s. In the chase that followed Lt Bosch (SAAF) succeeded in closing with a 109 and claims a damaged. In this chase he dove his a/c until he was off the clock and got a confirmed gun panel from his own kite. Not too bad a show at all.

Two more patrols were carried out but no contacts.

Facing page:

LT BOSCH – ME 109 – DAMAGED. ✠

Sunday 27 June
"B" Flt did the practice flying in the morning. "A" Flt put up 8 Mk IXs as top cover for Spit bombers, bombing Gerbini near Catania. No action.

Later in the day Sgt Millward crash landed at Luqa. He was OK. Four of the IXs were airborne on a scramble after 2+ und*[er]* the CO. Although they sighted the enemy they failed to catch him. F/Lt Willmott landed at Luca.

Monday 28 June
"A" Flt did sweet FA this morning.

"B" Flt went as escort to Spit bombers to Comiso. Eight of the IXs were airborne but no luck was to be had. Later on they put up a patrol over the island but again nil results.

Tuesday 29 June
"B" Flt put up a few a/c on camera gun aerobatics and formation flying this morning.

"A" Flt in the afternoon flew 8 IXs as top cover to fighter bombers bombing Comiso again. This time we had a decidedly better time. Although flying the IXs at a very low altitude (11–12000´) our boys managed to destroy 2 and damage 2. F/S Nadon getting 1 destroyed and one damaged. Very good show. Other boys from 229 and 249 got a damaged (one from each Squdn.)

Facing page:

F/S NADON:-   MACCHI DESTROYED ✠
                   ME 109 DAMAGED   ✠
SGT MEAGHER:-   ME 109 DESTROYED   ✠
SGT HENDERSON:-   ME 109 DAMAGED   ✠

Wednesday 30 June
"A" Flt came out and did practice flying which proved rather costly.

P/O Baxter was very unfortunate in writing off a IX. As he was landing his air pressure gave out and he had no flaps or brakes after touching down and didn't know it till it was too late. He went off the end of No 2 runway. Sgt Russum had a burst tire but landed very well at Luca.

Facing page:

✠ SCORE FOR JUNE ⚙

1 x FW 190 – DESTROYED.	2 x ME 109 – DESTROYED.
2 x ME 109 – PROBABLY	2 x MACCHI 202 – DESTROYED
3 x ME 109 – DAMAGED.	

185 Sqdn – 1-7-43.
– Sqdn/Ldr MACDOUGALL DFC –

"A" FLT.	"B" FLT
F/LT WILLMOTT DFM	F/LT McKEE
P/O WEBSTER	F/LT CHAPPELL
P/O SINCLAIR	F/O IRELAND.
P/O BAXTER	F/O SCHUREN (USAAF)
F/S SINCLAIR (UK)	LT BOSCH.
F/S NADON (UK)	P/O WYNDHAM
F/S THOROGOOD. (UK)	F/S MERCER (UK) P/O
F/S ROBERTS	F/S CROSS
F/S CRUICKSHANK	F/S LOWRY (KILLED)
SGT MEAGHER	F/S ERSKINE
SGT HENDERSON	SGT McRAE (UK)
SGT HARRIS	SGT BUCHANAN
SGT RUSSUM	SGT WILSON
SGT MILLWARD.	SGT STEWART.
	SGT SCOTT.

Thursday 1 July

"B" Flt for a change did a little bombing, sending up four a/c to bomb Biscari. However they did pattern bombing, not diving, because of enemy a/c. They were engaged by top cover of 72 Sqn and one was damaged. All returned safely.

"A" Flt came on and after practice flying all afternoon put up four IXs on island patrol. No excitement.

Friday 2 July

"A" Flt put up four a/c practice flying. And that was all for the morning.

"B" Flt came on and of course immed[*iately*] went out on a fighter sweep over Sicily. Unfortunately we lost one of our new pilots F/Sgt Lowry who crashed into the sea. F/Sgt Mercer got one Me 109 destroyed. They then did some practice flying and called it a day.

Facing page:

F/SGT MERCER – ME 109 DESTROYED ✠

Saturday 3 July
SFA.

Sunday 4 July
"B" Flt put up nine a/c as escort to Libs bombing Gerbini. Rendezvous was not made and a/c returned without any action. Later on five of our Mk IXs were airborne again to escort Libs. No action.

"A" Flt came on and 4 were sent up on practice flying. It turned out to be rather expensive practice however. One of the section, Sgt Millward, crashed on take-off and P/O Webster crash landed at Hal Far for engine failure. No one was seriously hurt.

Three of our IXs were later scrambled after 2+. No fun.

Monday 5 July
No flying in the morning. However "B" Flt put up six Mk Vs as close escort to Mitchells bombing Biscari. Other sqdns supporting had fun but our boys saw nothing. Sqdn Ldr White of 229 was shot down.

Tuesday 6 July
"A" Flt had a crack at flying and put up four IXs and six Mk Vs as escort, along with other squadrons, to Mitchells bombing Comiso. No action was had, not even flak.

Wednesday 7 July
"A" Flt put up six Mk nines as target support for Fortresses bombing Gerbini. But as usual nothing was had.

"B" Flt had SFA.

Thursday 8 July
"B" Flt took a flip up to Gerbini to watch the Fortresses drop their load and then came back in time for dinner.

"A" Flt SFA.

Friday 9 July
Four of the officers of "A" Flt were scrambled out of bed to do an air sea rescue. They looked and looked but nothing was cooking. So they came back. Then two more F/S went and escorted the Walrus out and back.

That was all.

"B" Flt then did another flip to Gerbini in five Mk Vs and five Mk IXs as target support for Mitchells. This time the boys in the IXs had some fun getting a prob. and two destroyed (as indicated on opposite page) *[see below]*. All returned safe *[sic]* Sgt Cross got shot up a bit but was OK landing at Hal Far. Then an uneventful scramble.

F/LT McKEE   – 1 FW 190 – PROB. DEST.   卐
SGT BUCHANAN – 1 FW 190 – DESTROYED.   卐
F/SGT MERCER   – 1 MACCHI 202 – DESTROYED ⊕

During Operation 'Husky' – the Allied invasion of Sicily – Malta played a prominent role as Allied Headquarters and as a forward air base with no fewer than twenty-three Spitfire fighter squadrons, one Spitfire photo-reconnaissance squadron and a Spitfire tactical reconnaissance squadron.

Saturday 10 July

185, represented by "B" Flt, did its first patrol over the ships of the forces invading Sicily. And greatly to our surprise and disappointment no action was had.

"A" Flt then carried on with the same job in the afternoon also seeing no action. Later on "A" Flt put up 8 Mk Vs and four Mk IXs as target support to Libs bombing Catania – no fun was had.

Sunday 11 July

Up bright and early "A" Flt again put up 12 a/c on patrol over the shipping off Sicily and again no action. We seem to be in the wrong places at the right time.

In the afternoon "B" Flt did their bit over Sicily. In fact they did it twice.

Monday 12 July

"B" Flt did two patrols over ships off Sicily but no enemy action.

"A" Flt carried on with one patrol – no action.

Tuesday 13 July

"A" Flt took off to go as escort to Forts bombing Catania but changed over to a sweep around Catania. We chased a few but no luck at all.

"B" Flt then came on and of course did two shows, one freelance and one patrol over shipping.

Wednesday 14 July

In the morning "B" Flt patrolled south of Catania and stayed a little too long. Five of the boys had to land at Pachino, Sicily. They didn't just refuel their kites either.

"A" Flt came on in the afternoon and escorted Mitchells to Paterno under W/Cdr Drake. No action. Later on we patrolled shipping off Sicily.

Thursday 15 July

"A" Flt took a flip over to Catania for a spot of sight seeing. But only succeeded in chasing spots in the sky. All returned.

"B" Flt flew along with a dozen Mitchells to watch them bomb Paterno. Very good bombing.

Friday 16 July

"B" Flt boys escorted an a/c carrier early in the morning. Then they again went with the Mitchells to watch them bomb.

When "A" Flt took over we did a sweep around Catania and Gerbini with usual results of SFA.

Saturday 17 July

Once again "A" Flt stooged around Catania and Gerbini but as usual nothing happened. A couple more air tests finished us for the morning.

"B" Flt came on and escorted naval units for a change. But again SFA.

Sunday 18 July

"B" Flt got a scramble early in the morning but it was too early, nothing was had. They then swept around Catania and Gerbini.

Monday 19 July

"A" Flt started the afternoon with a few air tests and ended up with a sweep around Catania. Nothing as usual.

Tuesday 20 July

"A" Flt did a sweep around Catania–Gerbini area again, with no results. F/Lt Willmott almost got knocked down by flak. But all returned safely.

"B" Flt came on and two IXs were scrambled. No connections made. To-day practice flying started and "B" Flt started it.

Wednesday 21 July

Again "B" boys had a scramble after 1+ but no fun. Practice flying followed.

"A" Flt came on for their dose of practice. Later on two of our IXs were scrambled after an [sic] Ju 88 PRU but only succeeded in chasing it back. Bad job of controlling on opps [sic: ops, i.e. operations] part.

Thursday 22 July

Practice flying by both flts. "B" Flt got a couple of island patrols also.

Friday 23 July
Same again – practice flying for "B" Flt with one scramble to patrol.
Sqdn released 13:00 hrs.

Saturday 24 July
"A" Flt came on and did practice flying.
"B" Flt of course got some opps time on a couple of convoy patrols and one scramble.

Sunday 25 July
Practice flying all around. "A" Flt had two island patrols.

Monday 26 July
Practice again for both flights.

Tuesday 27 July
Same again.

Wednesday 28 July
Practice and one scramble – no fun.

Thursday 29 July
Practice and one island patrol.

Friday 30 July
Practice – one scramble – no luck.

Saturday 31 July
Practice again.

Facing page:

✠ SCORE FOR JULY ⊕

1 x 109 – DESTROYED	1 x FW 190 – PROB. DESTROYED
1 x FW 190 – DESTROYED	
1 x MACCHI 202 – DESTROYED	

– 185 SQUADRON (1-8-43) –
– SQDN/LDR MACDOUGALL. DFC –

"A" FLT	"B" FLT.
F/LT WILLMOTT DFM	F/LT McKEE
P/O SINCLAIR	F/LT CHAPPEL

P/O WEBSTER
P/O BAXTER
F/LT CLEMENTS
F/O RAMSAY
P/O DUNSMORE
F/S ROBERTS
F/S CRUICKSHANK
SGT HARRIS
SGT RUSSUM
SGT MILLWARD.
SGT DYER

F/O IRELAND.
LT BOSCH
P/O WYNDHAM.
F/O CRYDERMAN
P/O MORRISON
P/O DOUGLAS.
F/S CROSS
SGT BUCHANAN
SGT WILSON
SGT STEWART
SGT SCOTT
F/S HARROP
F/S OSBORNE

P/O MORRISON
P/O DOUGLAS
W/O HARROP } arrived 1-8-43
F/SGT DYER
P/O DUNSMORE

Sunday 1 August
   PRACTICE.

Monday 2 August
   A convoy patrol by "B" boys. Then more practice.

Tuesday 3 August
   Practice flying again. An Island patrol by "A" Flt.

Wednesday 4 August
   Practice. "B" Flt did the island patrol.

Thursday 5 August
   One scramble by "B" Flt and then practice.

Friday 6 August
   Practice by all.

Saturday 7 August
   One scramble early in the morning. They managed to contact the 88 but P/O Wyndham was unfortunately the receiver of some Jerry lead and was forced to bail-out, and the 88 got away with slight damage. P/O Wyndham was picked up and suffered only slight burns. Sqdn stood down 13:00 hrs.

Facing page:

7-7- [*sic*] 42
P/O WYNDHAM – Ju 88 DAMAGED.

Sunday 8 August
Practise by both.

Monday 9 August
Practise again.

Tuesday 10 August
"B" boys had an uneventful scramble then practise.
"A" Flt also   „   „   „   and practise.

Wednesday 11 August
"A" Flt had one scramble but SFA then practise. "B" boys continued the practise.

Thursday 12 August
More practise flying. Stood down 1300 hrs.

Friday 13 August
More practise still.

Saturday 14 August
Practise flying.

Sunday 15 August
Practise flying. S/Ldr Rabone borrowed one of our Vs and hacked down an [*sic*] Ju 88.

Monday 16 August
Practise flying. "B" boys had two island patrols.

Tuesday 17 August
One scramble for "B" Flt.

Wednesday 18 August
Practise again.

Thursday 19 August
Practise flying and one scramble for "B" boys. However the scramble was more profitable for Adolf as one of the boys pranged on landing.

Friday 20 August

Practise flying. Four of "A" Flt went on an offensive stooge north of Sicily and managed to shoot down a Cant 506 off Capri. Some fun and very encouraging after this long period of practise. "A" Flt also had a scramble but no luck.

Facing page:

S/LDR MACDOUGALL ⎫
F/LT WILLMOTT   ⎪ CANT 506 – DESTROYED. ⊕
F/O BAXTER   ⎬
P/O DUNSMORE   ⎭

Saturday 21 August

One uneventful scramble and the rest practise.

Sunday 22 August

Practise flying again (Boring, isn't it?)

Monday 23 August

Same again.

Tuesday 24 August

More practise and one scramble for "B" Flt. We often wonder who is going to win out in this battle of nerves (practise flying), the aircraft or us. Right now the a/c are pretty clapped but it is too close a race for comfort.

Wednesday 25 August

Something wrong here. We had two convoy patrols and very little practise.

Thursday 26 August

In the groove again, practise flying.

Friday 27 August

Ditto

Saturday 28 August

Not even practise. (Three cheers!!!)

Sunday 29 August

Right back at it again.

Monday 30 August
Practise by "A" and "B" Flts. Mostly air to air firing.

Tuesday 31 August
"A" Flt had one convoy patrol then more practise.

Wednesday 1 September
"B" boys came on and did an air to air. Then came a scramble but no luck. Squadron stand down 13:00 hrs.

Thursday 2 September
F/O Ireland went to Scordia to visit Lt Schuren (ex 185) USAAF. "A" Flt had a convoy patrol but it was uneventful. F/O Ireland returned from Scordia. How he did [so] is an unsolved mystery. It must have been the spirit he was in or spirits that were in him.

Friday 3 September
Practise flying by "A" Flt. "B" Flt as usual got the convoy patrols.

Saturday 4 September
For a change to-day "B" Flt got a scramble. No fun. Then came Island patrols all day.

Sunday 5 September
More Island patrols. One thing the Navy does is to give us some opps time.

Monday 6 September
One island patrol and practise flip by "B" boys.

Tuesday 7 September
More island patrols by "A" Flt and a ferry trip from Luqa to Krendi by yours truly.

Wednesday 8 September
Opps really shook us up to-day by scrambling both the IXs on the line and fives in the pens. But "A" Flt shook them right back by getting airborne before they knew what they wanted us to do. However the plot was only 18+ and turned out to be 24 Libs.
"B" Flt came on and escorted the fleet. F/O Baxter, however decided he wanted "to be alone" and took off on the other runway all by his lonesome. Thank, God, he remained alone until we were airborne.

There are no entries for 9 September in either the diary or squadron ORB.

238

Friday 10 September

"B" Flt did little pansy formation to Pant. Then Sqdn Ldr MacDougall left them and put down on Pant for the day. "And the rest came home.

> Left all alone,
> Dragging their a/c with them."

On 3 September three brigades of British and Canadian infantry of the Eighth Army had landed north of Réggio di Calábria in southern Italy. Italy capitulated five days later. On the 9th Allied troops also started to come ashore at Salerno. On 10 September the Italian Naval Fleet began to arrive under escort at Malta, the triumphant occasion prompting a delighted Admiral Sir Andrew Cunningham to signal the Admiralty:

> *Be pleased to inform their Lordships that the Italian Battle Fleet now lies at anchor under the guns of the Fortress of Malta.*

For the heroic Maltese and all who had defended their islands, it was a fitting tribute.

Saturday 11 September

"B" boys had a practise flip then came stand down.

Sunday 12 September

"A" Flt did a practice flip, then another one.

Monday 13 September

"A" Flt had a convoy patrol and the CO went to Lampedusa.
"B" Flt did air tests all afternoon.
The CO came back and we had fish for a super supper.

Tuesday 14 September

Both flts did practise.

Facing page:

14 SEPT – F/SGT LIVERSIDGE ⎤
             W/O NOBLE. ⎦ ARRIVED.

Wednesday 15 September

More convoy patrols for "A" Flt.

Thursday 16 September

Practise again by "B" boys. Lt Bosch went to Sicily visiting. Squdn released 13:00 hrs.

Friday 17 September
Practise by "A" Flt.

Saturday 18 September
Practise by "A" Flt and naval escort by "B" Flt.

Sunday 19 September
"B" Flt practice flying.

Monday 20 September
"A" Flt practiced and Sqdn Ldr MacDougall went to Africa.

Tuesday 21 September
CO came back [and] "B" Flt started 8 a/c on an interception practise and 6 a/c finished it.

Wednesday 22 September
"A" Flt did some air to air firing.

Thursday 23 September
Practice by both flts.

Friday 24 September
Pre-dawn readiness.
Stand down 13:00 hrs.

Saturday 25 September
After a terrific party in the mess, the night before, the officers were escorted from Krendi to Hal-Far by the Sgts. All managed to arrive safely, except P/O Dunsmore who was too anxious to touch down to [sic] high up. However it was only an oleo leg change. F/O Baxter rather shook the boys in close formation. Must have been dodging the gin spots. At last we are off the stationary a/c carrier and on an aerodrome again.

Sunday 26 September
Practice again. (No rest for the wicked) by "A" Flt.

Monday 27 September
Practice by "B" Flt led by the CO.

Tuesday 28 September
Practice by "A" Flt.

Wednesday 29 September

Lt Bosch went to Sicily for a visit.

The flts were switched around and mixed up. "B" Flt got a new flt Commander F/Lt Gervais from 249 Sqdn.

Thursday 30 September

Practice by all.

Friday 1 October

Practice by both flts. F/Sgt Dyer pranged on an attempted formation landing. He was pretty badly hurt and his condition serious.

Saturday 2 October

More practice bombing and strafing.

Sunday 3 October

More practice.

Monday 4 October

Practice by both flts. The adj [adjutant] went for a flip in the Maggie with the CO. When he came down he was actually able to carry his kit back to dispersal!!!

Tuesday 5 October

More dive bombing and strafing practice.

W/Cmdr Drake and the CO went night flying.

Wednesday 6 October

"A" Flt got some air to air firing off. W/O Weaver formerly of 185 Sqdn, who was shot down over Sicily and captured [on 9 September 1942], arrived here to-day to do some flying. He walked from his PoW camp to southern Italy and was brought back to Malta. However he isn't staying with the Sqdn this time.

Facing page:

F/Sgt Dyer, better known in the Sqdn as "Scruffy" died last night. Scruffy was one of the gayer types on the Sqdn and he will definitely be missed by one and all.

Thursday 7 October

One air test.

Friday 8 October

Same old practice. F/Sgt Stewart pranged – dusk X wind landing.

Saturday 9 October

More and more practice flying.

Facing page:

F/O LORD
F/S SCHOOLING
F/S BALLANTINE   }   arrived on Malta 9-10-43.
SGT BOTSFORD
F/SGT HOLLIMAN

Sunday 10 October

Practice again. F/Sgt Russum found flying above the sea rather boring so he tried to go underwater. However his a/c wasn't equipped for it and he was forced to return. As a matter of fact he was a lucky lad to be able to get back. From now on Filfla will have a satellite known as Russum's Rock.

Monday 11 October

Practice flying and one air sea rescue which proved fruitless. Three new boys were flying and had to land at Luca on account of cross wind. Later on 3 of our "aces" went to collect our a/c and after landing here retraction tests were carried out on said a/c. (?)

Tuesday 12 October

Practice flying, affiliation with Wellingtons.

Wednesday 13 October

Nothing at all.

Thursday 14 October

One practice flip.

Friday 15 October

Practice flying. "B" Flt did some co-op with the Nelson.

Saturday 16 October

More of the same.

Sunday 17 October

SFA.

Monday 18 October
New runway was opened.

Tuesday 19 October
More practice flying. F/Sgt Cruickshank had an engine cut on take off and in the resulting crash was instantly killed. This is the worst blow the Sqdn has received for many a month. Not only was Bill a good pilot but one of the best liked fellows on the Sqdn among ground crews and air crews.

Wednesday 20 October
LT Bosch arrived back from Africa. More of the same.

Thursday 21 October
"B" Flt did a sqdn formation. This is the first time for awhile that we have had enough a/c serviceable. This would never do, so yours truly and P/O Dunsmore immediately go up for colds.

Friday 22 October
F/LT Willmott and F/S Millward went to Lampedusa and escorted a doubtful Spit back to Malta.

Saturday 23 October
Air to ground firing all around.

Sunday 24 October
Usual thing – practice.

Monday 25 October
Just a couple of air tests. F/LT Willmott bogged off to Foggia.

Tuesday 26 October
W/O Palliser flew for the first time and unfortunately pranged. One more flip finished the day.

Facing page:

W/O PALLISER
F/SGT NEHORAI ⎬ arrived 26-10-43

Wednesday 27 October
F/Sgt Russum air tested his submarine Spit and got away with it.

Thursday 28 October
Air tests and a couple of interceptions made up a busy day.

Friday 29 October
Rather busy day of practice.

Saturday 30 October
More of the same.

Sunday 31 October
Air to ground firing and formation.

185 SQUADRON
– SQDN/LDR MACDOUGALL DFC –

"A" FLT	"B" FLT
FLT/LT Willmott DFM	F/LT Gervais
F/O Ramsay	LT Bosch
F/O Sinclair	F/O Wyndham
F/O Douglas	F/O Lord
P/O Dunsmore	P/O Cross
F/SGT Roberts	P/O Morrison
F/SGT Millward	W/O Noble
F/SGT Stewart	F/SGT Buchanan
F/SGT Schooling	F/SGT Russum
F/SGT Nehorai	F/SGT Osborne
SGT Botsford	F/SGT Liversidge
W/O Harrop	F/SGT Holliman
W/O Palliser	F/SGT Ballantine

Monday 1 November
Practice flying – F/O Ramsay went to Catania.

Tuesday 2 November
G.C. Millar took one of our a/c to Palermo. A section of "A" Flt did some co-op with HM Cruiser. F/O Ramsay came back – lucky to get back. Also G.C. Millar came back. "B" Flt did very little.

Wednesday 3 November
A couple of air tests made up a busy day of bridge.

Thursday 4 November
After dawn readiness "A" boys managed a practice flip. "B" Flt of course put up a squadron formation and a strafing do.

Friday 5 November
Same practice only "A" Flt had the edge to-day.

Saturday 6 November

F/O Ramsay, the prodigal son, went out to Catania again.

Sunday 7 November

Prodigal son returns bearing gifts of fruit and nuts.
"B" boys did another sqdn show.
"A" Flt did some practice interceptions.

Monday 8 November

One section airborne.

Tuesday 9 November

Both flts threw a lot of lead at Filfla again to-day.

Wednesday 10 November

Practice firing and navigation flips.

Thursday 11 November

Practice interceptions and navigat[ion].

Friday 12 November

Practice firing and interceptions. Co-op with cruiser. F/SGT NEHORAI pranged the gramophone.

Saturday 13 November

Exactly nothing happened.

Sunday 14 November

One air test by flt commander.

Monday 15 November

Ops shook us by scrambling us from 30 minutes on air sea rescue flip but we shook 'em right back by getting off in four minutes flat. However nothing was seen as a/c in trouble managed to reach base.

Tuesday 16 November

"A" Flt just couldn't resist a squadron formation flip seeing as we had so many a/c serviceable. Actually we were damn mad at having to get 14 pilots up a [sic] pre-dawn for nothing. Ops seem to delight in causing a lot of work for nothing. Later the IXs did a practise interception.

"B" boys had an escort job in the afternoon taking 8 a/c to escort a D.C. 3 [DC-3/Douglas Dakota]. Must have been loaded with beer.

Wednesday 17 November
"B" Flt decided to reciprocate and also did a squadron formation. In fact they flew so late in the morning that the a/c were still warm when "A" Flt came on at 1300 hrs to escort the battle wagons headed this way. However as we got 2 hrs in we didn't mind. Two IXs and 2 Vs were also out on a patrol. So much excitement never has been had by us for soooo long. The CO returned from his air firing course also.

Thursday 18 November
Only one flip by "A" Flt.

Friday 19 November
No flying to-day.

Saturday 20 November
Both flts flew on air tests, rhubarbs and practice flying. The CO took a section up.

Sunday 21 November
One practice rhubarb by "B" Flt.

Monday 22 November
"A" Flt did firing at poor old Filfla.

Tuesday 23 November
"B" Flt did some practice and air tests.

Wednesday 24 November
Six separate formations were flown by both flts for a big day of practice.

Thursday 25 November
Another big day of practice, must be an epidemic, or the wind is right down the runway.

Friday 26 November
Formation has changed back to line abreast again. Practice flying and air test by the CO. Both flt commanders bogged off to Catania yesterday [and] came back to day.

Saturday 27 November
Practice formation, rhubarbs and strafing flips were done by both flts.

Sunday 28 November
Battle and pansy formation mixed with a little local flying and

aerobatics completed the menu for the day.

Monday 29 November
The main course for the day was camera gun practice mixed with a teaspoonful of battle formation and flavoured with a drop of pansy.

Tuesday 30 November
"B" Flt managed to scrounge a convoy patrol to ease their boredom, while yours truly and F/O Ramsay toured Sicily on a mail run.

Wednesday 1 December
Cine gun practice was clamped on again by "B" boys and "A" Flt promptly shot away a drogue. Formation and strafing finished off our work (?).

Thursday 2 December
F/Lt Willmott and myself did a practice rhubarb on Sicily.
"A" Flt did cine gun and air to air firing.

Friday 3 December
P/O Cross, F/S Russum, F/O Sinclair, F/S Roberts went to Catania to take over readiness section from 229 Sqdn. Practice rhubarb and battle formation and one dog fight finished flying.

Saturday 4 December
F/O Douglas dashed to Catania to make arrangements for himself and three others to follow, to stay for the night. They went, as reinforcements for the four already there, under Sqdn Ldr MacDougall.

Sunday 5 December
Bit of formation by "B" boys.

Monday 6 December
Little formation by "A" Flt. The three returned from Catania but the CO had engine trouble and force lobbed on Catania aerodrome. He had a few hard knocks but nothing broken. He is in 5th [or 8th] Canadian General – Catania. Lucky blighter.

Tuesday 7 December
"B" boys had a convoy patrol and landed at TK on account of weather. The IXs were scrambled after a 6+ plot which turned out to be 5 D.C. 3s.
"A" Flt did the egg run to Borizzo and a couple of flips locally.

Wednesday 8 December
"A" Flt had a scramble to patrol a convoy and also did an island patrol. And the "Wandering Flight Commander" (B Flt) wandered again to Catania. He also wandered back the same day.

"B" boys also did an island patrol.

Thursday 9 December
SFA.

Friday 10 December
Four more went to Catania thru' blinding rainstorms to relieve the besieged readiness section. F/Lt Willmott showed them the way in his sturdy Hurricane. The other four weary pee-los returned with the Hurry and Flt commander.

"B" Flt, as usual, got a convoy patrol. They should be operationally tired [?] now or at least convoy cautious.

Saturday 11 December
"B" Flt again did convoy patrols. "A" Flt sent F/O Sinclair and F/Sgt Millward on a practice rhubarb to Bir Rizzo [sic] but they failed to return owing to heavy ground attacks by Gremlins of the Bowser Division and Starting Battery. Cannon tests completed the day.

Sunday 12 December
Sinclair and Millward overcame the hostile attacks of the Gremlins and managed to return to base without loss. F/Lt Gervais took the "Doc" (F/Lt [name probably reads] Grant) for his monthly trip in the Maggy.

Monday 13 December
A weather test, a flip to Catania and back and the return of Peter Bosch all by "B" Flt was all the flying done to-day.

Tuesday 14 December
F/O Douglas hopped up to Catania in the Hurry and back again of course. "A" Flt also sent a section practice flying.

Wednesday 15 December
Gervais (F/LT) does it again, however he restricted himself to Catania and only one day. F/O Ramsay soloed in the Hurry. Camera gun practice continued all afternoon and F/LT Willmott practiced drogue towing.

Thursday 16 December
Most of the flying was done between Hal Far and Catania and vice versa, the rest was camera gun practice.

Friday 17 December
"B" boys again did a convoy patrol.
Four more went to Catania and four returned.
Four of the IXs were flown to keep them in trim.

Saturday 18 December
Four IXs airborne again.

Sunday 19 December
SFA.

Monday 20 December
"A" Flt did one flip. Then "B" boys of course, had a convoy to watch over. LT Bosch and F/Sgt Nehorai left for Italy.

Tuesday 21 December
F/O Lord, f—— off, I mean went to Catania and return[ed]. Outside of a couple of flips, one by each flt that was all.

Wednesday 22 December
Yours truly and F/Sgt Millward again went on an extended rhubarb and navigation trip. All went well except the eggs, they went 2 days ago. LT Bosch returned without Nero (??).

Thursday 23 December
"B" boys had a bit of convoy duty. F/Sgt Nehorai returned from his trip to Italy after one of 229's rogue a/c had given up the ghost and delayed him.

Friday 24 December
F/LT WILLMOTT took a flip to Catania and back.
An air test and local flying finished the day for us but F/O Douglas and Morrison came back for the Xmas doings.

Saturday 25 December
Even on Christmas day "B" Flt get convoys. Then two of B Flt went out looking for F/O Dunsmore who was supposed to have been lost but he was in Catania all the time with his finger well-in.

Sunday 26 December
"A" Flt did some local flying and an air-test, W/Os Noble and Harrop returned from Catania.
"B" boys also did some local flying and an air test or two.

Monday 27 December

"B" Flt did battle formation and a height climb. This time one of the pilots (F/Sgt Liversidge) went u/s, well it's a change anyway.

LT Bosch and Ballantine F/Sgt did the egg run to Bo-Rizzo. A night flying test was did [sic] but that's as far as it went.

Tuesday 28 December

To-day we flew more hours than that. Convoy patrols, air to air firing, practice flying and circuits and bumps by F/Sgt Schooling made up the grand total.

Wednesday 29 December

"B" boys did more convoy patrols and air to air on the drogue. "A" Flt did practice rhubarb and flying.

Thursday 30 December

Air to air was continued by "A" Flt in the morning and "B" Flt in the afternoon.

Friday 31 December

Odds and ends were caught up by a variety of flying. And that ended 185 Sqdn's flying for 1943.

Let's hope we see more action in '44.

After the Allied landings at Salerno in September 1943, the Germans withdrew to defensive positions north of Naples. Allied units continued to arrive in Italy where both sides became bogged down in a drawn-out battle of attrition. In the meantime, Army and Air Force units in Malta were redeployed as required. In early 1944 detachments of 185 Squadron operated out of Italy in the Táranto area and carried out attacks across the Adriatic in Albania.

1944

185 SQUADRON (1-1-44)
– S/LDR WILLMOTT. DFM –

"A" FLT	"B" FLT
F/[sic] RAMSAY	F/LT GERVAIS
F/O SINCLAIR	P/O CROSS
F/O DOUGLAS	P/O BUCHANAN
P/O STEWART	F/O WYNDHAM
P/O DUNSMORE	F/O LORD.

F/SGT ROBERTS   F/O MORRISON
F/SGT MILLWARD   F/SGT RUSSUM
F/SGT SCHOOLING   F/SGT OSBORNE
F/SGT BOTSFORD.   F/SGT LIVERSIDGE
F/SGT NEHORAI   F/SGT BALLANTINE
W/O PALLISER   F/SGT HOLLIMAN
W/O HARROP   W/O NOBLE

Saturday 1 January

After a hectic and very enjoyable New Year's Eve flying was entirely out of the picture.

Sunday 2 January

Two sections of 2 a/c were airborne on practice and cine gun exercises. The weather was certainly not fair and the X wind very strong but all managed to get down OK.

Monday 3 January

"B" Flt once again did convoy patrols. It is becoming a very bad habit with "B" Flt getting all the "OPPs" (?) trips as they do.

Tuesday 4 January

"B" Flt again put in the hrs on practise rhubarbs.

"A" Flt did a little practise flying and had a scramble which resulted in precisely f.a. F/O Douglas and Sinclair hopped over to Tunis and back with a message from AOC to a Groupy [Group Captain].

Wednesday 5 January

One cine gun flip. Exciting isn't it?

Thursday 6 January

"B" Flt did a little battle formation and then escorted the AOC, in his Mosquito, part way on his trip to —— (?). Well, anyway some people leave the island. Maybe there is still hope for us yet?

The intrepid pilots of "A" Flt braved the elements and did a couple of cine trips.

Friday 7 January

Air to air firing on the drogue was carried out by "A" Flt and F/O Douglas spoiled our record and our drogue by hitting it. What a blow! (What a bit of luck!)

"B" Flt didn't do much, "Just another convoy patrol!!!"

Saturday 8 January

"B" Flt followed suit and fired at the drogue. Our prodigal F/LT Gervais nipped off to Gela and Borizzo with F/Sgt Russum for eggs. F/Sgt Nehorai (Nero to you) f—— off to Catania. "A" Flt did a little practise and cine gun. The wandering "Egg-Men" returned.

Sunday 9 January

"A" Flt got reckless with the "Hurri" and let W/O Palliser fly it. He didn't do too bad actually. Yours truly (F/O SINCLAIR) and P/O Stewart bogged-off to Catania. Another futile attempt at getting eggs. However we arranged for future collection. Otherwise there was no flying worth mentioning. Of course we returned same day. (Must have been pay day or something!)

Monday 10 January

185 Sqdn moved over to Luca for a few days while works and bricks try to make the best of a bad job on the runway (?) they built a while back. Island patrols were flown by "B" Flt and they were also scrambled after 3+. Of course opps knew about the reccos last night but that only gave them more time to think up some way of making a balls of it. Our a/c already up on patrol was vectored after Mr Jordan's shadow and the other two scrambled were vectored after something or other, anyway they never found it. 229 scrambled about 10 min. later actually contacted the enemy and had a squirt. Either opps don't like 185 or their finger is so far in they are licking their lips with it!

More island patrols for "A" Flt.

Tuesday 11 January

"A" Flt had a couple of convoy escorts and an island patrol. Mr Douglas must have been sick because he flew on his afternoon off. He did a quick egg run to Catania.

Wednesday 12 January

"A" Flt had a very quick scramble for 10 mins. after SFA. We then returned to Hal Far.

Thursday 13 January

"A" Flt did some cine gun and a convoy patrol.
"B" Flt carried on with the convoy and did some cine gun.

Friday 14 January

More island patrols and air to air firing were done by "B" Flt. "A" Flt did cine gun and one or two patrols.

Saturday 15 January

"A" Flt did six island patrols, had one scramble, and did a navy co-op and smoke screen test, a pretty busy morning. "B" Flt did just about the same to add to "A" Flt's flying for a fairly good total.

Sunday 16 January

Island patrols, an air to air, and one pansy formation trip, occupied both flts for the day.

Monday 17 January

"A" Flt did a-to-a and patrols, "B" Flt did patrols.

Tuesday 18 January

Air to air and cine gun.

Wednesday 19 January

"A" Flt tried to get a drogue off but failed so cine gun was done instead. The egg rhubarb was done on Comiso and we got about 200 confirmed. "B" Flt did cine gun too.

Thursday 20 January

More cine-gun with an interception by "B" Flt.

Friday 21 January

Cine-gun by both flts and interception by "A" Flt.

Saturday 22 January

More cine gun by "B" Flt.

"A" Flt almost did a co-operation with Wellingtons but the weather closed in.

Sunday 23 January

F/O Douglas and F/S Botsford went to Comiso. F/O Ramsay and F/S Schooling were scrambled [but] no contact was made. F/S Schooling had engine trouble and had to bale out. The Vs and IXs were scrambled at the same time and got kind of mixed-up. However the IXs were fortunate enough to make contact. F/O Sinclair shot the Ju 88 (recco) into the sea. No survivors were picked up. F/S Schooling was eventually picked up and was no worse for wear.

W/O Harrop was scrambled on his own but had no luck. Ditto F/O Ramsay and F/S Nehorai.

Egg-run pilots returned safe and sound.

Facing page:

253

23-1-44
    F/O SINCLAIR – 1 JU 88 DESTROYED ⚙

Monday 24 January
  More cine gun. F/O Wyndham went to Catania to look for another IX but had no luck.

Tuesday 25 January
  One cine gun flip by "A" Flt. W/C Hanks borrowed one of our kites for the day.

Wednesday 26 January
  Boys returned from Mt Etna and two more went away. No flying was done by either flt.

Thursday 27 January
  Cine gun, air test and an air sea rescue made up to-day's flying.

Friday 28 January
  "B" Flt did some dive bombing and more air sea rescue. "A" Flt did cine-gun [word unreadable].

Saturday 29 January
  P/O Roberts and W/O Palliser took off in the grey of dawn on a convoy patrol over a convoy that wasn't there (wizard camouflage). Air to air finished the morning off.
  "B" Flt did a convoy patrol and a couple of air tests.

Sunday 30 January
  A terrific session of air firing was done by both flts. "A" Flt lost more drogues than enough.

Monday 31 January
  F/O Douglas (the egg man) again went to Comiso. Four of our IXs went to Italy to do some opps led by the CO.

Tuesday 1 February
  A couple of checks and tests by both flts.
  "B" Flt had one uneventful scramble.

Wednesday 2 February
  Three of the "opps" types came back, one had a u/s u/c and had to stay. They had a bit of luck and their score is recorded on opposite page [see below]. P/O [sic] Douglas took spare part to Grottaglie and returned.

S/LDR WILLMOTT		
P/O BUCHANAN	1 SCHOONER	DESTROYED 1 SCHOONER –
F/SGT OSBORNE	1 TRUCK	PROB. DEST.

Thursday 3 February
Started Met Flt on our Sqdn. F/S Holliman had the doubtful honour. Little more flying for the day.

Friday 4 February
Met Flt – F/LT TEKLOOT. Air tests and dive-bombing and AA co-op. Yours truly slipped up to Torigno in a PRU Spit. P/O Buchanan returned.

Saturday 5 February
SFA.

Facing page:

5-2-44 F/LT QUINE – arrived from 87 Sqdn

Sunday 6 February
Met Flt – F/O Douglas. Practice flying included cine gun and dive bombing. Yours truly returned from Torigno.

Monday 7 February
Met Flt – F/Sgt Liversidge. Very little done to-day. F/LT Gervais gave F/LT Tekloot dual on a Fairchild.

Tuesday 8 February
Met Flt – F/Sgt Schooling. – Egg run cracked-off. Practice flying of AA co-op, GL co-op, scrambles. P/O Noble chased a balloon and never found it.

Wednesday 9 February
Met Flt – P/O Noble – Four of our a/c went to Catania to do readiness. (229 went to Grottaglie.)

Thursday 10 February
Met Flt – F/LT Quine. – AA coop, practise interception, air tests was all practise flying *[sic]*. One scramble by "A" Flt no fun.

Friday 11 February
Very little flying, one uneventful scramble, practise flying and return of NCOs from Catania and P/O Buch. Roberts nipped up to Palermo.

Saturday 12 February
Practise flying and one interception was all for to-day.

Sunday 13 February
Besides a little practise flying "B" Flt had a scramble with no joy and a patrol over *[Cape]* Passero. Roberts returned again.

Monday 14 February
F/O Wyndham went to Palermo. The odd practise flip and convoy patrols made up flying for the day.

Tuesday 15 February
Egg run cracked off early. AA co-op, and other co-ops with dive bombing practise made up an exciting day. Egg run returned.

Wednesday 16 February
Two NCOs went to Catania. CO and Harrop went looking for a pontoon. CO got ambitious and flew again looking for a dinghy.

Thursday 17 February
Purely practise.

Friday 18 February
Ptce *[sic]* flying. Four more went to Italy to do some work (?).

Saturday 19 February
One naval co-op and rest ptce flying.

Sunday 20 February
A couple of practise interceptions and targets.

Monday 21 February
One ptce intercept. Three boys returned.

Tuesday 22 February
Ptce flying, egg run and the fourth from Italy returned.

Wednesday 23 February
"B" Flt, as usual, had convoy patrols, "A" Flt ptce flying. NCOs returned from Catania. Two officers to Cat.

Thursday 24 February
Five more pushed off up north to Grottaglie.

Friday 25 February
Ptce flying.

Saturday 26 February
"A" Flt escorted a Warwick [and] "B" Flt ptce flying.

Sunday 27 February
Ptce flying.

Monday 28 February
F/Lt Quine went on a search over Sicily.

Tuesday 29 February
Four returned from Grottaglie. The sqdn heard the news of Morrison's death and we all felt rather shaken. Ken was one of the more experienced lads and also one of the more popular ones in the Sqdn. His death brought a serious loss to the Sqdn. He was a type of fellow hard to replace.

Facing page:

F/O Morrison – killed in action over Albania

Entries for the first half of March are largely uneventful with terse references recording mainly practice flights and training. On Monday 13 March Flight Sergeant F.T. Holliman took over the diary after Flying Officer Sinclair was posted.

Monday 13 March
Section set out for BRENDISI [sic: BRINDISI] to do "BIG OPs", landed at CATANIA. Bad weather.

Tuesday 14 March
No flying.

Wednesday 15 March
Detachment at BRENDISI did shipping recce and bombing and strafing, had good results. "B" Flight had two scrambles today.

Thursday 16 March
Practice flying.

Friday 17 March
The section at BRENDISI went on a rhubarb and pranged several trucks and damaged two schooners.

At base we had a day of convoy patrols. The BRENDISI section returned in the evening, full *[of]* joy.

Saturday 18 March
Bags of practice flying.

Facing page:

SGT BROWN. arrived 18.3.44.

Entries for Sunday 19 March to Thursday 23rd are again uneventful.

Friday 24 March
Another section set out for BRENDISI. Practice flying only at base. Section did two shows when arriving at BRENDISI, good results.

Saturday 25 March
Practice flying.

Sunday 26 March
'B' had convoy patrol. Section at BRENDISI did two shows.

Monday 27 March
The BRENDISI section returned today.

Facing page:

S/LDR WILLMOTT	
P/O BUCHANAN	7 trucks destroyed
F/O WYNDHAM	11 „ damaged
P/O PALLISER.	2 Staff cars damaged.
F/SGT RUSSUM	

During the next few days there was a continuation of practice flying.

Saturday 1 April
'A' Flight detached at PALERMO. 'B' Flight is the only defence the "Gem of the Med" has, it's in good hands!!

Little of note occurred for much of April as practice flying continued interrupted only by convoy patrols on the 11th and occasional uneventful scrambles. During the month the following new arrivals were recorded:

F/O BROOKS. arrived from 249 SQDN 7.4:44

F/O HILTZ arrived from 73 Sqdn 7:7.44
LT PENTON (SAAF) arrived 7.4:44.

SGT ROBERTS arrived 10.4.44.
W/O MORRIS arrived from   [sic] 13:4:44.

F/LT BULL arrived from 73 Squadron 22:4:44.

Thursday 27 April
And Practice.
Section set for GROTTAGLIE to dice with the Hun.

Friday 28 April
Practice flying.

Saturday 29 April
Section returned from GROTTAGLIE minus two, great loss to squadron.

Facing page:

20 P/O BUCHANAN   } Shot down by ground fire over
28 F/SGT SCHOOLING } ALBANIA. Bailed out OK.

S/LDR WEBB
P/O BUCHANAN
P/O NOBLE
F/SGT SCHOOLING
F/SGT BALLANTINE.

Again, practice flying predominated during May. On the 9th a section set out for Grottaglie. Three new arrivals were recorded the following day:

10:5:44 SGT PROCTOR
          SGT WEEDON   arrived. Proctor and Weedon have only
          SGT SLEIGH.   3 hrs on Spits; Sleigh has 40.

Thursday 11 May
Scramble today intercepted friendly D.C.3 (very dangerous). There was also an egg run to COMISO, all egg[s] returned unharmed.

Friday 12 May
All GROTTAGLIE section returned today with good results. Only practice flying took place here.

Facing page [presumably the Grottaglie section]:

F/LT BULL.
F/O LORD
F/SGT HOLLIMAN
LT PENTON.

Three days of practice flying followed.

Tuesday 16 May

Big 'opps' today, two convoy patrols and one scramble, work at last! The new boys flew today, two 'kites' had to have leg changes. "They did well."

Wednesday 17 May

Two more scrambles but still no joy, the Hun is getting shy, he won't come near the island.

For the rest of May the squadron flew mainly practice flights with just two uneventful scrambles recorded. There were two new arrivals on Thursday 25th:

LT ROWE   } Arrived 25/5/44.
LT RITCHIE } SAAF.

A day later:

P/O BUCHANAN returned today the 26:5:44 after three weeks walking in Albania and Jugoslavia, he managed to get through 3 pairs of boots in his travels

The pilots' frustration at the lack of activity is evident in the month's final entries:

Tuesday 30 May

New boys flew again, had another leg change, watching these fellows land is the only excitement we get these days.

Wednesday 31 May

Finished the month with practice. What a life!!

Thursday 1 June

Started the month well with practice flying. We have just got the gen that there is an Air Day coming up on the 21st of the month, so we are doing bags of Formation, there is some talk about us doing aerobatics in formation. What a horrible thought!

Friday 2 June
More formation today, we did a loop, it's not as dangerous as we thought it would be.

With the exception of some uneventful scrambles the first three weeks of June were spent rehearsing for the forthcoming air display.

Wednesday 21 June
Air Day, crowds of people turned *[out]* to see the big show, *[and]* it went off OK without a hitch except for the 'last act' *[when]* F/O Cross and F/O Brooks almost had a head on crass *[sic]* whilst beating up the 'drome, *[but]* the crowd thought it was pretty good and wanted an encore.

Thursday 22 June
Back to the practice flying again, the excitement is all over, peace once again in the crew room.

Friday 23 June
Scramble, still no joy, "what a bind!!"

Saturday 24 June
Practice again.

Sunday 25 June
Practice.

Monday 26 June
And more practice.

Tuesday 27 June
The new boys have started dive bombing Filfla, we have got the gen that the squadron is heading North, spirits are very high at last.

Wednesday 28 June
More bombing, the boys are getting keen *[and]* three hit the target today.

Thursday 29 June
Two scrambles today the Hun is getting braver.

Friday 30 June
Two more scrambles today*[;]* the CO intercepted a JU 188 on the 'deck' leaving trails in the water (very low!) S/LDR Willmott's cannons jammed

after the first burst, but he did a good job with his machine guns.

Facing page:

30.6:44. S/LDR WILLMOTT. 1 JU 188 DAMAGED.

Saturday 1 July
Sent out a recce to wait for the Hun, but he is not so keen after what happened on the 30th.

Sunday 2 July
All quiet on the MALTA FRONT practice again.

Practice flying including bombing and strafing predominated during July. There were a few fruitless scrambles. On Tuesday 18th low flying battle formation commenced prompting hope of a move to Italy.

Saturday 22 July
At last!!! P/O Ballantine and LT Rowe found a JU 188 90 miles out at sea and hacked him down. The rear gunner was a "gen lad", he shot LT Rowe down and damaged P/O Ballantine. LT Rowe was picked up by an HSL and returned after a night at sea none the worse for his experience.

Facing page:

22:7:44 P/O BALLANTINE } JU 188 DESTROYED ✥
       LT ROWE

Sunday 23 July
Another scramble but the Hun is not so keen today, he turned back 150 miles away.

Monday 24 July
The squadron has been stood down today prior to posting to Italy. Good show!
That night beer flowed freely over the bar.

Tuesday 25 July
And so we say goodbye to this beautiful "gem set in the blue Mediterranean" for we are taking our aircraft up north to join in this war which is going on, (so they tell us) Grottaglie first stop.

Wednesday 26 July
No flying [as] we are getting organised on the camp.

Thursday 27 July

The CO flew up to DAFHQ to get the full gen on our posting. Spirits are very high on the Squadron now.

Overleaf:

SQUADRON STRENGTH ON ARRIVAL IN ITALY. 25.7.44

S/LDR WILLMOTT. DFM	RAF	
F/LT BULL	RCAF	
F/LT BROOKS DFM	RAF	
F/O CROSS	RAF	KILLED. 23.8.44
F/O LORD	RAF	
F/O STEWART.	RNZAF	
F/O BUCHANAN	RNZAF	
F/O HILTZ.	RCAF	
F/O ROBERTS	RAF	
F/O OSBORNE	RNZAF	
F/O PALLISER	RNZAF	
P/O BALLANTINE	RAF	
P/O HOLLIMAN	RAF	
LT PENTON.	SAAF	
LT RITCHIE	SAAF	
LT ROWE.	SAAF	
LT WEST.	SAAF	
W/O LIVERSIDGE	RAF	
W/O MORRIS	RAAF	
W/O NEHORAI	RAF	
F/SGT BOTSFORD	RAF	
F/SGT GEORGE.	RAF	
F/SGT JONES.	RAAF	
SGT ROBERTS.	RAF	
SGT BROWN.	RAF	KILLED 1.9.44
SGT WEEDON	RAF	
SGT PROCTOR	RAF	
SGT SLEIGH.	RAF	
SGT MEDLICOTT	RAF	
SGT JEANS	RAF	KILLED 12.9.44.
SGT MORGANS	RAF	
SGT JOHNSON	RAF	
SGT MATHER	RAF	
SGT HOUSE	RAF	

Friday 28 July

We are doing "gash" flying now pending further orders. We did three convoy patrols today.

Saturday 29 July
  No flying.

Sunday 30 July
  No flying.

There is no diary entry for 31 July and nothing of significance in the squadron ORB.

In August Number 185 Squadron moved to the Italian front for fighter-bomber missions in support of the Allied armies where it remained until the end of the war.

Tuesday 1 August
Started the month well with two convoy patrols, and we got the gen that we are going north tomorrow.

Wednesday 2 August
  No move.

Thursday 3 August
  No move.

Friday 4 August
All our aircraft took off and headed north destination Perugia, we all landed without any incidents.

Saturday 5 August
  The CO flew to Malta to organise the beer.

Sunday 6 August
The CO returned with everything under control, good show. Two armed recces went out, no transport on roads so they attacked bridge west of Rimini, no hits scored.

Monday 7 August
Three aircraft went out to bomb road junction, one hit junction [and] the other two hit the road.

Tuesday 8 August
Two bomb line recces went out, nothing sighted. Hurricane set out for Malta to collect the beer.

Wednesday 9 August

Two shows bombing road targets. Too much cloud about for any big shows.

Thursday 10 August

Hurricane Beer Waggon returned, 'bags of Grog'.

Friday 11 August

One show went out to bomb a heavy gun position and scored near misses.

Saturday 12 August

Section went out to bomb rail junction, and scored two direct hits. They found quite a lot of flak over the target. LT Penton had one aileron put out of action but he landed all in one piece. An armed recce went out later in the day but had no joy.

Sunday 13 August

Another section went out to bomb the bridge which we went after a week ago, when they returned they returned [sic], they informed us that the bridge is still intact.

Monday 14 August

Two sections out after their bridge again, they are getting nearer but they haven't hit it yet. 87 Sqdn have been out after it and they have had no luck either, there must be a troop of gremlins that move it when the bombs are falling.

There is no entry for Tuesday 15 August. The squadron ORB states:

No operational activity took place.

Wednesday 16 August

No flying [as] weather u/s.

Thursday 17 August

One section out on an armed recce, found nothing to bomb so they vent[ed] their anger on a railway line west of Rimini and scored two direct hits. Three other recces went out but had no joy. The beer Hurricane set out for Malta.

Friday 18 August

It's that bridge again, a section of four attacked it and scored hits on the road. The CO led another section later in the day and hit the supports on the embankment *[but]* the other bombs fell wide, they have experienced no flak on these shows yet!

Saturday 19 August
Weather duff.

Sunday 20 August
Two sections bombed railway bridge at Rimini, hits were scored. They had quite a bit of flak to contend with, this is the first the new boys have seen, I think it shook them a little.

A section of six went out on a recce and found nothing to bomb so they decided to go after the much-attacked bridge, and pranged it, at last!! It was rather unfortunate for the Hun, he decided to move some AA guns around this particular eyesore today, but they did no damage.

Monday 21 August
Big escort day, Marauders in the morning and Kittyhawks in the afternoon, quite a rest.

Tuesday 22 August
The boys found another bridge to play with today. A section of six went out this morning and pranged it first time, good show.

Another section of six went out this evening and pranged the railway between FORLI and FAENZA. (The Italian "Bradshaws" can't be very reliable these days). On the return journey they spotted a tanker (Hun) hugging the coast off Rimini, so they bombed up after landing and took to the air again. No hits were scored, but some very near misses were observed. A lot of flak was encountered from the shore batteries and the ships' own defences, but nobody was damaged.

Wednesday 23 August
Eight aircraft took off and landed at Falconara to do an escort job. F/O Cross got stuck on the runway and another aircraft ran into the back of him. This will be quite a loss to the squadron, he was well liked. The escort went off without a hitch.

Six aircraft went out strafing and pranged a hay cart, a shaky do!

Facing page:

23:8.44 F/O CROSS KILLED.

Thursday 24 August
Four aircraft escorted Kittyhawks. The rest of the day was filled in with air-tests, we have just received six Spit VIIIs and everybody is happy.

Friday 25 August

Another day of escorts and movement. Six aircraft provided cover for Marauders bombing Forli. After the show they landed at the new base (LORETO). In the afternoon six aircraft escorted the PM and Gen Alexander in a D.C.3., they landed at our base to inspect.

Saturday 26 August

One section went out on recce and strafed power station.

Sunday 27 August

Col Moody led six aircraft to bomb barges at Bellaria scoring direct [sic] in centre of concentration, light flak was experienced.

Monday 28 August

First show out bombed and strafed MT workshops at Forli and destroyed one truck and damaged several buildings.

The next show attacked a bridge all near misses, a Hun truck got in the way of one bomb and "had it", an engine and a truck were strafed on the way home [and] strikes were observed.

The last show bombed marshalling yard at Faenza [and] all bombs fell in target area, bags of flak with nobody hit. This was quite a good day's "opps".

Tuesday 29 August

Six aircraft took off this morning at 0600 hr, led by Col Moody they did a recce near Bologna and clobbered a railway line. On returning they strafed five trucks damaging two and destroying one. The Hun gunners in a nearby town [were] annoyed at being woken up so early [and] put up a good barrage damaging one aircraft.

On return journey P/O HOLLIMAN'S (the diarist) engine cut through lack of fuel, he tried to force land but a tree got in the way, and he was carted off to hospital slightly injured.

Three other shows went off that day, bombed and hit three railway lines and destroying one staff car. Quite a good day's work.

Wednesday 30 August

A section of four led by Col Moody bombed railway bridge, two scored near misses [and] the other two fell on small huts near railway, very little flak was experienced.

Another section went after the same railway and scored near misses, they strafed and destroyed 3 ton truck.

Thursday 31 August

One section went out on armed recce and bombed railway, two hits were scored.

Another section were out after gun positions, one direct hit was scored and strikes were observed on strafing. Bags of flak but nobody was hit.

Friday 1 September

A section went out and bombed gun positions west of Cattolica [*and*] all bombs fell in target area[*;*] not much flak was experienced.

The next show to go out attacked bridge near Rimini, no hits were scored but they were very near. They strafed a 15 CWT truck on the way out and received heavy flak from Rimini which accounted for Sgt Brown's glycol leak, he tried to bail out but appeared to get caught up in the cockpit.

This was Sgt Brown's 2nd opp trip.

Two other shows went out and pranged a bridge near Rimini.

Facing page:

1.9.44 SGT BROWN KILLED IN ACTION.

Saturday 2 September

Two sections were scrambled for three plus coming in from Rimini area. They patrolled Rimini at 10,000 ft for some time but had no joy, the only thing they saw was 88mm flak.

The CO led a section at dusk to cover Rimini area looking for these bandits but had no joy.

Sunday 3 September

The CO led six aircraft into Rimini area and attacked a railway bridge at Faenza, three bombs fell on the embankment very close to the bridge [*and*] the others scored near misses. No flak over target.

Two other shows went out after bridges and pranged one. One Hun 3 ton truck accidentally got in the way of one of our bombs.

Monday 4 September

Nine aircraft did a Rover David (support to army)[*;*] they were split up into two sections, one section was directed to a bridge in the fighting line and scored one direct hit [*while*] the other section bombed a bridge at SANT ARCANGELO, three direct hits were scored and one bomb fell in the town starting large fire. Heavy and light intense flak was encountered, but no damage was inflicted on our aircraft.

After this show the aircraft moved up to our new base (FARNO) [*sic: Fano*]. We are getting quite used to this packing, unpacking and moving off at a moment's notice.

Tuesday 5 September

Only two short shows went out today*[;]* the first pranged a bridge and the other found a small Fiat car out on a pleasure run and ended it abruptly.

Wednesday 6 September

The CO led four aircraft on an armed recce and bombed a bridge without success, they pranged a staff car on the way home. The weather is getting duffer each day.

Thursday 7 September

No flying *[as]* p——ing with rain.

Friday 8 September

Same as yesterday.

Saturday 9 September

Stopped raining but the 'drome is u/s.

Two photographs – not reproduced here – are affixed to the facing page. One is of pilots apparently at standby and the other shows three individuals in a posed interior shot. Written at the bottom of the page:

9.9.44. F/LT GARNHAM. arrived from 241 SQDN.

Sunday 10 September

The 'drome has dried up a little so we started flying again. Col Moody led six aircraft on a Rover Jimmy*[;]* they were directed onto a field gun position but they could not see it. They hung around for twenty minutes for the gun to fire so that they could position it but the Hun wouldn't play, so they had to bomb a pin-point. All the bombs fell in the target area.

The rest of the day was fill*[ed]* up with air tests.

Monday 11 September

The beer Hurricane set out early this morning for Malta heavily loaded with empty bottles and letters to the "types'" various "bints".

A section of six did a good spot of bombing on a railway bridge at Bellaria *[and]* scored *[a]* direct hit. Later they recce'd the roads in the Ravenna, Mass Lomarda *[and]* Imola area and pranged two trucks at Bagnana. P/O Roberts chased a motor cyclist and pranged him. They pranged another truck and strafed some tanks scoring hits but no other results.

Six Spits led by the CO went out on the next show bombing field gun positions at the northern tip of San Marina*[;]* all the bombs fell in target area. LT Rowe had rather a twitch when he saw 10/10 flak ahead but they did not go through it.

Tuesday 12 September

Four aircraft set out to bomb train near Bagnavallo *[Bagnacavallo?]* but did not find it owing to duff weather so they bombed a railway line at Russi and pranged it. Sgt Jeans's wing came off in the dive, he had no chance to get out. This was his third opps trip, for the short time he was on the squadron he became quite popular in the mess.

The CO led a section to bomb transport yard (a small triangular field) *[and]* all the bombs fell in the target. A nice spot of bombing!

Facing page:

12:9.44 SGT JEANS. KILLED IN ACTION.

Wednesday 13 September

Had a big day of Opps today. Col Moody led bombing attack on village, the section got pooped at by rockets and were severely shaken.

All told today we did 25 sorties, which is good for six aircraft[;] we pranged a couple of railways.

P/O Palliser dived on what he thought was a truck and received a 40mm shell through his wing so he changed his mind and came home.

Thursday 14 September

We had only three serviceable aircraft first thing to day so "Opps" found us a nice bridge to prang[;] the first show had no joy but put some nice bombs on the railway line.

The next section to take off were briefed to bomb a train but Kittyhawks beat them by a short lead and pranged it. Finding nothing else to bomb they went after the rail bridge again, but had no luck.

In final desperation we sent another section out after the bridge and as luck would have it the lads led by P/O Ballantine clobbered it. Good show!!

Friday 15 September

Four close support shows went off today with good results against field gun and mortar positions. An armed recce led by F/O Palliser destroyed 5 trucks in the route 9 area

Saturday 16 September

The CO led a close support and made rather a mess of a village which was being used as an enemy strong point. The Hun is not playing the game these days[;] he is using rockets against us which is rather worrying on a bombing run.

Later in the day we moved all our aircraft and equipment to Brugnetto [sic: Borghetto;] we are joining 8 SAAF Wing, with 3 SAAF Sqdn [and] 11 [?] SAAF Sqdn and 87 Sqdn.

COL DU TOIT is the CO and LT COL Moodie is the wing leader.

Sunday 17 September

Two close support shows went out bombing field gun positions, Jerry guns are getting rather a pounding these days.

Monday 18 September

The weather was not too good today[;] there was a lot of low cloud. One section went dive-bombing from 3000 ft, Lt Rowe was hit by flak and went straight in.

Facing page:

18.9.44. LT Rowe Killed in action.

Tuesday 19 September

More close support[;] today three sections went out after heavy gun positions and shook the gunners considerably, the bombing has improved 100% in the last few weeks.

Wednesday 20 September

Another day of bombing troop concentrations and field guns. The Hun must be quite used to us being over all day now.

Thursday 21 September

We gave the army a miss today and carried out armed recces up to Ravenna. Sgt Medlicott vanished on one of these, nobody even saw him go, he must have got hit strafing and gone straight in, It's a mystery to us!

Facing page:

21.9.44. SGT MEDLICOTT. MISSING.

Sergeant Donald W. Medlicott did not survive and is buried at Cesena War Cemetery in the Province of Forli.

Noted by Pilot Officer D.S. Weedon:

21:9:44 S/Ldr Christopherson arrived to take over the squadron from S/Ldr Willmott, who is posted to UK.

1945

Wednesday 28 March

Owing to the fact that the diary was borrowed, some time has elapsed since it was last written. P/O Holliman, now F/LT Holliman, has handed the keeping of it to myself, P/O Weedon. I shall endeavour to record all the doings of the mighty 185th Squadron!

During the lapse, the squadron has been doing some excellent work, and has lived up to its old reputation.

Towards the end of September and onwards the boys' bombing was such that Close Support work was getting really close. November 5th was the big day when our a/c attacked buildings on the north side of Forli aerodrome, with our troops on the other side, some 200 <u>yards</u> away. Needless to say, all our bombs were on the target! Most of the close support was done under the directions of a ground controller, who went under the title of Rover David or Rover Paddy.

In November, 185 Squadron (with 8 SAAF Wing), bid [sic] a sad farewell to the 8th Army and moved over to Florence. Actually, it was because of the Wing's good close-support work that we were moved across to support the 5th Army around the Bologna area. The runway at Florence was a lot shorter than at Fano, but was concrete and very wide. It took the boys some while to get over the beauty of the Florence "sights". They are certainly beautiful <u>AND</u> well-dressed. Several members of the Officers and Sgts Messes were soon organised.

Not very much flying was done from this airfield, as the weather had definitely clamped. Still, a number of close support jobs were carried out with great success, directed by a ground control[ler] called Rover Joe. Also, targets of many descriptions, from guns to Jerry billets were attacked from the coast to Bologna.

Christmas was happily spent by all and a couple of glorious "parties" were had by the pilots. (and some actually <u>flew</u> on Xmas day!).

On New Year's Day the squadron moved to its present 'drome, Pontedera. The runway is 1800 yds long (should be enough for anyone.)

The squadron now really went into action. Most of the attacks these days were centred against guns and messages of congratulations were soon pouring in from the Army.

One show was rather out of the ordinary. The CO led 12 a/c to attack a German Rest Camp at Massa. Seven direct hits did not improve it and the Jerries must have needed a rest after we'd finished.

January ended well with an ammo dump exploding, sending smoke and dust up to 3000´. This was done by strafing and the a/c doing it was badly damaged by the explosion. We learnt a lesson; don't get <u>too</u> reckless in strafing.

February was mostly uninteresting from our point of view, mainly bombing guns and Rover Joes. The trouble with this type of work is that you can't <u>see</u> any results. The army thinks differently and we get quite a few reports of guns wiped out and Jerries killed, when we only claim near misses.

About this time F/Lt Holliman set up a record. He was hit by flak on <u>EIGHT</u> consecutive trips. In one, a shell passed through the door, behind his head and out through the hood, without exploding. A shaky do!

An ammo dump was successfully attacked by 8 a/c and <u>seven</u> small buildings exploded, sending white smoke up to 1000 feet.

March has seen us bombing and strafing a great variety of targets with excellent results. We are now operating further afield and doing practically no close-support.

We have now 4 a/c with Gyro gun-sights and have two teams picked, one from "A" and one from "B" Flight, to train with these sights. As soon as their training is complete, they will go on sweeps way up north with 90 gall. over loads. We might then be able to add a few more a/c to the "line-shooting" board. We all hope so, anyway!

That just about brings the diary up-to-date in a general sort of way. Many of the old-timers have left, but the newcomers are just as keen for the squadron, as have been all its members since the squadron was formed.

SQUADRON STRENGTH ON MARCH 28th 1945.
S/LDR CHRISTOPHERSON.Officer Commanding.

A FLIGHT.		"B" FLIGHT.	
F/LT GARNHAM.	RAF.	F/L HOLLIMAN.	RAF
P/O LIVERSIDGE	RAF.	F/O STRETCH	RAF
LT RITCHIE.	SAAF	LT ROSENSTEIN	SAAF
LT PENTON	SAAF	P/O WEEDON	RAF
LT WEST.	SAAF.	W/O JONES	RAAF.
W/O BOTSFORD	RAF	F/SGT PROCTOR	RAF
W/O LYNCH	RAF.	F/SGT ROBERTS	RAF.
SGT PICKERSGILL	RAF.	SGT MAYNE	RAF
F/SGT YARRANTON	RAF.	SGT NISBET	RAF.
		SGT KURREIN	RAF.

Wednesday 28 March
No flying owing to bad weather.

Thursday 29 March
The day started early and well. 4 a/c took off at 05:55 to attack Jerry billets near Aulla. Two DHs *[direct hits]* or VNMs *[very near misses]* were obtained and the building was badly damaged by many strafing runs.

Quite a bit of flak was encountered which is not surprising, considering the situation of the target.

8 a/c set out at 0835 to attack a gas plant at Firenzuola. Six bombs fell in the target area and the other two were near misses, which is pretty good bombing. One of the two buildings in the area was completely smashed.

4 a/c took off at 1035 and escorted 3 C47s [C-47/Douglas Dakota] north of Genoa, where the latter dropped supplies for the partisans. (We do one of these nearly every day and what a bind they are!)

8 a/c attacked the remaining building at the Gas plant and scored 2 or 3 DHs and several near misses. After 20 strafing runs had been carried out, the building was completely wrecked. No flak was encountered on this or the other show (which is a very good thing!)

The last show of the day nearly ended in disaster! 8 a/c set out to bomb two targets in an oilfield at SALSOMAGGIORE. The bombing in both cases was good, DHs being obtained.

During his strafing, Sgt Nisbet was hit (apparently by heavy machine-gun fire) and black smoke started pouring out of his engine. In spite of the fact that his windscreen and cockpit (and himself) were covered with oil and his engine was _very_ rough, he brought the a/c back and landed safely, which was a wizard effort. His kite had nine holes in it (one in the oil tank.) Two other a/c also had holes in the wings, but nothing serious.

Friday 30 March

6 a/c, led by F/Lt Garnham, attacked a Fuel storage dump at   [sic]; although the bombing was good, no fires or explosions were obtained.

8 a/c, led by F/Lt Holliman, went after the same target at 13:30 and this time had more luck. The first bomb caused an explosion and seven more bombs helped to stir it up. The boys went in strafing and added a couple more fires to help things along. F/LT HOLLIMAN spotted a train with a few trucks in the station and he and his section gave it a good going over.

Saturday 31 March

F/LT HOLLIMAN led 8 a/c to attack a condenser in the oilfield at Vallezza. P/O Liversidge's bomb was a direct hit and caused a large explosion, followed by a big fire.

W/O Botsford led 4 a/c on a patrol of Florence airfield. It's a binding job doing these patrols and we're all hoping we shan't get many of them.

F/LT GARNHAM led 8 a/c, TO [took-off] 14:50, to another part of the oilfield at Vallezza and although the bombing was good and 2 DHs were obtained, there were no explosions or fires. On both this and the other show, moderate 20 and 40mm was encountered, but no one was hit.

The coming of the three new pilots to the mess was duly celebrated. What the first chaps on in the morning will feel like, remains to be seen.

Facing page:

<u>31st MARCH</u> Three new pilots arrived:-
        F/O McFARLANE (RSAF)
        F/O BAMFORD (RNZAF).
        F/O BROWN (RNZAF).

Overleaf:

F/LT GARNHAM	"GEORGE"	F/LT HOLLIMAN	"CHUTNEY"
P/O LIVERSIDGE	"BLONDIE"	F/O STRETCH	"BILL"
LT RITCHIE	"TOM"	LT ROSENSTEIN	"ROSEY"
LT PENTON	"OSSIE"	P/O WEEDON	"DOUG"
LT WEST	"BERN".	W/O JONES	"CLEM"
W/O BOTSFORD	"DROF"	F/SGT PROCTOR	"JIM".
W/O LYNCH	"SQUIRE"	F/SGT ROBERTS	"ROBBIE"
SGT PICKERSGILL	"PIGGY"	SGT MAYNE	"PETE"
F/SGT YARRINGTON	" [sic] `	SGT NISBET	"JOCK"
F/O BAMFORD	"BAM"	SGT KURREIN	"KURRY"
F/O BROWN	"BROWNIE"	F/O McFARLANE	"MAC"
		F/SGT NICKOLSON [sic].	"NICK"

Sunday 1 April

The "Gyro" teams being ready, the squadron was put on fighter readiness for the first time in months. Chutney and Jock had a scramble and were vectored after a jet a/c (the first time in the sqdn's history!) They got within 7 miles of it, but made no contact. Doug and Pete went on a weather recce and got one staff car; it went up with quite a bang.

Bill, Jim and Robbie attacked an oil collecting tank at Villazza. One DH (Bill's) badly damaged the tank. They found moderate accurate LAA *[light anti-aircraft]* from the TA *[target area]*.

Blondie, Hayman, Tom and Piggy then went after a power house at Villazza oilfield. One bomb in the TA. The lads made one strafing run apiece and scored multi strikes. This time there was intense acc*[urate]* LAA which hit Tom in the wing and elevator. In spite of no ASI he landed it OK.

The day ended with George and Ossie doing a dusk patrol of highway 65. They found no EA and landed just after dark. Hmmm? Very shaky!

Monday 2 April

The squadron again went on readiness again *[sic]* at 6:30 and soon after Chutney and Jock were scrambled but had no joy.

Bob and Bernard were scrambled soon after but again no joy.

Blondie, Hay, Tom, Yarr, Rosey and Kurry went after a Methane Gas Plant. Blondie scored a DH on the compressor bldg and that and two NMs pretty well wrecked it. Rosey's a/c burst into flame at the beginning of his dive and he went straight in. He will be greatly missed by all in the mess.

Doug (that's me) and Pete were scrambled in the afternoon but again no joy.

Bill[,] Clem[,] Jim and Robbie went after [a] troop concentration in a wood. Only one bomb was seen, and that fell on the edge of the wood. The lads strafed and got bags of strikes, and no flak!

Chutney and Jock finished the day off with a dusk patrol over highway 65. No joy, but they saw about a dozen enemy transport[s] (which they were not allowed to strafe).

What a war!

Facing page:

2nd APRIL LT ROSENSTEIN ~~KILLED IN ACTION~~ Missing

Lieutenant Ernest W. Rosenstein was killed and is buried at the Milan War Cemetery.

Tuesday 3 April

On readiness again from 0630, but nothing all day.

Bob and Bern went on a weather recce and reported weather OK for bombing.

So Bill, Mac, Jim and Clem went after a "gas field" south of Parma. Owing to the fact that no photograph of the TA was available, the lads just bombed a map pin point. Nothing startling happened, except that while they were strafing they were joined by Thunderbolts, also strafing. Very shaky!

Blondie, Bam, Tom and Brownie went off to the same place a bit later. Apparently the bombing was not too hot but they got bags of strikes on two derricks whilst strafing.

George and Ossie started a new racket today! Dropping leaflets! We have an amazing effort rigged up, a 90 gall overload, with "bomb-doors". They got south of Bologna and pulled the effort, but nothing happened apart from the cables coming adrift from the "bomb-doors". We'll have to have a few mods. on them!

Wednesday 4 April

Chutney and Jock started the day's flying with a weather recce with nothing unusual happening.

Sgt Hayman, a new lad, went on an air test and disappeared! He took off OK and that was the last we've seen or heard of him. Jolly hard luck!

Bill and Jim took off later and searched for him, but it was no use. Blondie and Bam scrambled after a bogey, which was friendly (as usual.)

Doug and Pete did the dusk patrol, while George and Ossie again tried dropping leaflets, this time successfully. Hope the Jerries use them!

Facing page:

4:4.45. SGT HAYMAN. MISSING, PRESUMED KILLED.

Sergeant William P. Hayman was killed. He has no known grave.

Thursday 5 April

Chutney, Mac, Doug and Clem started the day with an attack on a compressor building at Valleria oilfield. Although one bomb hit the building and the whole area was well strafed, no fires resulted.

Bob, Brownie, Ossie and Bern went after an oil well in the same field a little later, and although they got no fires, they managed to knock down a derrick. It's something anyway!

Chutney again returned to the oilfield, this time with Nick, Jock and Pete. At last some results were obtained and a small fire was started.

Blondie and Bam carried out the dusk patrol, while Tom and Piggy dropped Jerry his daily news.

Friday 6 April

Jim and Robbie carried out a weather recce; nothing unusual. Blondie, Yarry, Bern and Ossie went out after a stores depot and scored three very near misses on the building. There was intense accurate LAA from the TA (very dangerous) but the lads gave it a good strafing. The wall and roof on one side were seen to be badly damage[d].

Bob and Bam had a scramble; friendly again.

Ossie, Mac and Brownie escorted 6 C' 47s [*sic*: C-47s] dropping supplies and everything went off OK.

Chutney, Jock, Doug and Pete went on a Rover Joe and were directed by "Horsefly" (a 'pisser' [?] directing operations) to bomb and strafe the village of Capanelle. Two bombs hit the village, throwing up showers of brick dust. 20 strafing runs were made scoring bags of strikes and lots of dust. Horsefly was very enthusiastic about it. There was some scant inaccurate LAA.

Bill and Clem did the dusk patrol and Jim and Robbie the leaflet.

Saturday 7 April

Squadron was released, so most of the pilots visited Florence, where a good time was had by all and everyone returned in a happy condition quite late.

Sunday 8 April

Squadron released again owing to bad weather.

Monday 9 April

Chutney, Mac[,] Doug and Kurry went on the first show, which was an unusual one. Forty a/c from this wing alone took part and the whole show was run to a very strict time schedule. The whole thing went off very well and all the bombs good. Kurry reported glycol trouble and landed at Cervia.

A little later George, Bam, Drof and Bern went on another of these shows (known as SUZY) and again it went very well. Three bombs among the buildings, sending up showers of dust. They were greeted with a large amount of very intense and very accurate light AA from the TA.

Tuesday 10 April

The day started with another SUZY, this time with 8 a/c from 185. The target was the Jerry Para Corps HQ. We had about five different bldgs to attack and all were damaged by bombs. We are still doing readiness and two scrambles resulted, both friendly.

Chutney led 8 a/c to attack a compressor bldg. at Monticelli oilfield. Although all bombs fell in the TA and many strafing runs were made, no fires or explosions were obtained.

Drof, Bam, Squire and Mac did an armed recce of Area 5. As nothing was observed, they bombed a bridge.

Bill and Clem dropped the leaflets and Jim and Robbie carried out an uneventful dusk patrol.

This is the last diary entry. The squadron ORB records mainly bombing and strafing attacks and armed reconnaissance flights until 26 April. Two days previously the squadron also began to relocate from Pontedera to Bologna. At the end of the month the squadron moved again, this time from Bologna to Villafranca. In summing up the month's events, the commanding officer, Squadron Leader M.V. Christopherson, noted:

April has been a most satisfactory month for the Squadron, as it has for the forces in Italy as a whole. Communications and close-support bombing was steadily intensified, culminating in the route [sic] of the German Armies during the last 10 days of the month.

Apart from many bridges and railway communications destroyed or damaged, the Squadron destroyed 46 M.T. and damaged 30 others. In flying over 500 sorties, the Squadron established a record.

Four Pilots are missing, two of them believed killed, and F/Sgt. Nisbet, G.Y. has been awarded the Distinguished Flying Medal for a very good show put up on March 29th, 1945.

Flying Officer Robert A. Bamford was killed on 12 April. Flight Lieutenant Frank T. Holliman was lost on 23 April, less than two weeks before the end of the war in Europe. On 3 May the ORB recorded:

> Information was received announcing that all German resistance in
> Italy had ceased. The Commanding Officer, S/Ldr. M.V.
> Christopherson ordered that a Squadron Party be held tonight at the
> Airmen's Mess for all members of the Squadron. An emergency
> meeting of the P.S.I. Committee was called, and it was voted that all
> drinks will be free of charge for the party.

The next day Pilot Officer R.H. Botsford and Flight Sergeant K.R.
Pickersgill undertook one final mission before the end of the war in Europe.
In the squadron ORB the commanding officer's remarks for the month of
May read:

> On May 4th the Squadron carried out its last operation of the European
> War, when a reconnaissance was carried out over the surrendered
> German Armies from the Brenner Pass to the Austrian Border. This
> operation was a quiet close to the campaign in Italy from the Gothic
> Line days of last July, during which the Squadron has taken a full share
> in making possible the advance of the 8th and 5th Armies.
>   Almost a year ago the Squadron, brought up from Malta to Perugia,
> dropped its first bombs in the Senegallia [sic: Senigállia] area. Since
> then it has dropped 2,266 bombs weighing 1,133,000 lbs., and has fired
> well over 500,000 rounds of ammunition in almost 3,000 sorties
> against enemy targets. To summarise the the [sic] results of these
> operations would be impossible, since like every close-support
> Squadron, our targets were of a widely different nature, and in any case
> many of the results will never be known. Together with the Squadrons
> of Desert Air Force, we consider that our efforts and losses have not
> been in vain, and we can pride ourselves with the fact that on not one
> occasion has a bomb or round landed on the wrong side of the lines.
>   The future of 185, the Malta Squadron, is at present unsettled, and
> for the past three weeks we have been engaged solely on practising for
> the Desert Air Force Fly-Past, which took place on May 28th.

In August 1945 all remaining aircraft were transferred to Number 11
Squadron South African Air Force. On 11 August:

> The Squadron had their final "Get Together" today. All ranks were
> present and a good time was had by all.

Number 185 Squadron was disbanded at Campo Formido three days later.
The final entry in the ORB, dated 14 August, reads:

Official date of disbandment. Posting instructions have now been received for all personnel, and it is anticipated that work will finally be cleared up within the next few days.

Toward the back of the diary the Australian SNCO John W. 'Slim' Yarra had begun to compile a list and tallies of squadron pilots based on that prepared previously by Sergeant J.R. 'Jock' Sutherland. This is followed by another list by an unknown hand. (In the original diary the latter runs to several pages with names grouped according to their initials.)

LIST OF 185 PILOTS.

ORIGINAL SQUADRON

F/LT P O W [sic] MOULD. DFC AND BAR: CANT Z 506 DES. 1 PROB. 1 DAM. MC 200 DESTROYED: KILLED IN ACTION 1/10/41. FINAL SCORE: 2 DESTROYED 1 PROB 1 DAM

F/O ELIOT: POSTED OFF OPS 6/6/41 FINAL SCORE ZERO

F/LT JEFFRIES: 1 JU 88 PROBABLE. MC 200 DESTROYED. CANT Z 506 DESTROYED, ONE PROBABLE, 1 DAMAGED. (SYRACUSE) MC 200 DESTROYED 1 DAMAGED. MC 200 PROBABLE. POSTED ME 27/10/41. FINAL SCORE: 3 DESTROYED. 2 PROBABLE 1 DAMAGED

P/O HAMILTON: 1 PROBABLE JU 87 KILLED IN ACTION 14.5.42. [sic] FINAL SCORE: 1 JU 87 PROB.

P/O INNES: POSTED 5.4.41. FINAL SCORE: ZERO

P/O HALL: 2 JU 88 PROBABLE INJURED IN ACTION POSTED HQ (CONTROLLER) POSTED UK 14/5/42. FINAL SCORE: 2 PROBABLE

SGT BAMBERGER: POSTED UK 6.6.41. NO SCORE

SGT OTTEY: KILLED ON ACTIVE SERVICE 2.5.41. NO SCORE

SGT WALMSLEY: POSTED OFF OPS 1.5.41. INJURED. NO SCORE

SGT WYNNE: KILLED IN ACTION 15.5.41. NO SCORE

SGT BURTON: POSTED UK 26.8.41. NO SCORE

F/O WESTMACOTT: 2 HE 111s SHARED POSTED TO MNFU

F/LT HANCOCK: 2 HE 111s (SHARED) DAMAGED: 2 E BOATS DESTROYED (SHARED): 1 SM 79 DES. POSTED ME 17.9.41. FINAL SCORE. 1 DESTROYED 2 E BOATS: 2 DAMAGED

P/O BAILEY: 2 HE 111 DAMAGED (SHARED). MC 200 DESTROYED (SHARED) MC 200 DAMAGED. ⅛ BR 20 DESTROYED. KILLED IN ACTION 9/11/41. FINAL SCORE ⅛ + ¼ DES 3 DAM

P/O THANSON: NO INFORMATION. [*Pilot Officer Thanson, also mentioned on 30 April 1941, should probably read Pilot Officer Thompson.*]

P/O DREDGE: INJURED IN ACTION: POSTED OFF OPS NO SCORE

SGT BRANSON: ⅛ BR 20 POSTED ME 7.9.41. FINAL SCORE: ⅛ DES.

SGT HODSON: NO INFORMATION

SGT JOLLY: 1 MC 200 DES. 1 MC 200 DES. 1 MC 200 DAM. POSTED ME 20.2.42. FINAL SCORE: 2 DESTROYED. 1 DAMAGED.

P/O GRAY: POSTED UK 23.7.41. NO SCORE

PILOTS POSTED AS REPLACEMENTS

SGT VARDY: FROM 261 SQDN 5.5.41. POSTED ME 20.2.42. NO SCORE

SGT SHEPPARD: (RAAF) 6.5.41. FROM 261 SQDN. ½ MC 200 POSTED ME 20/2/42 FINAL SCORE: ½ DESTROYED

P/O ALLARDICE: FROM 52 OTU UK 27.6.41 1 ME 110 DES. 1 JU 88 DAM. KILLED IN ACTION 22.3.42. FINAL SCORE: 1 DESTROYED 1 DAMAGED

SGT ALDERSON: FROM 52 OTU UK 27.6.41. ⅛ BR 20. POSTED 10.4.4.2. FINAL SCORE: ⅛ DESTROYED

P/O BARNWELL: FROM 607 SQDN UK 30/6/41. ⅛ BR 20. ⅕ 2 "E" BOATS. POSTED MNFU 1.8.41. 2 BR 20s DESTROYED (NIGHT.) AWARDED DFC 5.9.41. CZ 1007 DESTROYED, MC 200 DESTROYED. KILLED IN ACTION 14 10 41 FINAL SCORE 4⅛ DESTROYED ⅕ 2 "E" BOATS

SGT BATES: FROM 52 OTU UK 27/6/41. PROBABLE MC 200 POSTED HQ MED. 20.3.42. FINAL SCORE: 1 PROBABLE

SGT COUSENS: 245 SQDN UK 30.6.41. KILLED IN ACTION 21.11.41 NO SCORE

SGT COMFORT: FROM UK 13.9.41. POSTED ME 25/9/41 NO SCORE.

SGT ELLIS: FROM No 1 SQDN UK 30/6/41 1 BR 20 (SHARED WITH 8 OTHERS) ¼ PROBABLE JU 88. ½ JU 88 DESTROYED. FINAL SCORE: ⅛ ½ DES. ¼ PROB.

SGT FORTH: FROM 52 OTU UK 27.6.41. SHARED SM 79. SHARED 2 "E" BOATS SHARED SM 79. KILLED IN ACTION 29.12.41. FINAL SCORE: ½ DES ½ DES 2 "E" BOATS SHARED

SGT HUNTON: FROM 59 OTU UK 30.6.41. 1 MC 202 DES. ⅕ JU 88 DES. – JU 88 PROB. POSTED HQ MED. 20.3.42 FINAL SCORE: 1. ⅕. ¼. DESTROYED

SGT HAYES: FROM 607 SQDN UK 30.6.41. KILLED IN ACTION 21.2.42 NO SCORE.

SGT HORSEY: FROM 52 OTU UK 30.6.41. POSTED ME 25.9.41. NO SCORE

SGT KNIGHT: FROM 258 SQDN UK 30.6.41. KILLED IN ACTION 25.10.41. NO SCORE

SGT LILLYWHITE: FROM 242 SQDN UK 30.6.41. 2 "E" BOATS SHARED. 1 SM 81 DES.

185 SQUADRON

PERSONNEL

as at 30/4/42 onwards

Book 2

Broad SGT   from 234 UK 2/3/42

BECKETT P/O   from 605 MALTA 18/3/42
½ ME 110, ¼ ME 110 DAM. 21/3/42,

BOYD SGT   from 242 MALTA

DODD SGT (RCAF)   from 126 Spitfires MALTA

FINLAY SGT   from 605 MALTA 18/3/42

FERRABY SGT   from 126 MALTA (Spits) 5/4/42

LLOYD F/LT   from 130 UK 16/12/41

LAWRENCE F/LT   from 91 UK 17/2/42

LESTER P/O (RAAF)   from 605 MALTA 18/3/42

MORTIMER-ROSE S/LDR (DFC & BAR) from Fighter Control MALTA
17/3/42
1 ME 110 23/3/42

McKAY P/O (RCAF)   from 605 MALTA 18/3/42

NOBLE P/O   from 605 MALTA 18/3/42

SIM SGT   from 249 MALTA 5/4/42 (RNZAF)

TWEEDALE SGT (RAAF) from 43 UK 2/3/42

283

Select Bibliography

While no single publication has focused solely on the activities of Number 185 Squadron, much has been written about other squadrons and the battle of Malta in general.

Agius, John A. MBE and Galea, Frederick R., *Lest We Forget, Royal Air Force and Commonwealth Air Forces Servicemen Lost in the Defence of Malta*, Malta Aviation Museum Foundation, 1999.

Bailey, Captain E.A.S. CBE DSC Royal Navy (ed.), *Malta, Defiant & Triumphant, Rolls of Honour, 1940–1943*, EAS Bailey, 1992, and *Addenda & Amendments* (as at 31 December 1997).

Barnham, Denis, *One Man's Window, An illustrated account of ten weeks of war Malta, April 13th, to June 21st, 1942*, William Kimber, 1956.

Bekker, Cajus, *The Luftwaffe War Diaries*, Macdonald, 1968.

Bellows, Jim, *"When in Doubt, Brew Up"*, ELSP, 2002.

Beurling, Flying Officer George F. DSO, DFC, DFM and Bar, and Roberts, Leslie, *Malta Spitfire – The Story of a Fighter Pilot*, Hutchinson, 1943.

Bonner, Robert A., *The Ardwick Boys went to Malta. A British Territorial Battalion during the siege 1940–1943*, Fleur de Lys Publishing, 1992.

Borgiotti, Alberto and Gori, Cesare, *Gli Stuka Della Regia Aeronautica 1940–45*, Stem Mucchi Modena, 1976.

Brennan, Pilot Officer Paul DFC, DFM, Hesselyn, Pilot Officer Ray DFM and Bar, Bateson, Henry, *Spitfires Over Malta*, Jarrolds, 1943.

Caldwell, Donald, *The JG 26 War Diary, Volume One, 1939–1942*, Grub Street, 1996.

Cameron, Ian, *Red Duster, White Ensign, The Story of the Malta Convoys*, Frederick Muller, 1959.

Cull, Brian, *249 At War, The Authorised History of the RAF's Top-Scoring Fighter Squadron of WWII*, Grub Street, 1997.

——, with Malizia, Nicola and Galea, Frederick, *Spitfires Over Sicily, The Crucial Role of the Malta Spitfires in the Battle of Sicily, January – August 1943*, Grub Street, 2000.

——, and Galea, Frederick, *Hurricanes Over Malta, June 1940 – April*

1942, Grub Street, 2001.

Douglas-Hamilton, Squadron Leader Lord David, 'With a Fighter Squadron in Malta', *Blackwood's Magazine*, April and May 1944.

Douglas-Hamilton, Lord James, *The Air Battle for Malta – The Diaries of a Fighter Pilot*, Mainstream Publishing, 1981.

Franks, Norman, *Buck McNair, Canadian Spitfire Ace, The story of Group Captain R W McNair DSO, DFC & 2 Bars, Ld'H, CdG, RCAF*, Grub Street, 2001.

Galea, Frederick R., *Call-Out, A wartime diary of air/sea rescue operations at Malta*, BIEB BIEB, 2002.

Gibbs, Wing Commander Patrick DSO, DFC and Bar, *Torpedo Leader*, Grub Street, 1992.

Hamlin, John F., *Military Aviation in Malta G.C., 1915–1993, A comprehensive history*, GMS Enterprises, 1994.

Hay, Ian, *The Unconquered Isle, The Story of Malta G.C.*, Hodder & Stoughton, 1943.

HMSO, *The Air Battle of Malta*, 1944.

Holland, James, *Fortress Malta, An Island Under Siege 1940–1943*, Orion, 2003.

Hughes, Jimmy Quentin MC, *Who Cares Who Wins*, Charico Press, 1998.

Johnston, Wing Commander Tim DFC, *Tattered Battlements – A Fighter Pilot's Diary*, William Kimber, 1985.

Lucas, Laddie, *Five Up – A Chronicle of Five Lives*, Sidgwick & Jackson, 1978.

——, *Malta – The Thorn in Rommel's Side, Six Months that Turned the War*, Stanley Paul, 1992.

Lloyd, Air Marshal Sir Hugh, *Briefed to Attack, Malta's Part in African Victory*, Hodder & Stoughton, 1949.

Mahlke, Helmut, *Stuka, Angriff : Sturzfleug*, Verlag E.S. Mittler & Sohn, 1993.

Malizia, Nicola, *Inferno su Malta*, Mursia, 1976.

McAuley, Lex, *Against All Odds, RAAF pilots in the Battle for Malta 1942*, Hutchinson Australia, 1989.

Mifsud, Richard, *Flames over Malta*, Richard Mifsud, 1989.

Neil, Wing Commander T.F. DFC*, AFC, AE, RAF Ret'd, *Onward to Malta, Memoirs of a Hurricane pilot in Malta – 1941*, Airlife, 1992.

Nolan, Brian, *Hero: The Falcon of Malta*, William Blackwood, 1982.

Oliver, R. Leslie, *Malta at Bay, An Eye-Witness Account*, Hutchinson, 1942.

——, *Malta Besieged*, Hutchinson, 1944.

Perowne, Stewart, *The Siege Within the Walls, Malta 1940–1943*, Hodder & Stoughton, 1970.

Poolman, Kenneth, *Faith, Hope and Charity, Three Planes against an Air Force*, William Kimber, 1954.

——, *Night Strike From Malta, 830 Squadron RN and Rommel's Convoys*,

Janes Publishing, 1980.

Prien, Jochen, *Chronik des JG-53 Pik-As Band 1*, Flugzeug Publikations GmbH.

——, *"Pik-As", Geschichte des Jagdgeschwaders 53, Teile 2 and 3*, Struve-Druck, 1990 and 1991.

——, *Geschichte des Jagdgeschwaders 77, Teile 3 and 4*, Struve-Druck.

——, *Messerschmitt Bf 109 im Einsatz bei der II/Jagdgeschwader 3*, Struve-Druck, 1996.

Radtke, Siegfried, *Kampfgeschwader 54*, Schild Verlag, 1990.

Rae, Flt Lt J.D. DFC and Bar, *Kiwi Spitfire Ace, A Gripping World War II Story of Action, Captivity and Freedom*, Grub Street, 2001.

Ramsey, Winston (ed.), *After the Battle* (magazine), number 10, Battle of Britain Prints, 1975.

Rogers, Anthony, *Battle over Malta, Aircraft Losses and Crash Sites 1940–42*, Sutton Publishing, 2000.

Rolls, Flight Lieutenant W.T. DFC, DFM, AE, *Spitfire Attack*, William Kimber, 1987.

Scott, Stuart R., *Battle-Axe Blenheims, No 105 Squadron RAF at War 1940–1*, Sutton Publishing, 1996.

Shankland, Peter and Hunter, Anthony, *Malta Convoy*, Collins, 1961.

Shores, Christopher, *Aces High, Volume 2*, Grub Street, 1999.

——, and Cull, Brian with Malizia, Nicola, *Malta: The Hurricane Years 1940–41*, Grub Street, 1987.

——, and Cull, Brian with Malizia, Nicola, *Malta: The Spitfire Year 1942*, Grub Street, 1991.

——, and Williams, Clive, *Aces High*, Grub Street, 1994.

Smith, Peter C., Pedestal, *The Malta Convoy of August 1942*, William Kimber, 1987.

Spooner, Tony DSO, DFC, *Warburton's War, The Life of Wing Commander Adrian Warburton, DSO*, DFC**, DFC (USA)*, William Kimber, 1987.

Stones, Donald, *Operation "Bograt" – From France to Burma*, Spellmount, 1990.

Vella, Philip, *Malta: Blitzed But Not Beaten*, Progress Press, 1985.

Index